SOLDIERS
OF THE
QUEEN

SOLDIERS
OF THE
QUEEN

VICTORIAN COLONIAL CONFLICT IN
THE WORDS OF THOSE WHO FOUGHT

STEPHEN MANNING

SPELLMOUNT

To David Brown and Robert Taylor of Dallas, Texas.
Partners in Crime.

First published 2009 by Spellmount,
an imprint of The History Press
The Mill, Brimscombe Port
Stroud, Gloucestershire, GL5 2QG
www.thehistorypress.co.uk

© Stephen Manning, 2009

The right of Stephen Manning to be identified as the Author
of this work has been asserted in accordance with the
Copyrights, Designs and Patents Act 1988.

Maps on pages 177 and 179 from Thomas Pakenham – *The Boer War*,
courtesy of Weidenfeld & Nicolson, part of the Orion Group

British Library Cataloguing in Publication Data.
A catalogue record for this book is available from the British Library.

ISBN 978 0 7524 4984 5

Printed in Great Britain

CONTENTS

ACKNOWLEDGEMENTS

I must first thank all the 'Soldiers of the Queen' whose letters, diaries and journals have left such a vivid picture of what it was like to serve in the numerous campaigns of Victoria's reign. I am indebted to the following institutions and individuals for allowing me to access research material: Alastair Massie and his staff at the National Army Museum, the archivists at the Somerset Records Office, the staff at Stirling Castle and the Bankfield Museum, Halifax. Also, the volunteers at the Devonshire Regimental Museum, Exeter, Major White at the Duke of Cornwall Light Infantry Museum, Bodmin and the staff of the Royal Artillery Museum, Woolwich. I would like to thank Mr and Mrs McNaught of Edinburgh for allowing me to stay with them during my research in Scotland.

For their help, support and encouragement I would wish to thank Professor Jeremy Black, Dr Huw Davies, Mr Cliff Cogger, Mr Sam Hudson and Dr Matthew Potter. As ever, I am more than grateful to my wife Michaela, for her patience and proof-reading skills and I would also like to thank my two young sons, Alexander and Dominic, for allowing me to 'disappear' for hours on end to write this book. Finally, I would like to express my gratitude to David Brown and Robert Taylor for all the interest and encouragement they have shown to me throughout the process of researching and writing. It is to these two great friends that this is book is dedicated.

ABBREVIATIONS

ASHM	ARGYLL & SUTHERLAND HIGHLANDERS, MUSEUM, STIRLING CASTLE
DCLIM	DUKE OF CORNWALL LIGHT INFANTRY MUSEUM, BODMIN
DRM	DEVONSHIRE REGIMENTAL MUSEUM, EXETER
EIC	EAST INDIAN COMPANY
NAM	NATIONAL ARMY MUSEUM
RAM	ROYAL ARTILLERY MUSEUM, WOOLWICH
RMDWR	REGIMENTAL MUSEUM DUKE OF WELLINGTON REGIMENT, BANKFIELD MUSEUM, HALIFAX
SLI	SOMERSET LIGHT INFANTRY. RECORDS HELD AT THE SOMERSET RECORDS OFFICE, TAUNTON
SRO	SOMERSET RECORDS OFFICE, TAUNTON
WO	WAR OFFICE RECORDS HELD AT THE PUBLIC RECORDS OFFICE, KEW

LIST OF MAPS

INTRODUCTION

For the vast majority of the British public in the nineteenth century, their understanding of the campaigns in which their soldiers were engaged was obtained from newspapers. Often such reports focused on what the editors considered to be the unique imperial qualities, such as selflessness, bravery and determination. Whilst the British may have been thrilled, excited and even revolted to read of such disastrous defeats as Isandlwana (1879) and Maiwand (1880), these reversals did not detract from the overall impression that their forces were engaged in a glorious civilising crusade to install peace and order throughout the world, whilst at the same time extending the Empire.

However, such newspaper coverage was to give, and leave with us even today, a misleading and unrealistic understanding of what it was like to serve in colonial campaigns. Many of the letters that appeared in both the national and provincial press were concerned with great engagements rather than the possibly more mundane aspects of campaigning, and the editors had a tendency to edit their length and content, being more interested in reproducing 'graphic' or 'sensational' accounts. Such editorial interventions devalued many of the original letters. In addition, some less scrupulous papers showed a limited concern for accuracy. An examination of letters home printed in British newspapers has already been undertaken by Frank Emery in his two works, *The Red Soldier* (1977) and *Marching over Africa* (1986), and more recently by Edward Spiers in his books *The Victorian Soldier in Africa* (2004) and *The Scottish Soldier and Empire, 1854–1902* (2006). A simple repetition of this technique would, I believe, offer nothing new, yet an analysis of the original letters and diaries would hopefully provide an interesting and rewarding comparison.

It was not only newspaper editors that emphasised the nobility of colonial warfare. Writers also stressed that such wars were the test of the country's virtue. Winston Churchill wrote in the introduction to his book, *The Malakand Field Force*, published in 1897, that he was to record a story which told of 'the stubbornness of the British soldier, and the jaunty daring of his officers', and of 'occasions of devotion and self-sacrifice, of cool cynicism and stern resolve.'[1] Juvenile literature, particularly from the late 1870s onwards, had prominent themes of foreign adventure and imperialism. George Henty was a prolific and widely read writer of schoolboy yarns which told of the daring exploits of imperial adventurers and campaigning soldiers. Similarly, Dr Gordon Stables wrote nearly one hundred tales, many of which centred on a young Scottish lad who would travel to far off lands to help expand the Empire. All Stables' tales possessed an aggressive militarism centred round 'muscular Christianity'. Such themes could also be found in the *Boy's Own Paper*, which in 1879 could proudly claim a circulation of 200,000.[2] Sir Henry Newbolt in his famous poem of 1897 'Vitai Lampada' even compared the virtues needed to win on the sporting field to those that were required on campaign. Whilst it may have been true that pluck, selflessness and determination were required to fight a successful colonial war, readers of such works would have surely acquired an erroneous opinion of what it was like to serve in such campaigns.

The Victorian war artist also had a tendency to glorify or romanticise warfare, and throughout Victoria's reign a number of artists attempted to capture and recreate specific events within colonial battles. One of the earliest, painted in 1858, was Frederick Goodall's rather fanciful *The Campbells are coming: Lucknow, September 1857*, which depicted Jessie Brown, a corporal's wife, hearing the sound of the bagpipes which told of the arrival of the relief force at Lucknow. The Scottish painter Robert Gibb frequently captured images of Scottish, particularly Highland, troops in battle and his first canvases portrayed scenes from the Crimean War. His somewhat sentimental *Comrades* (1878) depicts a dying Highlander lying in the Crimean snow who is supported in his last moments by a fellow Highlander, whilst *The Thin Red*

Line (1881) dramatises the stand of the 93rd Highlanders against the rampaging Russian cavalry at the Battle of Balaclava (25 October 1854). Gibb was even able to use some of the veterans of the battle as models in the painting, although the positioning of the fallen enemy was perhaps over dramatised. Similarly, Lady Butler went to great lengths to achieve accuracy in her paintings, and was even able to pose many of the actual survivors of the Battle of Rorke's Drift (22–23 January 1879) in her painting of that name. However, even here realism ended with the depiction of only the British troops, for the attacking Zulus were confined to the shadows of the painting.[3] When Butler did truly capture the shock and realism of defeat, as in her painting *Floreat Etona* (1882), which illustrates an incident during the unsuccessful attack on Laing's Nek on 28 January 1881, she was roundly criticised for producing an image of a debacle in which, unlike her earlier *Balaclava* (1876), there was no honour for British arms.[4]

Later artists such as Vereker Hamilton and Richard Caton Woodville were able to incorporate a degree of grittiness into their works. Woodville was to first gain recognition with his painting *Maiwand: saving the guns* (1882) which, despite illustrating a defeat, was able to capture the 'spirit, or rather the fire and energy'[5] of the British troops in adversity. Over the next twenty years Woodville produced numerous works with a colonial war theme, many of which did not always focus on British military success, such as *'All that was left of them'*, a typically dramatic painting of the last stand of the 17th Lancers at Modderfontein, South Africa in 1901. All of these artists, however, managed to depict the gallantry and honour of British troops.

In a similar fashion, the newspaper war artists, such as Melton Prior of the *Illustrated London News* and Charles Fripp and Frederic Villiers, both of *The Graphic*, produced images direct from the battlefront depicting the bravery and fortitude of British troops. Like many of the reports from the special correspondents attached to the advancing British columns, and even those letters from the soldiers involved, close proximity to the battlefield occasionally led to inaccuracies, as the artists, correspondents and soldiers were simply too closely involved to capture the overall picture of the action. For this very reason, Captain Alfred Hubbard, who was present at the Battle of Omdurman (2 September 1898), complained in a letter to his wife that the newspaper reports and illustrations were full of 'gross mistakes and inaccuracies'.[6] Another reason for inaccuracy was that sometimes the illustrator was not even on the battlefield; Melton Prior produced images of the Zulu War Battle of Gingindlovu (2 April 1879) from sketches made by serving officers.[7]

Inaccuracies could of course result when there was a desire on the part of the illustrator to magnify or glorify the role of British troops. Melton Prior – when covering the Ashanti campaign of 1873–4 – produced a fanciful image of the 42nd Highland Regiment advancing shoulder to shoulder and firing at the enemy during the Battle of Amoaful (31 January 1874), when the reality was that the men, as directed by their officers, advanced from tree to tree and fired prone on the ground to avoid the withering fire from the Ashantis.[8] Similarly, the newspaper illustrators were sometimes guilty of over-emphasizing the role of a particular individual or regiment in a battle, much to the annoyance of others involved. For example, many newspaper images appeared of Piper Findlater, who although wounded in the advance to capture the Dargai Heights (20 October 1897) continued to play the pipes and encouraged his comrades on. These images, along with numerous paintings of the incident such as Vereker Hamilton's *Piper Findlater at Dargai* (1898), helped to make the piper an imperial hero who was then able to enjoy a successful career as a music hall act.

Such media coverage naturally focused on the role of Highland troops during the battle, at the expense of the Gurkas and those men of the Dorset and Derbyshire regiments that had played such an important part, and was to cause some disquiet at the time. Likewise, the illustrators of the *Illustrated London News* and *The Graphic* had earlier dwelt upon the role of Highland troops at the Battle of Tel-el-Kebir (13 September 1882), with *The Graphic* even producing a coloured supplement entitled 'The Highland Brigade at Tel-el-Kebir'.[9] Not only did such coverage annoy the men of the other regiments present, but it presented an inaccurate account to the readers of such papers.

During the First World War (1914–1918) it was the poets who best captured the horrors and reality of the conflict. It was no coincidence that the likes of Siegfried Sassoon and Wilfred Owen were men who had served at the battlefront. In contrast, during the nineteenth century, the American poet Walt Whitman worked as a hospital orderly throughout the American Civil War (1861–65) and he warned that 'real War' would 'never get in the books' for he concluded that language itself was incapable of capturing war's practicalities and its 'minutiae of deeds and passions'.[10] Whitman believed that those who had actually known war had already provided the glimpses, the details that mattered, and that no historian could ever capture that experience. Whitman in his *Memoranda During the War* may have produced the most atmospheric writing of the American Civil War, and for the British it was left to another poet, Rudyard Kipling, to capture best the soldier's experience of colonial service.

Whilst living in Lahore, Kipling made a point of getting to know those British soldiers of all ranks who were stationed at the cantonments of Mian Mir, notably the men of the 5th Northumberland Fusiliers, from 1886 to 1888. The more Kipling witnessed the stoicism of the troops as they endured hardships, so his respect for them grew. In such poems as *The Young British Soldier*, *Cholera Camp* and *The Widow's Party*, Kipling sang their praises and described their hardships more evocatively than any newspaper report. He was able to catch the vernacular of the soldier quite brilliantly and in his poem of 1887, *The Three Musketeers*, Kipling's characters of the Irishman, the cockney and the dalesman from the West Riding of Yorkshire spoke in a language which was convincing and which made them seem very real and alive. However, not even Kipling could completely capture the minds and thoughts of those that served. Only the troops themselves could do this in their own words.

Historians have always been guilty of stressing the role of politicians or of commanders at the expense of those who fought, something that has begun to be redressed in recent years. As the nineteenth century rolled on, military needs took the soldier ever farther from home, and his fortitude largely passed unnoticed. In this book I aim to help to restore that balance, to give an understanding of what it was like to be engaged in a colonial campaign. I have tried to do this by recording the words of those soldiers from their letters home, from their diaries and in their reminiscences, so as to gain a glimpse of a history not told in official reports or regimental histories. The individual stories convey powerful images, and are not simply orders of battle or lifeless remnants, although their limitations as accurate historical documents are recognised and described, as they were by the men who wrote them. Even so, I hope they will leave a lasting impression of what it was like to serve in Victoria's campaigns.

Notes

1. W.S. Churchill, *The Story of the Malakand Field Force*, (Longmans, Green & Co., London, 1898), p.1.
2. E. Spiers, *The Scottish Soldier and Empire, 1854–1902*, (Edinburgh University Press, 2006), p.115.
3. Ibid, pp.10 & 15.
4. P. Usherwood & J. Spencer-Smith, *Lady Butler Battle Artist, 1846–1933*, (Alan Sutton, Gloucester, 1987), p.84.
5. Ibid, p.173.
6. P. Harrington & F. Sharf (eds.), *Omdurman 1898: The eye-witnesses speak*, (Greenhill Books, London, 1998), p.67.
7. E. Spiers, p.45.
8. Ibid, p.32.
9. Ibid, p.82.
10. CR. Bonner, *The Soldier's Pen: Firsthand Impressions of the Civil War*, (Hill & Wang, New York, 2006), p.235.

CHAPTER ONE

VICTORIA'S SOLDIERS

During the nineteenth century, literacy, and therefore the ability to record one's experiences, was to be found only in a minority of those in the ranks of the British Army. Only the Royal Engineers and a few specialist corps expected new recruits to know how to read and write. Most officers were well educated and had sufficient leisure time to write home on a regular basis, and the surviving correspondence reflects this. However, as the century progressed more letters survive from those in the ranks and this reflects 'the increased access to education both in the community at large and within the British Army itself'.[1] By 1856, schools operated in nearly every permanent detachment of troops, and Army regulations specified a minimum school attendance of four hours per week. However, the compulsion to attend such lessons was removed in 1861 and for the next ten years the effectiveness of the provision depended on the individual commanding officers.

It has been stated that 60% of the soldiers in the Crimean War (1854–56) line infantry regiments were illiterate.[2] In 1860, Sergeant Gowing of the 7th Royal Fusiliers would regularly write letters home for his comrades. Troop Sergeant-Major Mole of the 14th Hussars was the only one in his barracks of fifteen troopers who could read and write. In return for his literary services, Mole had his comrades clean his kit for him.[3] Soldiers with such skills even managed to get into print. Private Charles Wickens of the 9th Regiment wrote an *Indian Mutiny Journal*, in which he took exception to some of the reports seen in the British newspapers. Even the famous reporter William Russell of *The Times* did not escape Wickens' criticism. Wickens can, however, be viewed very much as an exception.

In 1861 the government gave an indirect boost to the education of soldiers by setting literacy and arithmetic standards that were required for promotion. The Third Class Certificate was necessary for promotion to the rank of corporal. This required the candidate to read aloud and to write down a dictated passage, as well as to work examples in arithmetic and show a complete understanding of the use of money. The Second Class Certificate was necessary for promotion to sergeant and this entailed writing and dictation from a more difficult text, familiarity with all forms of regimental accounting and an understanding of fractions, interest and averages. The First Class Certificate was aimed at those wishing to rise from the ranks and obtain a commission and was a great deal more difficult. Whilst these Certificates did succeed in motivating men of ability to advance their education and career, they did little to resolve the high levels of illiteracy amongst the ranks.

To tackle this issue the Army introduced a new Fourth Class Certificate for all soldiers in 1871, as well as the compulsory attendance at classes of five hours per week for all new recruits. The Certificate was designed to reflect a level of reading and writing that an eight-year-old child was expected to achieve. At first the Army made meteoric claims as to the success of the new Certificate and in 1889 the director-general of military education claimed that 85% of the rankers possessed 'a superior level of education',[4] which only meant that they had reached the very low standards of the Fourth Certificate. However, it soon became clear that even this claim was wildly optimistic, when it was reported that over 60% of the rank and file were either unwilling to even sit for the Certificate or unable to pass it.[5] The lack of participation resulted in the demise of the Fourth Class Certificate, as well as the end of compulsory schooling. It was now expected that each regiment would make provision for voluntary schooling. At the same time, the standards required for promotion were raised, such that the possession of a Second Class Certificate was required for promotion to corporal and for promotion to sergeant the First Class was expected. Such a voluntary approach appeared to be successful with the number of rankers who passed the Third Class Certificate rising by over 30% from 1870–1896.

Illiteracy – defined as the inability to read or write one's own name – diminished dramatically by the end of the century to virtually nothing. However, despite modest improvements, fewer than 40% of the rank and file had achieved more than the barest level of literacy and the 'standard reached by the majority of those in the ranks was elementary at best'.[6] Despite all the efforts of the Army, it was probably Forester's Education Act of 1870 – which provided the guidelines for compulsory elementary education – that resulted in improvements in literacy in the Army and across the country.

Thus the aptitude for reading and writing amongst the rank and file of the Victorian Army was far from widespread. Yet, the reluctance or inability to pass the Fourth Class Certificate did not necessarily mean that soldiers were unable to correspond with their loved ones back home. The erratic spelling and grammar in many of the surviving correspondence did not stop letters being written and sent, and where such letters are quoted in the text I have resisted the temptation to correct errors and misspelt placenames, and have remained faithful to the original.

The practicalities of finding the time and the tools to write home whilst on active service were a severe limitation. George Milman of the Royal Artillery was forced to suspend his Crimean War diary on 30 December 1854 on account of 'ink frozen, no means of writing. Have no pencil.'[7] Milman resumed his diary on 16 January 1855, presumably when his ink had thawed. Soldiers begged, borrowed or stole in order to find materials with which to write. As Private George Morris of the 1st Battalion, 24th Regiment explained in a letter to his father from South Africa in March 1878, 'For the last four months I have been unable to procure either stamp, pen, ink or paper ... I am getting this paper and stamp from a Volunteer captain, or God knows when I shall be able to write.'[8] If paper could be bought it was often expensive; 6*d* a sheet in Egypt in the 1880s was not uncommon. Troops pleaded in their letters home for more paper to be sent out to them, and some even resorted to writing on clothing or knapsacks.[9] Finding the time to write home whilst on campaign was also sometimes difficult. In a letter to his brother, Private J. Davies, who served in the Duke of Edinburgh's Own Volunteer Reserve during the Basuto War in South Africa in 1880, wrote that he was 'filled with regret for not writing to you oftener, but there is much work here, one night picket another guard duty, the day, drill, clothes washing, cooking etc, etc.'[10]

Yet when soldiers did find the time, writing often became the main leisure pursuit. In his masterful work on the Boer War (1899–1902), Thomas Pakenham described how British troops would write at every opportunity and that letters 'littered the veld at every camp site.'[11] Similarly, Archibald Forbes, the special correspondent of the *Daily News* during the Zulu War (1879), recorded that letter-writing was the chief relaxation of the men in their encampments.[12]

Brigadier-General F.P. Cozier had been a corporal in Thorneycroft's Mounted Infantry and fought at the Battle of Spion Kop (24–25 January 1900). He was one of those rare individuals who rose from the ranks to a senior position in the officer corps and as such he could claim to have a real understanding of what motivated the British soldier. In his memoirs of 1930 he wrote

> No officer can possibly realise the lack of interest which the private soldier displays in the 'big ideas' of a commander unless he has been a private himself. The cleaning of arms, ammunition and equipment, the care of horses, the drudgery of fatigues and working parties confront him and he does them. The variation of his diet interests him at the time, and a dry bed (or a soft one, if he can get it) appeals to him much; beyond that nothing matters. He marches, counter-marches, deploys, goes into action, comes out of it and then does the hundred and one things which soldiers do collectively without question. It is the only way; if it were otherwise, battles could never be fought or wars waged.[13]

An examination of soldiers' letters supports Cozier's assertion, for they do indeed reflect the everyday obsession with diet and comfort; but the letters also demonstrate the importance soldiers placed upon letters from home. Writing to his brother from the Zulu campaign of 1879, William Fitzwilliam Elliot wrote

> very many thanks for writing so often, it is a great event in this camp when the English Post arrives and a great disappointment to those who get no letters. Newspapers also are much wanted, if I stay here I shall ask you to send me the *Pall Mall Gazette* or *Public Opinion*.[14]

Lieutenant H. Pope-Hennessy, who served in the 1890 campaign in Somaliland, described the receipt of two copies of *The Spectator* magazine from his family as being 'as refreshing as a cool spring in a desert!'[15] Likewise, Lance-Corporal William Eaton, who served with the 14th Regiment in Afghanistan in 1880, wrote to his brother and sister to express his gratitude for their frequent letters.

> I got your letter yesterday but I got the paper 4 days since and was thankful for it for I am very lonesome when I have nothing to read. I hope you will send me another and a song paper and when I come home I will not forget you.[16]

Private Milton's diary entry for 19 June 1900 suggests the importance of letters from home. It simply reads 'Glorious news. Mail arrives several letters.'[17] Writing later in the 1880, Eaton was clearly very homesick.

> I hope you will send me a paper regular and a book now and then. I would be glad if you would send me a *Yorkshire Post* now and then with plenty of cricket matches in it. It reminds me of home to read about all the old clubs.[18]

When letters were not forthcoming from home or were delayed for whatever reason, the sense of frustration and disappointment is clear. Writing to his sister from India in 1843, Private Samuel Clunie writes that

> it is now four months since I received a letter from you. I have been anxiously watching every mail expecting to receive a letter but I am always disappointed. I have not received a letter from Andrew [presumably his brother] since I was at Ferozeepore, tell him that if he does not send me a letter by the next mail I shall begin to talk very serious to him.[19]

Ensign C. Bourne, writing to his mother from Hong Kong in 1845, illustrated that the weather played an important part in the receipt of mail from home:

> Here we are still in Status Quo; no news, nothing going on and terribly dull – we have been expecting the May and June Mail for the last week and as it has been very stormy weather of late are beginning to get rather anxious about them.[20]

It was not until the 1880s that the Army fully realised the importance of both letters sent from home and correspondence written by the troops to their loved ones. On their journey to Egypt in 1882, the men of the 1st Battalion of the Black Watch were delighted to find over a thousand letters waiting for them when their troopship called at Gibraltar. The Army first utilised the services of the newly established Army Post Office Corps, which was composed of volunteers from the 24th Middlesex (Post Office) Rifle Volunteers and six post offices, during the 1882 Egyptian campaign. Two of these offices accompanied the 1st and 2nd Divisions on the line of march, thus speeding the despatch and receipt of mail.[21]

Most soldiers realised that one crucial need was to write to reassure loved ones. Arnold William, who served in the Royal Artillery during the Crimean War, wrote to his mother to put her mind at ease:

> I have to undergo hardships but not half so hard as you think – I have always had plenty to eat and drink and better coffee than ever I had in England. We are only short of grog, but the infantry fared different to us. I am quite well at present never fatter in my life you would not know me and I only hope that I may continue so.[22]

In battle, the Victorian soldier obeyed orders; he faced the enemy, loaded, fired, reloaded, and fired until ordered to do otherwise. His view was soon obscured by black powder smoke and he often had little idea whether his firing was having the desired result. For example, at the Battle of Bida (1897) in Nigeria, the officer in command of a Maxim gun stated that he could not even see his target, due to the smoke created by the weapon.[23] Thus many authors of letters, particularly when writing about combat, were well aware of their own limitations as chroniclers of events. This is clearly seen in a letter Captain Alfred Edward Hubbard of the Lincolnshire Regiment wrote to his wife, describing the Battle of Omdurman (2 September 1898).

> This battle, is, I shd. imagine one of the most difficult to write an account of – partly because of the numbers engaged on both sides, & partly because of the nature of the ground, wh. made it impossible to see what was going on except in your own immediate front – I propose merely to say what I saw myself – so that my account will deal entirely of the part taken by my own regiment, & the 1st British brigade.[24]

Likewise, Captain John Charles Ramsden, Royal Artillery, wrote in his diary, of service in both the Crimea and the Indian Mutiny, that 'I can now only describe my own actions, being too much engaged to have observed others – a diary must be egotistical.'[25] Captain Henry Marriot Paget of the Royal Engineers, who was present at the Battle of Tamaai (13 May 1884) attempted to write a description of the action to his wife. He too was aware that his descriptive powers could not do full justice to what he had experienced and thus he resorted to sending home a sketch of the battle. Even so, in trying to describe the combat, Paget admitted that the sketch 'gives a faint idea. You must have the fearful dim and dust and smoke and the smell of blood and powder and the ghastly wounds to make the thing complete.'[26]

There was, no doubt, an element of self-censorship in letters home; we cannot know how many soldiers refrained from writing of their experiences of conflict so as not to upset their loved ones, but the number of surviving letters in which combat was vividly described suggests that the Victorian soldier was not particularly reluctant to write of such incidents. Certainly swear words were avoided in print and there is very little mention of sexual liaisons, indeed the only such mention that I have found was in a letter from an officer serving in Egypt to a colleague in England. Also, it can be imagined that, if a soldier required the assistance of a literate comrade to write his letter home, then he would have been somewhat reluctant to fully express his feelings and experiences.

Although censorship was never officially imposed upon letters home, in extreme circumstances action was taken. Lance-Corporal Eaton recorded whilst serving in Afghanistan in 1880, 'A private of the 25th [sentenced to] 15 lashes last week for sending word home how we were treated, sometimes letters are opened.'[27] Many soldiers, particularly officers, were well aware that if any adverse comments that they had written home were to appear in the British newspapers, then their careers were very likely to be jeopardised. Lieutenant Percy Marling, who served with the Mounted Infantry during the attempted rescue of Gordon from Khartoum and who fought at the Battle of Abu Klea (17 January 1885), wrote home to his parents and described the terrible conditions the troops had to endure. However, he finished his letter with the instruction, 'Please keep this letter, but whatever you do, do *not* send it to the papers.'[28]

Newspaper editors, particularly those in the provincial press, were more than happy to receive letters either directly from soldiers serving on campaign, or second-hand from their friends or relatives, especially if the soldiers were engaged in one of the then conflict hotspots of Zululand or Afghanistan.

This could cause some controversy if the letter reported a failing in the Army's logistical planning or atrocities carried out by British troops. For example, Private Snook, who served in the 13th Light Infantry throughout the Zulu War of 1879, wrote to his uncle in Tiverton and described the apparent slaughter of wounded Zulus after the Battle of Kambula (30 March 1879). Snook's uncle decided to send the letter to his local newspaper, the *North Devon Herald*, whose editor printed the letter in full. The report was brought to the attention of the Aborigine Protection Society and, through their lobbying and that of Mr O'Donnell MP in the House of Commons, the Army were forced to hold a full enquiry into the claims.[29]

For many Victorians who did not have husbands or sons serving in the Army, such printed letters from soldiers were the only way for them to gain any appreciation of the hardship and the nature of the campaign. It was rare, but not unknown, for candid letters to appear in newspapers. For example, on 4 April 1879 the *Daily Western Times* of Exeter published a letter from an Ashburton man who was serving in Zululand, which described in graphic detail the British dead found on the battlefield of Isandlwana (22 January 1879).[30] Yet the majority were printed simply to give some local connection to the events in far distant countries. Editors clearly felt that their readers would be far more interested to read of the exploits of a local man, rather than national news stories. Again, during the Zulu War, the editor of the *Dawlish Times*, William Cornelius, printed letters sent to the local vicar by his son who was serving in South Africa, at the expense of wider coverage of the war.[31]

Both London and provincial newspapers were more than happy to print letters from soldiers, and many papers went even further and actively employed serving officers. Throughout the Zulu conflict, the *Western Morning News* of Plymouth regularly printed 'Our Natal Letter', which reported on events from South Africa and appears to have been written by an officer on the British staff.[32] Similarly, Henry Brackenbury, who served on Wolseley's staff during the Ashanti

Expedition (1873–74), produced copy on the campaign for the London based *Daily News*, and he would eventually write the official history of the war.[33]

Such writings can be viewed in the same context as those written by the numerous 'special correspondents' who were employed by London newspapers to report upon Victoria's campaigns. It was normally the case for both serving officers and the newspapermen to focus on the bravery of British troops and their ability to overcome any obstacle. However, if logistical failings were bad enough, the correspondents did not hesitate to make their readers, and thus the British government, aware of them, as for example in the Crimea. Both serving officers and the 'specials' rarely reported total reality; small successes were heaped with praise, while insignificant reverses could be viewed as great disasters. Thus, with such attitudes to reporting in mind, Archibald Forbes' copy for the *Daily News* on the aftermath of the Battle of Isandlwana can be viewed as striking.

> In all the seven campaigns I have been in ... I have not witnessed a scene more horrible. I have seen the dead and dying on a battlefield by hundreds and thousands; but to come suddenly on the spot where the slaughtered battalion of the 24th Regiment and others were lying at Isandlwana, was far more appalling. Here I saw not the bodies, but the skeletons, of men whom I had known in life and health, some of whom I had known well, mixed up with the skeletons of oxen and horses, and with wagons thrown on their side, all in the greatest confusion, showing how furious had been the onslaught of the enemy. Scattered over the field of carnage were letters from wives or parents at home to their husbands or sons in the field, & portraits of babies and children sent by mothers to loving fathers – one was signed 'dear darling Dadda.' I could not help the tears coming into my eyes.[34]

Such a poignant newspaper report was unusual. Editors generally assumed that their readers did not want to read of defeat, disaster or hardship, but of bravery, fortitude and success. Thus the reading public, particularly those who had no relative serving in the forces, were given a false impression of the realities of colonial campaigning.

So who were these Victorian 'Soldiers of the Queen' who journeyed to distant lands to fight for Queen and Country? Well just as the soldier became gradually more literate as the century progressed, so the composition of the Army altered throughout the Victorian period, as did its size. When Victoria came to the throne in 1837, the British Army was roughly 100,000 strong and was principally composed of infantry line regiments, three Guards regiments, the cavalry, artillery and engineers. More than half this number were to be found overseas, where the troops garrisoned various parts of the expanding Empire. By 1840, of the hundred infantry battalions in the Army, only twenty were to be found in Britain, as the rest were stationed in the colonies. So stretched were the battalions that Victoria's first government, headed by Lord Melbourne, was forced to propose an increase in the Army's strength to 120,000 when it introduced the Army Estimates in 1840. By 1859, with the threat of war with France a possibility and forces still mopping up opposition in India, the Army's strength had risen to 237,000, with 130 infantry battalions, of which 50 were to be found in India, 37 in other colonies such as South Africa, and 44 at home.[35]

By 1890, the Army had reached a size of 201,848 non-commissioned officers and men, with an addition of 54,136 men in the 1st Class Army Reserve. The combined figures represented 1.4% of the total male population under arms, and this percentage was never to exceed 1.6% throughout Victoria's reign.[36] The scale of commitment the Empire imposed upon Britain's Victorian Army meant that any infantry ranker could expect several years of his service to be overseas, either on garrison duty or on active campaign.

In 1830 more than half of the rankers derived from the 'Celtic Fringe' (42.2% Irish, 13.5% Scottish), but by the end of the century this demographic imbalance had been eliminated. In 1890 only 14.2% of the men in the army were Irish, just slightly above their 12.5% representation in the UK as a whole; Scots made up 8% of the army compared with 10.5% of the entire population.[37] The reasons for this change in the composition of the army are many and varied. Irish enlistment declined significantly after the Irish Potato Famine of 1846, both because of the mortality the famine inflicted on the population, and also due to the large scale emigration from Ireland, primarily to the United States. Over 5,500,000 Irish emigrated to America between 1846 and 1911, including many young men who would have otherwise enlisted in the British Army. In contrast, Scotland never provided as many soldiers as Ireland and her proportion of the total fell steadily throughout Victoria's reign. By 1879, 7.7% of the Army came from Scotland, despite the Scots comprising 15.4% of the total British population.[38]

By the 1870s the pattern of recruitment from Scotland had undergone considerable change. In 1878, of the nineteen nominally Scottish regiments, only the 42nd, 79th and 92nd Highlanders were able to claim that over 60% of their officers and men were recruited from Scotland. Five other Scottish regiments, the 1st, 25th, 73rd, 75th and 99th, recruited less than 15% of its non-commissioned officers and ranks from Scotland. H.J. Hanham has argued that emigration to America – particularly from the eastern and northern Highlands – and competition from better paid industrial employment, led to recruitment difficulties in Scotland.[39] Although the strong traditions and illustrated histories of the Highland regiments guaranteed that the bagpipe playing, kilt-wearing Highland soldier remained very much a battlefield reality from the Alma (20 September 1854) to Dargai Heights (20 October 1897), many artists such as Robert Gibb and war correspondents like Bennett Burleigh ensured that their battlefield achievements would reach almost mythical status.

The shortfall in recruitment from Ireland and Scotland was partly met by a corresponding increase in the number of rankers recruited from urban England. Whilst both officers and non-commissioned officers claimed that the rural recruits were to be praised for their strength and health as compared to those found in city slums, and that they were more malleable and obedient than their urban counterparts, the century witnessed a slump in the number of rural recruits. This no doubt reflected the rapid urbanisation of Britain throughout the nineteenth century, which saw tens of thousands of rural workers leave the land to find work in industrial cities. By 1860 former rural workers comprised 15.5% of the total army strength of 202,508 men, whereas industrial workers, by definition from urban areas, made up 37.6% of the total.[40] In his attempts to localise recruitment, the Secretary of State for War, Edward Cardwell, no doubt hoped to attract more of the rural population to the colours, yet the Army was trying to focus on a depleting resource and by the 1870s was forced to concentrate its recruitment drives in urban areas.

To meet the needs of expanding commitments, with a corresponding fall in recruitment from rural areas, Ireland and Scotland, the Army was forced to turn to the industrial towns of the Midlands and the North, as well as London. Throughout the century recruitment failed to meet the demands placed upon the Army, and it was repeatedly forced to lower its physical standards in an attempt to reach its recruitment targets. The height restrictions for infantry recruits was altered sixteen times between 1820 and 1859 and after 1861, when it reached 5 feet 8 inches, it declined steadily until 1900, when it was a mere 5 feet 3 inches.[41] Until 1871, the minimum age for enlistment was seventeen, rising to eighteen in that year, and the maximum 25, but as recruitment shortages continued the War Office resorted to 'special enlistments'. By this measure boys were enlisted who were considered likely to make efficient soldiers, despite the fact that they had failed to meet the minimum age or height. By the 1890s, over 30% of recruits were classified as 'special enlistments', in that they were either underage or underdeveloped teenagers.[42] By 1898 the percentage of the Regular Army who were under eighteen years of age had risen to nearly 50%, from 34% in 1861, and the percentage 5 feet 5 inches or less had risen to 35% from 21% in 1861. At the other end of the scale, the percentage of soldiers over twenty years of age had decreased from nearly 40% in 1861 to under 20% in 1898, and the percentage over 5 feet 6 inches had fallen from nearly 80% in 1861 to 65% in 1898.[43] Thus there was a significant increase in the proportion of younger, lighter and smaller recruits towards the end of Victoria's reign.

Although the size and composition of the army altered throughout the nineteenth century, the reasons for a man to enlist changed little. The most frequently quoted reason for a man to join up was commonly believed to be economic necessity. In 1865 Brigadier-General George Campbell, a commander at Aldershot, stated that 'men who have no option left them go into the army'.[44] However, although numerous Royal Commissions on the recruitment issue voiced the belief that the number of new recruits swelled when unemployment was high and fell in times of economic prosperity, there is no direct statistical evidence to support these assumptions, only conjecture and the words of rankers who testified at recruitment Commissions. The Army did require that every new recruit state his last employment before he signed up, yet it did not enquire whether the new soldier was employed at that time. From the information that was recorded, it is clear that the vast majority of recruits classed themselves as labourers. In 1862, of the total number of recruits in that year, 52.8% considered that they had been labourers before enlistment, and this rose to 65.7% in 1898.[45] A more detailed breakdown of the occupation before enlistment of men serving with the British Army in 1860 showed that, as we have already discussed, the highest percentage, 37.6%, thought of themselves as 'industrial workers', with 15.5% as 'rural workers.' Other significant occupations included 'semiskilled tradesmen' at 14.8% and 'domestic workers' at 6.3%.[46] This confirms that the Army drew the majority of its recruits from the ranks of the labouring and semiskilled workforce, precisely those groups which would have been most susceptible to periods of economic downturn and unemployment.

Those rankers who gave evidence at the various Recruitment Commissions that were convened throughout the nineteenth century gave anecdotal evidence as to the reasons behind their enlistment which seems to confirm that economic necessity was a strong reason to join up. Sergeant Taffs, who served in a number of campaigns from the Crimea onwards, claimed in his memoirs that it was clear unemployment was the main driving force behind recruitment. 'I found myself by force of circumstances, starving in the streets of London, and determined to tramp to Chatham and enlist as a soldier.'[47] Robert Blatchford claimed that his penniless and unemployed state forced him towards the recruiting sergeant in 1871.[48] Sergeant Robert Edmondson claimed that by the end of the nineteenth century up to 80% of the British Army was drawn from the unemployed and he stated that 'empty pockets and hungry stomachs are the most eloquent and persuasive of recruiting sergeants'.[49]

While it is evident that unemployment did force many unskilled men into the Army, this is not the complete picture of recruitment. Throughout the Victorian period the Army continually struggled to meet its manpower requirement despite high levels of unemployment. Between 1859 and 1888 the largest number of recruits in any one year was just under 40,000 men, yet during this period there were never fewer than 745,000 paupers in any particular year.[50] Although it is true that many men in this figure would have been too old or unfit for army service, it is also true that there existed a vast number of men that the Army simply failed to attract. Despite the harsh situations that many of these paupers must have experienced, their hardship could still not force them to join, for the poor pay, the low esteem in which the

Army was held by society and the conditions of service were enough to deter many.

Some recruits used the Army as a place of refuge to escape from domestic circumstances. Once in the ranks, the soldier could not be arrested for leaving his wife and children at the mercy of the parish, or for debts under £20. Others escaped the boredom of menial occupations or the sameness of their civilian lives. Many joined up simply on a whim, or for the opportunity to travel, and even for the glamour that the newspaper writers told them that they could expect on colonial service. There was also a large number of men who enlisted to be with family or friends in the ranks, or who had relatives that had previously served. Boy soldiers who had been schooled at the Royal Military Asylum and the Royal Hibernian Military School would have been more willing recruits. The reasons for enlistment were many and varied and, whether the new recruit was indeed unemployed on signing up, it can be said that the majority of those in the ranks of the Victorian Army came from a background of manual labouring and, as a result, they would not have been natural letter writers, as the known literacy rates seem to confirm. That so many letters written by Victorian soldiers survive is remarkable.

The reforms introduced by the Gladstone government of 1868–74, and in particular the work of Edward Cardwell, the Secretary for War, had the most far-reaching impact on the composition of the Victorian army. In his reforms, Cardwell established the 'linked battalion' system. This reform rearranged regiments according to geographical districts, so that volunteers would serve in units in which the same dialect was spoken. British regiments developed a peculiar family atmosphere, which offered support to all, so that a man posted from one battalion to another found himself in an equally familiar background. Lord Wolseley, commander-in-chief of the British Army from 1895, wrote that to the rank and file 'the Regiment is mother and sister and mistress … That its fame may live and flourish he is prepared to risk all and die without a murmur. To the soldier, the Regiment is his country.'[51] This particular love of regiment, and the comrades who served alongside, was to carrying the British Army through many hardships and conflicts in both the nineteenth and twentieth centuries.

Furthermore, Cardwell introduced a system of short-term enlistments, designed to provide Britain with an army of young professional soldiers who would serve for a limited number of years and then return to civilian life, settle down to a trade and spend additional time in the reserves. Although these changes can be overplayed, and due consideration must be given to social changes in society such as urbanisation, which had an impact upon recruitment, there is no doubt that the one-time army of Irish or Scots and elderly worn-out men evolved out of all recognition, although improvements in education were somewhat slow to be realised. The average British soldier came to be a tough volunteer serving on a short-term contract, supported by a regular army reserve, youthful, well trained, and capable of being instantly called to the colours. This was important as the Army was designed primarily for 'imperial policing' – for fighting small wars and minor campaigns on the frontiers of the ever-expanding Empire.

A tour of any American Civil War battlefield will encompass a number of specific monuments, whether they show the direction of a particular charge, or the placement of the artillery on the day of the battle, or even where an individual fell. The battle site of Gettysburg (1–3 July 1863) is a fine example over which the tourist or historian can walk across mowed, even manicured, fields to view General George Pickett's charge at the Union Army centre, or see the spot where a Confederate sharpshooter shot dead General John Reynolds. Furthermore, by journeying across small town America, the traveller will see numerous statues to specific regiments of men who left their town or county to fight in the Civil War. The care such monuments receive today – over one hundred years after they were first erected – is a clear testament to how important the Civil War still is to American culture and the country's sense of itself. Yet, writing at the time, Walt Whitman, in describing the National Monument erected to the 12,100 men buried at Salisbury, North Carolina, questioned whether any 'visible, material monument can ever fittingly commemorate the spot'.[52]

In contrast, most of the monuments that are seen today in Britain are not to those soldiers who fought in nineteenth century colonial wars, but to those that lost their lives in the conflicts of both the First and Second World Wars. Whilst plaques to commemorate battles or regiments can be viewed in many of England's provincial cathedrals, often demonstrating a county association with a regiment, for example the memorial to those soldiers of the 13th (Somerset) Light Infantry who fought in the Zulu War which is to be found in Wells Cathedral, monuments to colonial wars are rare. One impressive exception is the Maiwand Lion in the Forbury Gardens in Reading, Berkshire, the base of which lists the names of 328 officers and men of the 66th (Berkshire) Regiment who lost their lives in Afghanistan, particularly at the Battle of Maiwand (27 July 1880). Another commemorative exception is the obelisk to the men of the 24th Regiment who fell at the Battle of Chillianwallah, 13 January 1849, during the Second Sikh War, and which can still be seen in Chelsea Royal Hospital Gardens. More generic monuments to specific regiments are more common. These include the Cameron Monument which was unveiled in Inverness in 1893 and the memorial cairn to the Black Watch at Aberfeldy. When, in 1887, the Marquis of Breadalbane unveiled the 35-foot-high cairn, surmounted by a life-size figure of a fighting Highlander, he described it as a means to inspire young men to serve in such a distinguished regiment.[53]

It was not until the Boer War (1899–1902) that the use of statues or plaques became more widespread across the country and that the names of individuals who fell in a colonial war were recorded. Towns as geographically widespread as Penzance in Cornwall and Girvan in Ayrshire have statues and crosses listing the names of those inhabitants of the various towns who died serving in South Africa. Most were erected between 1902–1906, and some, such as the memorial in the Morrab Gardens in Penzance, have had to be refaced or re-erected following serious damage by vandals in recent years.

The battlefields of Victorian conquest are to be found in distant lands and although some sites are marked with monuments to the fallen, such as Ulundi (4 July 1879) and Isandlwana, many, particularly those of the early Sikh wars, have become overgrown, neglected or even forgotten. In addition, while it is possible for comrades and relatives of soldiers who fell in France, Belgium and Holland in the twentieth century to visit these countries to view the immaculately kept cemeteries and monuments, this was never an option for the grieving widow of a British ranker who fell in South Africa or Afghanistan in the nineteenth century. Thus the memorials for those who fought in Victoria's wars are hard to find. No better monument now exists than the words the soldiers recorded in their letters and diaries, and which have left us with a vivid picture of their experiences.

Their writings reveal to us today that these soldiers were vulnerable, that they were often scared, lonely and homesick, but were also hardworking, resolute and brave. Their writings display all the characteristics of human nature and demonstrate that they were not very different to us. In his last letter home to his mother before his death in the Crimea, Arnold William of the Royal Artillery wrote,' I hope and pray to God that we may all live to see each other again and that soon, so in case that this should be my last letter let me beg of you not to cry for me, and now I bid you all Goodbye and may God Bless you.'[54] Not only do we gain an understanding of what Arnold William thought and experienced as a 'Soldier of the Queen', but his letters, and those of the other soldiers that are quoted in this book, function as a memorial to those who served in Victoria's armed forces.

Notes

1. P. Boyden, A. Guy, M. Harding, *'Ashes and Blood': The British Army in South Africa 1795–1914*, (NAM, London, 1999), p.131.
2. D. Featherstone, *Khaki & Red: Soldiers of the Queen in India and Africa*, (Arms & Armour Press, London, 1995), p.21.
3. Ibid.
4. A. Skelley, *The Victorian Army at Home: The Recruitment and Terms and Conditions of the British Regular, 1859–1899*, (Croom Helm, London, 1977), pp.89–90.
5. E. Spiers, *The Victorian Soldier in Africa*, (Manchester University Press, 2004), p.3.
6. A. Skelley, p.98.
7. Diary of George Milman, RA, 30 December 1854, REF: RAM MD 2697.
8. F. Emery, *Marching Over Africa: Letters from Victorian Soldiers*, (Hodder & Stoughton, London, 1986), p.54.
9. E. Spiers, p.4.
10. Pvt. J. Davies, letter to his brother, Richard, 9 November 1880, REF: NAM 9309-98-5.
11. T. Pakenham, *The Boer War*, (Weidenfeld & Nicolson, London, 1979), p.376.
12. E. Spiers, p.3.
13. Brig.-General F.P. Cozier, *Impressions & Recollections*, (T. Werner Laurie Ltd, London, 1930), p.25.
14. William Fitzwilliam Eliot, letter to his brother Arthur, from Ulundi Camp, 18 August 1879, REF: ASHM N-C93-ELL.

15. Pope-Hennessy Papers, REF: NAM 7610-7.
16. Lance-Corporal William Eaton, letter to brother and sister, 22 May 1880, REF: NAM 1992-04-115-4.
17. Diary of Pvt. W. Milton, 19 June 1900, REF:NAM 2006-04-09.
18. Lance-Corporal William Eaton, letter to brother and sister, 25 June 1880, REF: NAM 1992-04-115-5.
19. Pvt. S. Clunie, letter to sister, 1 August1843, REF:NAM 2002-07-12-3.
20. Ensign C. Bourne to mother, 8 September 1845, REF:NAM 2004-10-81.
21. E. Spiers, *The Scottish Soldier and Empire, 1854–1902*, (Edinburgh University Press, 2006), p.67.
22. Arnold William, letter to mother, 20 February 1855, REF RAM MD/2816.
23. L. James, *The Savage Wars: British Campaigns in Africa, 1870–1920*, (Robert Hale, London, 1985), p.171.
24. P. Harrington & F. Sharf (eds.), *Omdurman 1898: The eye-witnesses speak*, (Greenhill Books, London, 1998), p.67.
25. Diary of Capt. John Charles Ramsden, REF: RAM MD 1185.
26. Capt. H.M. Paget, letter to wife, 14 May 1884, REF: NAM 8811-28.
27. Lance-Corporal William Eaton, letter to brother and sister, 10 April 1880, REF:NAM 1992-04-115-1.
28. F. Emery, p.150.
29. S. Manning, 'Private Snook and Total War', *Journal of the Anglo-Zulu War Historical Society*, XIII, June 2003, pp.22–26.
30. Unpublished PhD, University of Exeter, 2005, S. Manning, 'Foreign News Gathering and Reporting in the London and Devon Press: The Anglo-Zulu War, 1879, A Case Study', p. 88.
31. Ibid, p.89.
32. Ibid, p.86.
33. H. Brackenbury, *The Ashanti War of 1873–4*, (Frank Cass, London, New Impression, 1968).
34. S. David, *Zulu*, (Viking, London, 2004), p.306.
35. J. Strawson, *Beggars in Red: The British Army 1789–1889*, (Pen & Sword, Barnsley, 2003), pp. 136 & 181.
36. E. Spiers, *The Army and Society 1815–1914*, (Longman, London, 1980), p.36.
37. L.H. Gann & P. Duignan, *The Rulers of British Africa, 1870–1914*, (Croom Helm, London, 1978), p.79.
38. E. Spiers, *The Army and Society*, pp.48–49.

39. H.J. Hanham, 'Religion and Nationality in the Mid-Victorian Army', in M.R.D. Foot (ed.), *War and Society: Historical Essays in Honour and Memory of J.R. Western 1928–1971*, (London, Paul Elek, 1973), pp.159–81.

40. Report of the Army Medical Department, P.P., XXIV (c3233), 1863, p.35, From A. Skelley, p.296.

41. E. Spiers, *The Army and Society*, p.40.

42. Report of the Inspector General of Recruiting, P.P.,C.6,597, 1892, XX, p.5, From E. Spiers, *The Army and Society*, p.40.

43. Annual Report of the Army Medical Department, P.P.1899, From A. Skelley, p.283.

44. Report of the Commission on Recruiting (1867), p.39, From A. Skelley, p. 248.

45. Annual Reports of the Army Medical Department, From A. Skelley, p.297.

46. Report of the Army Medical Department, P.P., XXIV (c3233), 1863, p.35, From A. Skelley, p.296.

47. E.M. Small, (ed.), *Told from the Ranks*, (Andrew Melrose, London, 1897), p.87.

48. R. Blatchford, *My Life in the Army*, (Clarendon Press, Oxford, circa 1870), pp.11–12.

49. R. Edmondson, *Is a Soldier's Life Worth Living?* (Twentieth Century Press, London, 1902), p.5.

50. E. Spiers, *The Army and Society*, p.45.

51. J. Duncan & J. Walton, *Heroes for Victoria*, (Spellmount, Tunbridge Wells, 1991), p.25.

52. W. Whitman, *Memoranda During the War*, (Oxford University Press, 2004), p.103.

53. E. Spiers, *The Scottish Soldier and Empire*, p.112.

54. Arnold William, letter to mother, 17 April 1855, REF RAM MD/2816.

CHAPTER TWO

THE JOURNEY TO WAR

At the time of her accession in 1837, Queen Victoria's army was involved in a number of colonial wars. The Sixth Cape Frontier War, in South Africa, had just been brought to an unsatisfactory conclusion, which would ensure that further conflict would be inevitable; tension in New Zealand between the Maoris and British settlers would see the engagement of British soldiers there, whilst a revolt amongst French settlers in Canada had broken out against British rule. Trouble on the North West Frontier in India would soon see the disastrous deployment of troops into Afghanistan. The beginning of the new reign was just the start of an almost continuous and seemingly endless series of conflicts across the world as the 'Soldiers of the Queen' were dispatched to calm trouble-spots or expand the Empire.

There were very few years during Victoria's reign in which British troops were not engaged in conflict in some part of the world. To the readers of Victorian newspapers, colonial warfare must have seemed like a seasonal occurrence. Whether the soldiers were required in the Crimea, India, Burma, New Zealand, Canada, Egypt or South Africa, they would have to be transported there. This meant lengthy periods of sea passage during which the men would have to endure both the perils of nineteenth-century ocean transfers and intense periods of boredom, as well as generally appalling conditions on board the troop-ships. Added to this was the even greater discomfort that would have to be endured when troops were carried on coastal transport vessels, most of which were completely unsuitable for such work, along and around the coasts of South Africa, India and China. In addition, the long months of a sea voyage eroded the period of time a soldier could expect on home service.

On numerous occasions, thousands of British troops had to be efficiently and speedily transported to various conflicts from Britain, as well as from India, and even South Africa. For example, the Second China War of 1860 saw the deployment of 14,000 men, with the bulk of the expeditionary force coming from India, although some troops were sent from England and South Africa. Around three-quarters of the force were British, including a Naval Brigade, and the rest were Native Indian troops.[1] The Ashanti War of 1873–4 was a much smaller affair, with only 3,500 troops involved. Half the contingent was despatched from England, the rest came from West Indian regiments and locally raised native troops.

The British commander of the force, Garnet Wolseley, and his special service officers, who included Evelyn Wood, Redvers Buller and Henry Brackenbury, boarded the steamer *Ambriz* at Liverpool on 12 September 1873 and all must have viewed the troopship in horror. Wolseley described her as 'the most abominable and unhealthy craft I ever made a voyage in'.[2] Wood described her as hardly seaworthy and stated that on more than one occasion he thought the ship would capsize in the heavy seas.[3] Henry Brackenbury was to write that the cabin floor oozed with bilge-water, the whole ship reeked of foul smells and that the discomforts suffered during the voyage in the Bay of Biscay exceeded any that the campaign itself inflicted.[4] Later in his long army career, Evelyn Wood would take great personal satisfaction when, in 1895, as Quartermaster General, he was able to authorise the scrapping of the most notorious troop steamers, such as the *Ambriz*, for which act he received much praise from Wolseley.[5]

In contrast to the Ashanti War, the Egypt Campaign of 1882 saw the despatch of 24,000 troops from England and a further 7,000 from India. Wolseley was again in command of British forces and the scale of the deployment can be measured by the fact that 71 transport ships were employed to ferry the troops from England and a further 54 were used to bring contingents of the Indian army.[6]

Even the scale of the routine movements of troops across the Empire was immense. For much of the Victorian period, Portsmouth was the principal port for troop embarkation and arrival and it was here, from

1860 until 1894, that the Royal Navy operated its five-strong transport fleet for the Indian Troop Service. From September 1868 to March 1869 the Service carried approximately 24,000 officers and men to and from India.[7]

For those British troops who were sent to fight in Iraq in 2002, the journey to war was at least of a comparatively short duration, compared to that of the Victorian soldier. One infantry officer, quoted in Richard Holmes' *Dusty Warriors*, described how

> The 'movers' of both services [RAF & Army] combine to make it the most painful, drawn-out and seemingly badly run affair. They have done so consistently throughout my time in the army and our move to Iraq was to prove no exception. Despite our base at Tidworth being little more than an hour away from the airfield ... we were to move there at least twelve hours prior to our flight. The reason for this was not explained to me or my staff. I still do not understand it to this day. Having taken our farewells of our families – in some cases tearfully – we sat at Brize Norton [RAF airfield] while nothing happened for hour upon hour.

Similarly, Major Chris James told of 'a quite dreadful thirty hours (when I got here it turns out thirty hours was a good run – others had much longer) travelling nightmare, courtesy of the RAF'.[8] In addition, the food given to the troops during the journey received some criticism. Major James Coote described a coach transfer to his forward base in Iraq during which he 'tucked into my packed lunch which comprised exactly the same sausage roll and inedible fruitcake that we get in the UK, no doubt specially flown in on a 747. I was amazed to see that the army had managed to produce sausage rolls in the middle of the desert that were still frozen. How do they do it?'[9]

Whilst the modern-day British soldier and his Victorian counterpart share the same ability to moan at their lot, the British soldier of today is designed to be part of a 'rapid reaction force' who can be flown promptly into the war zone, whereas the Victorians journeyed to war by sea, usually for weeks at a time. The transfer of troops was of course at its most tedious length on the journey from Britain to India. At the beginning of Victoria's reign the East Indiamen boats were taking anything between four and six months on the passage from England to

Bombay, via the Cape of Good Hope. As well as the time wasted while the troops were in transit, a reply to any correspondence could take up to a year. This was clearly no way to administer an Empire. In 1836, with the intention of improving transit times, the East India Company decided to acquire a steam fleet. The first to be sent out from England in 1837 was the *Atalanta*, of 617 tons, and she was followed three months later by the *Berenice* of 765 tons. These vessels had a dual function for they were a mixture of passenger ship and warship and from the following account concerning the *Berenice*, they do not seem to have been successful at either.

> the cabins were small and miserable, cockroaches abounded. Washing had to be done in a public room. Each passenger was expected to fit up his own stateroom ... sleeping accommodation consisted of a mattress placed on some trunks or boxes, while many slept on tables and benches. The rooms were hot and smelly, and servants lazy and indolent. Food was served in the common saloon, which also served the purpose of toilet room and lounge for both sexes. Piles of coal soot invaded everything.[10]

A typical early Army contract required the British India Steam Company (B&I) to 'provide and allow, free of freight under the hatches of the said vessel, clear of the 'tween decks, sufficient space for the baggage, arms and accoutrements, regimental and mess stores, according to the scale laid down by Her Majesty's regulations.' Beer and porter were to be supplied on a stated ration scale for the troops and their wives, whilst those who regarded such tipple as insipid stuff were allowed to consume rum instead. From the fourteenth day after embarkation until the end of the voyage, scurvy was to be averted by the daily issue of lime or lemon juice, water had to be available on a scale of one gallon per man per day for a period of twenty weeks, but this was to include washing as well as drinking. The ration of a married private soldier with his wife included three pounds of fresh beef or mutton a day 'with vegetables and oatmeal for the soup'. There was no stated scale of rations for officers' families, but it was stipulated that the messing of officers' wives and children over the age of sixteen was not to cost more than £40 for a voyage of 120 days.[11]

Alive to the commercial possibilities of providing a reliable service to India, and one that offered a higher degree of comfort than the East India Company vessels, the Peninsular Steam Navigation Company, later P&O, announced a new service in 1837. This offered steamship transfer from Falmouth to Vigo, Oporto, Lisbon, Cadiz, Gibraltar, Malta, Greece, the Ionian Isles, Egypt and India. The service left London on the 1st and 29th of each month, with passengers embarking on the Peninsular Company's steamships to Gibraltar, then continuing by Admiralty steamer to Alexandria via Malta. Egypt was crossed overland in two-wheeled horse-drawn vehicles and the sea voyage was then continued from Suez to Bombay in an East India Company ship.

The success of this service encouraged the Peninsular Company to commission the 2,000-ton steamship *Hindostan*, the largest ship of its time, so as to remove the reliance on the East India Company between Suez and Bombay. The design of the ship was revolutionary, with cabins located along the centre of the ship, thereby providing passengers with some relief from the effects of the rolling of the ship and the layout gave them some protection from the excessive heat experienced on the way. The maiden voyage from Southampton to Calcutta on 24 September 1842 experienced some teething problems when the ship ran out of coal in transit and took 91 days as a result. Subsequent sailings improved upon this time.[12] However, by the 1890s, even after the Suez Canal was opened in 1869, journeys to India still took three to four weeks.

In 1850, sailing ships were still in the majority by far, outnumbering steamships by about twenty to one both in quantity and tonnage, and the ratio of cargo capacity was even more in their favour, owing to the absence of engines and fuel. The 10th Hussars went out to India in 1846 by sailing ship. The regiment was stationed at Canterbury when it received orders to embark at Gravesend. On 30 April the first detachment, consisting of C & D troops, marched the eight miles to Herne Bay, where they were taken in steamers to Gravesend, from where they embarked in the *Brahmin*. On 5 May the regimental HQ, plus A, B, E & H troops, followed and embarked on the *Larkins*. The remaining two troops, F & G, followed on 7 May on board the *Persia*. Thus, by 8 May, the whole regiment was on its way to India. The *Persia* was actually the first to reach Bombay, arriving on 21 August, but all arrived by the 28th, a journey time of just under four months.[13]

Conditions, and the speed of voyages, generally improved throughout the nineteenth century and these improvements had been accelerated by the need to move large numbers of men during the Crimean War.

There was no shortage of potential troopships, for most of the early steamship companies had been subsidised by the government on condition that their ships were made available for military use at a low charge in time of war. There were also some larger sailing ships available which had been built to carry emigrants out to Australia during the gold rush, and these made good, roomy transports, which could be towed by steamships if necessary.[14] After the Battle of Balaclava (25 October 1854), Britain's French ally expressed a willingness to send another 20,000 troops, as long as British could supply the transport. However, the Foreign Secretary, the Earl of Clarendon, declared that the British could not spare even one steamer. Horrified by this predicament, the Queen herself offered the use of the Royal steam yacht to transport 1,000 men. The government declined this offer.[15] To ease the problem, the government purchased the *Himalaya* from P&O for £130,000, eleven other P&O ships were taken as transports. The company carried 62,000 officers and men during the war, together with 15,000 horses and a large quantity of military stores. The temporary loss of these ships, however, led to a drastic cut in the mail services, and those to Australia had to be suspended altogether.[16]

In 1858, as a result of difficulties experienced in the Crimea, it was suggested by Rowley Richardson of the Admiralty that the somewhat haphazard troop transport arrangements should be replaced by a regular service of troopships. It took until 1863 for final government approval, when the Navy was instructed to build and operate five steamships on behalf of the Indian government, which should be specially designed for trooping. The ships, built in 1866, were named *Crocodile*, *Euphrates*, *Jumna*, *Malabar* and *Serapis* and all were painted in the colours that distinguished troopships until the end of their day: white with a red ribbon round the hull and a yellow funnel; the ribbon colour varied from ship to ship. Each was designed to accommodate a full battalion of infantry with married families, or about 1,200 persons. The dimensions were such that they could pass through the Suez Canal, which was then under construction. Troop quarters were unattractive – below the water line, ill-ventilated and were soon christened 'pandemonium'. Most of the cabins were on the deck below the saloon. It was called the 'horsebox' deck because the cabins – each of which was supposed to accommodate three persons – were alleged to be no larger than railway horseboxes. The portion of this deck allotted to unmarried women and those without children was known as the 'dovecot'. Married ladies with children were in the 'nursery', a large cabin on the port side which opened off the saloon. Bullocks for slaughter, cows for milk, sheep and assorted fowl were stowed in any convenient place on the upper and main decks, in many cases close to the passengers' cabins. NCOs and men had a free daily issue of a dram of rum – officers also had a daily liquor issue, but they had to pay for it, whether they drank it or not.[17]

Before the opening of the Suez Canal the *Serapis* and the *Crocodile* ran between England and Alexandria, and the other three operated the service between Suez and Bombay. The *Crocodile* was particularly popular with the rank and file in the early days as she had a reputation for providing good food. The *Jumna* was the least liked as she was always having engine trouble. On 6 February 1884, the engines of the *Jumna* worked well enough, for she carried the 10th Royal Hussars from Bombay to Suakin in Egypt, together with M battery, 1st Royal Artillery and the 2nd Battalion of the Royal Irish Fusiliers. They arrived at Suakin on 18 February 1884.[18] The five troopships were in service for 30 years and in this time they conveyed tens of thousands of troops between England and India.

A mere five ships could not meet all the Empire's requirements for moving men and supplies across the world and the government continued to rely heavily on commercial shipping companies. Several famous lines competed for lucrative contracts: both the Bibby Line and B.I. (British India Steam Navigation Co.) became specialised troopship lines, whilst the ships of the Union and Castle lines fought for government troop movement contracts, as well as for the mail service between London and South Africa. Along with P&O, these shipping lines virtually monopolised regular troop movements across the Empire.

It was during periods of conflict – when additional troops had to be moved rapidly and at short notice to far-flung war zones – that the private shipping companies really demonstrated their value. It was in times of such crisis that the lines were also able to increase both their revenues and their profits. During the British Expedition to Abyssinia of 1867, nine B.I. vessels were chartered by the government to transport troops from India to the east coast of Africa. The ships not only carried troops, but all towed a sailing ship with additional supplies in their wake. Interestingly, three of the newer B.I. vessels utilised their engines to condense seawater into water fit for the consumption by both men and animals, at a rate of 30,000 gallons a day.[19] They were kept at this task for most of the campaign whilst the remaining six ships continued to convey men and supplies from India. A further six troopships were supplied by P&O and all were later used to condense seawater and over the duration of the campaign, these ships contributed 500,000 gallons. The success of the service provided by B.I. certainly bolstered the government's high opinion of the company and, in 1869, after the opening of the Suez canal, the B.I.'s finest steamship, the *Dacca*, was accepted for trooping between England and India, against strong competition from P&O.[20]

The shipping lines of the Donald Currie Line and the Union Steam Shipping Company – which in 1877 began a joint seven-year contract sharing the mail service between London, Cape Town and Natal – were both asked to supply additional shipping for the transportation of troops during the Anglo-Zulu War of 1879, and the extra passenger numbers, whether of military wives, administrators, or war correspondents, certainly increased their revenues. The Union Line's mail steamer *Pretoria* was converted into a troopship and sailed within nine days of the news of Isandlwana reaching London, with reinforcements from the 91st Highlanders.[21] Although no profit and loss accounts are to be found in the uncatalogued records of the Union Line held in the Royal Maritime Museum at Greenwich, two ledger books exist and they supply a detailed break down of the various voyages from Plymouth to Cape Town during the years 1876–1881. From these books it can be seen that in the months from 1 January 1879 to 1 February 1880 the Union Line made a very considerable profit from all its troopship sailings of £84,487.[22]

The First Boer War of 1881 brought a miscellaneous collection of ships to South Africa. The first reinforcements arrived in the *Calabria* of the Cunard Line, the *Hankow*, the *Lapland* and the *Balmoral Castle*, all of which had been requisitioned by the government as troopships.[23] The B.I. Line provided only one vessel during the Zulu War, but 22 of its ships were used to carry troops and stores in the Egyptian Expedition of 1882 and 29 were used in the Suakim campaign three years later. Also in that year the government chartered another ten B.I. ships to move troops for the 3rd Burmese War. In 1900 39 were required to carry the British contingent to China, to save the British Legation in Peking during the Boxer Rebellion.[24] It was, however, the

Boer War that placed the greatest strain on the resources of the private shipping lines.

The Boer War was the first great conflict in which troop transport was undertaken entirely by engine-driven ships, and practically every major British shipping company contributed its quota – Union and Castle lines, P&O, B.I. and the Bibby Line. Even Cunard was there with the 7,000- to 8,000-ton ships *Servia*, *Umbria* and *Aurania*. Three of the Castle liners were requisitioned as soon as war broke out: the *Roslin Castle*, *Lismore Castle* and *Harlech Castle*. Other Castle ships joined them, including the new 9,600-ton *Kildonan Castle*, which was completed on the Clyde when war broke out and was rapidly converted to a troopship. The first troopships left Southampton on 20 October 1899; of these, the first to disembark troops in South Africa was the *Roslin Castle*, which transported a battalion of The Duke of Wellington Regiment. A fortnight later the *Kildonan Castle* arrived at Cape Town with about 3,000 troops, which is said to have constituted a record for the number of persons carried in one ship.[25] With British reversals in late 1899, many of these ships returned to England with casualties on board and the Union and Castle liner *Spartan* was converted into a hospital ship.

Throughout the duration of the war 37 B.I. ships were used exclusively for troop movements to South Africa and over the same period the nine larger P&O vessels carried 150,000 troops.[26] P&O had built three vessels, named *Assaye*, *Plassy* and *Sobraon*, as specialist troopships; these were the first to be so designed by a private company. They were twin-screw steamers of 7,400 tons, with triple-expansion engines and a speed of 16 knots. Those troops fortunate enough to sail in these ships were blessed with a high degree of comfort and utility. They were designed with wide decks, clear of obstructions, for the parade and exercise of troops, and were airy and relatively spacious.[27] In other words, they were much improved from the vessels that had been used as troopships throughout the nineteenth century.

The journey to war began with the departure from the home barracks, either by a march to the embarkation port, or, as the century progressed, to the nearest train station for a train to take the troops to the docks. During this initial stage of the journey, most accounts tell of the rapturous send-off given to the troops by the local population. On 30 May 1879 the Royal Marines boarded a Donald Currie Line vessel at Dartmouth for the voyage to South Africa and the local newspaper reported that the inhabitants of the town lined the waterfront, that a salute was fired from Dartmouth Castle as the ship departed and that the mayor led the inhabitants in singing *Auld Lang Syne*.[28] When, on 7 August 1882, the 1st Battalion of the Black Watch left its barracks in Edinburgh Castle for service in Egypt, the troops received a tumultuous send-off from the people of the city and Bandsman Barwood recorded that the men 'encountered surging, cheering crowds all along the route from the esplanade to Waverley station'.[29] Private Grant of the 1st Battalion the Buffs recorded in his diary of February 1887, at the beginning of the regiment's journey to India, that

> ... on the road to the station we were played to by the band and the people of Dover gave us a hearty cheer and a hearty farewell for a pleasant and safe voyage. All the way down from Dover to Portsmouth and at every station we stopped at parents were wishing their sons goodbye and sisters were crying for their brothers as they left the station and lookers on gave us ringing cheers.[30]

Lance-Corporal Rose, of the Duke of Cornwall's Light Infantry, wrote in his diary of 4 November 1899, 'Received orders 7.15 pm proceed to Station to embark for Royal Albert Docks. It was raining hard all the time but not withstanding the bad weather we had a splendid send off from the people of Plymouth and Devonport.'[31]

Similarly, Private Ernest Stanton of the Somerset Light Infantry captured in his diary the moment his regiment left their barracks to journey to the Boer War (1899–1902).

> A lot of boys marched in front of the regiment when proceeding to the Station singing most heartily 'Soldiers of the Queen'. All kinds of people were waiting at Portland Station to bid us farewell, workpeople turned out of their shops, and the men we left behind accompanied us to the Station. On our journey to Southampton, the Union Jacks were flying in all directions and everybody as they saw the train full of soldiers' coats would wave their hands as a sign of farewell.[32]

Private Lasby of the 2nd Battalion of the Devonshire Regiment, barracked in Exeter, also described the regiment's departure for the Boer War, on 19 October 1899.

Mr Lloyd of Exeter, the tobacconist, gave every man 2oz. of tobacco, and wished every man God speed out and a safe return to our homes again. We then marched through the Town of Exeter to the Station, the Band being in attendance and some lively tunes were played. The route to the Station was thronged with the inhabitants of Exeter who cheered us the whole way to the Station. We then entrained for Aldershot at 10 am amid great cheering from the crowds who were assembled there to witness our departure. The train moved slowly out of the Station, the Band playing the National Ode 'Auld Lang Syne', then we were soon out of sight of Exeter.[33]

For many soldiers, this first part of their journey to foreign service was the most memorable, for, despite the fact that troop voyages were so lengthy, there are surprisingly few surviving first-hand accounts of this experience. Perhaps, for the vast majority of soldiers the voyage was simply too long and too tedious for them to put pen to paper, but where accounts do survive they tell of a floating world that has fortunately long since disappeared. Although conditions on board Victorian troopships did improve throughout the nineteenth century, this improvement was from a very low starting point. Lieutenant Jary of the 12th Lancers described the regiment's journey from Liverpool to Cape Town on the 700-ton *Charlotte* to take part in the 1846 Kaffir wars. 'Cut a walnut in two and you have our lives exactly. No convict ship was worse. Food we had none and the water was poisonous.'[34] The journey had, apparently, not improved six years later when Private John Pine, of the Rifle Brigade, sailed to South Africa. In a letter to his father, Pine described the misery of the 89-day voyage on board the *Megara*. 'We had nearly nine hundred souls on board altogether and we were all packed as close as herrings. We were miserable enough in fine weather but a great deal more so in rough.'[35]

Naturally the weather could have a major impact on the transit times of troopship sailings to South Africa, India and beyond. Not only would a rough crossing of the Bay of Biscay or a journey around the Cape of Good Hope hinder the voyage, but it could also be extremely dangerous. Further delays could occur in the Indian Ocean when a sailing ship became becalmed in the doldrums, where the wind necessary to fill the sails could be lost for days or even weeks at a time. In a chronicle of his service in India with the 32nd Regiment of Foot,

Private Henry Metcalfe described the regiment's voyage from England to Calcutta in 1848.

> Landed in Calcutta on 3 November 1848 after a stormy voyage, being in a severe storm off the Cape of Good Hope on the 15th, 16th and 17th August, in which we were what sailors term battered between hatches without food or drink the whole of that time. We lost on that occasion two of our boats, the bulwarks stove in, our jib boom taken away, also our fore and main top masts, with their running and standing rigging. There was 2½ feet of water on the Troop deck.[36]

For old sea hands this must have been a frightening experience, but for the men of the 32nd, for many of whom this voyage would have been their first trip to sea, this journey must have been terrifying. Adverse weather would also jeopardise the ship's supply of fresh meat, for with the cramped conditions below deck, and for health reasons, livestock were carried as deck cargo. The B.I. ship *India*, caught in a cyclone in 1867, lost overboard 23 sheep, three goats, three kids, 10 geese, 48 pigeons, 54 ducks, 132 fowl, 10 buckets of potatoes and six buckets of onions.[37] Meal times must have been very bland onboard the *India* after this upset.

Captain Thomas Knox of the Royal Artillery recorded his experience of bad weather during a voyage to the Second China War in 1857.

> Then the ship gives a lurch that sends the soup from the plates on one side of the table into the faces of those on the opposite side! The Captain says 'Oh that is nothing, wait till we are off the Cape; the last ship I passed the Cape in winter in the deadlights (that is the outside shutters) of the cabin windows were stove in and the ship was flooded and we had to ram them with bedding and blankets!' All these little anecdotes are rather cheering when the rain is coming down, not in drops or even streams, but in a dense mass and we are told that it is a mere trifle![38]

The description of the weather and its effects during the voyage did, at least, give the troops something to record in their diaries, beyond the normal tedium of the trip. Colour Sergeant John McGrath of the 33rd Regiment wrote of the rough weather he had experienced during the voyage to India, via Mauritius.

First [was] in Bay of Biscay when a couple of coops was washed overboard containing live sheep and fowls. The other was rounding the Cape,
13th April 1857, when ropes had to be fastened along the deck so that
the sailors and soldiers on watch could do their work. had three days
and nights of a terrible storm. One sailor of 30 years experience said he
never was in such a storm. I was on watch on one of the nights and was
on sentry in the Engine room; my duty was to take charge of a lamp. I
had not been long on my post when she shiped a sea. It seemed to me
that her stern went under water, at any rate some tons of water came
down the hatchway, put my lamp out, flooded the officers' cabins and I
need not say there was a nasty sensation throughout the ship. I shall never
forget an officer whose cabin was just opposite the lamp I had charge of.
He rushed out of his cabin in his night shirt, made for me as best he could
in the dark, and just as he was approaching the ship gave a lurch and we
were thrown into each other's arms, I treading heavily on his toes; I will
not mention here what he said but he certainly did not say his prayers.[39]

All the men that journeyed with McGrath would have heard of the
fate of the troopship *Birkenhead*, which, on 25 February 1852 sank off
Danger Point on the coastline of South Africa between Port Elizabeth
and Natal. Of the 648 persons on board, including troops of 60th, 73rd,
74th regiments and the 12th Lancers, who were destined for the Kaffir
War, only 193 were saved. When the ship struck the rocks the men were
ordered on deck in parade order, whilst the women and children were
placed in the only three boats available for evacuation and of these one
fell into the sea as its ropes snapped as it was being lowered, drowning
all in the boat. Another boat was found to be rusted into position and
could not be lowered, a situation which reflected the low level of main-
tenance on board troopships at this time. It was later reported that the
troops remained at their post as the ship broke in two and sank.[40] The
name *Birkenhead* became synonymous with bravery and duty. However,
for those troops who had subsequently to journey in troopships it must
have reminded them all too clearly of the dangers of sea voyages.

The dangers of bad weather were not simply restricted to sailing
ships for if the engines failed on board a steam-powered troopship the
men onboard could expect an uncomfortable time. Such was the experience of an unknown private of the Devonshire Regiment who sailed
with his battalion to South Africa in 1899.

We were busy all the day and left the harbour [St.Vincent] about 5 pm
and went on smoothly again for five days when our engines broke down.
We were in very rough sea at the time and the vessel tossed about from
side to side throwing everything and everybody about in a marvellous
manner from one side of the vessel to the other. Men, kits and dinner were
all mixed up together, rolling with the ship. If a man was lucky enough
to come in contact with a table he would hold on like grim death for if
he lost his hold he would find himself the other side of the deck so suddenly and then so quickly back again that he would not know that he had
received the bruises until he was able to lay hold of something again.[41]

Apart from the weather the other subject that dominated the diaries
and letters of the troops was food, its quantity and quality. With journey
times of several months aboard sail ships, large amounts of food and
water had to be carried and the Army resorted to that which could be
easily stored. Complaints about the poor food aboard troopships were
not confined to the early part of Victoria's reign, as these diary entries
made by Lance Corporal Rose illustrate. Writing on 11 November 1899
whilst on board the troopship *Somasa*, Rose complained, 'We are living
very bad indeed, hard biscuits and salt. Also very bad for water about
1 pinte per man being allowance during the day.' When Rose finally
arrived in Cape Town on 29 November to participate in the Boer War
he was still fixated on that aspect of the voyage from England.

pleasant as far as the weather is concerned but our food was awful.
Everything was rotten. We had hard biscuits every day they were too hard
to eat and no wonder we arrived here in a state of semi-starvation.[42]

Similarly, Private Charles Gibson of the 2nd Battalion of the Devonshire
Regiment recorded in his diary the battalion's voyage on board the SS
Manila to South Africa in 1899.

Routine of the Ship Reville sounded every morning at 6 am and every
man turned up on Deck to get a bath, stow Hammocks at 6.30 am.
Breakfast at 7 am the meal consist of three Biscuits and Half a pint of tea
with very little milk and sugar. Parade for Gymnastic at time appointed
every day eye full of lime juice at 11.30 am. Dinner bugle sounded at
12 Midday which consisted of Salt Pork two Pickles and one chilly and

a small drop of vinegar which was rolled into the plate as if it was served to pigs instead of human beings.[43]

Colour Sergeant McGrath also recorded the scarcity of food on board his troopship sailing to India in 1857.

We landed on Mauritius on the 5th May after being on board 91 days exactly, a happy release as the discipline on board was very severe, the food was also very bad; it consisted of biscuits throughout the voyage, salt pork and beef alternate days. It was said that 6 men had to live on 4 mens rations.[44]

Private Gray, of the 72nd Highland Regiment was rather more resigned to the fare he faced during the battalion's voyage to India in 1858.

The food we got was sufficient and after a short time we got an allowance of lime juice twice a week and a bottle of pickles for each mess. And, as every men got an allowance of porter, we fared not so badly. The allowances for the week for each man was something like 7lbs of good hard biscuits, 4 or 5 lbs of salt beef, 2llbs of salt pork, a small allowance of preserved potatoes and on a Friday pea soup. The pork or bacon was almost all fat and the greater part went to feed the flocks of birds following us.

Gray also recorded that his comrades also used their initiative to fish from the troopship and on one occasion, 'we caught one shark over five feet long. They made ready some of it and I got a little of the soup. It was very good.'[45]

In his diary of the voyage to the Second China War in 1857, Captain Thomas Knox of the Royal Artillery recorded that the livestock carried on board not only enriched the men's diet, but also supplied them with a welcome diversion.

Our live stock thrive well – the sheep are excellent, the pigs look uncommonly well. The turkeys are as fat and jolly as possible and have the privilege of walking about the deck which the other poultry have not – they are supposed to be better behaved than other fowls – in return for which indulgence some of them have taken to laying and we draw lots for the eggs. We have numbers of guinea fowl, they thrive better than anything else and are excellent eating. It is curious to see the way the soldiers pet the turkeys, being the only live things they can get at – I have frequently seen a lot of them lying on the deck, playing cards, with three or four turkeys sitting amongst them and they sticking the cards of the tricks under their feathers to prevent them blowing away.[46]

Soldiers could always enrich their diets out of their own pockets when the troopships called at islands or ports on route. Such stops were made to re-supply the vessel with fresh food and water, collect or deliver mail, receive the latest instruction from London via telegraphic links to such islands as Madeira or St.Vincent in the Atlantic, or to restock with coal. Such stops also allowed the men on board to witness exotic sights, such as the local inhabitants and the food and gifts they were trying to sell to the troops. It was very rare, however, for the soldiers on board to be allowed off the ship during such visits, although officers and their wives were often able to disembark for a few hours. Even as late as 1898 such scheduled stops offered real excitement to the men on board. Private Milton of the Buffs described in his diary the moments when the troopship called at Tenerife for fresh water and St. Helena for coal: 'at both places swarms of natives came round the ship in small boats selling fruit, tobacco, cigars, cigarettes and curios at St Helena. Officers and a few NCOs were allowed to go ashore, alas Tommy had to stay on deck.'[47] Private Grant recorded in his diary that when sailing to India in 1887 his troopship stopped at Port Said where only the officers and their wives were allowed ashore. Grant and his comrades were entertained by the natives who threw more that fifty oranges onto the deck as samples of the goods they were trying to sell to the troops. Grant claimed that the free oranges started a scramble amongst the troops.[48]

In his diary describing the voyage to China, Captain Knox recorded on 23 July 1857 that the troopship arrived in the Straits of Sunda and here the peoples of the island of Java sailed out to the vessel and held on to it so as to sell the men all sorts of foods. These included exotic fruits, eggs, fowl, monkeys (for eating) and turtles.

One or more of the men in each boat can talk English very well and the noise of bargaining is some thing fearful. The best fruits are bananas and green coconuts and we have all made beasts of ourselves when eating such a quantity of them and have enough of them to last five days – of course we pay a great deal more for everything than the regular traders prices but we must expect that – it is a great place for ships homeward bound to lay in stock and provisions of various costs, but then they stop a few days and have time to make their bargains – we have got 8 good sized turtle for 28/- that certainly is cheap – 6 dozen good chickens which will be about three weeks for 10/- those ready for immediate use are about 2 shillings a dozen – Monkeys 3/6 to 4/6 each.[49]

Malta was a frequent stop-off, both on the journey home or out to India or Egypt. Private Grant sailed to India in 1887 aboard the *Serapis* and he described in his diary his experiences of Malta when the troop-ship called to replenish its coal supplies. On entering the harbour

… beautiful coloured boats approached the ship selling oranges and other fruit which the Island produces – several natives came on board with Tobacco and figs things too numerous to mention, what talking and asking questions, there was quite a bauble of voices round the ship.

Grant even recorded his view of the quay side from his vantage point on the deck of the *Serapis*. He saw 'mosques and churches with minarets in all shapes and styles' and 'all along the quay is teaming with wagons and horses all loaded running to warehouses and different places of business, it was quite a change to watch them after gazing on the ocean for so long.' Once the coaling was over Grant thought that he and his comrades 'look like a lot of niggers instead of British soldiers. Now the soldiers and sailors are now cleaning the ship and cleaning themselves ready for our departure at 5 pm.'[50]

In his diary Lieutenant Percy Marling expressed a more jaundiced view of the island when he wrote on 10 April 1882 that 'Malta was a dreadful place for soldiers. The Tommies get blind drunk there on the most horrible stuff for a shilling. The barrack-rooms in the hot weather were frightfully hot and stuffy, and each company used to take it in turns to sleep on the roof.'[51]

It does seem that the experience of the voyage, whether good or bad, depended much upon the captain and crew of the vessel as well as whether the officers inspired their men to any activities while on board. Thus Private Milton found his journey of 1898 to South Africa monotonous no variety whatever save for seeing swarms of seagulls and flying fish occasionally … I spent most of my time under the coning on deck, reading, smoking and conversing with one and another.[52]

Yet Private Collett of the Middlesex Regiment, who travelled to the Boer War, found on board the *Arundel Castle* 'everyone in the best of spirits, we had two concerts every week which we could not finish as there was always a long programme to get through.'[53] Private Grant too wrote of numerous concerts and music evenings held during his 1887 voyage to India. One of the sailors owed a pianoforte which he played and the soldiers provided accompaniment on a tin whistle, a violin, two flutes and a fife. Recitations were also given and on one occasion, after a concert, Grant stated that 'all retired down below to sleep the sleep of the happy.'

According to Grant, the captain of the *Serapis* was very enterprising when it came to keeping the men busy. Every Sunday he would lead all on board in church service and he insisted upon frequent fire drills and exercises in which he would pretend that the ship had hit a rock, or that a man had fallen overboard, so as to keep the sailors and soldiers alert. The captain received the highest praise from Grant when he designed an obstacle race around the ship run between the sailors and soldiers, which 'caused roars of laughter as they had to go over the bridge from the deck by means of a rope which was well greased and to see them sliding down on the top of one another was very amusing and caused such roars of laughter that tears could be seen in the eyes of all on board.' There followed a duck race in which a sailor was pursued all over the vessel and the first to catch him received prize money from the captain.

Yet for all the colourful experiences, the happiness, laughter or even the hours of boredom, there was always the fear of sickness or even death whilst in transit. The poor overcrowded conditions on board the troopships inevitably contributed to illness. Grant claimed that the heat on the lower troop decks was unbearable, especially during the voyage across the Indian Ocean. The situation was aggravated by the men's inability to open the portholes to increase ventilation, for, unless the sea was flat calm, the water would pour in through the openings. Conditions for the officers were not much better. Lieutenant Marling described the heat in the subalterns' cabins during a troopship voyage from Durban to Egypt as 'appalling', and wrote 'the atmosphere down on the lower

troop deck is stifling.' In an earlier journey from Dartmouth to Cape
Town, on board the *Dunrobin Castle*, Marling stated that 'we had one
oil-lamp between two cabins, and only four bathrooms in the whole
ship.' The presents of vermin and pests added to the risk of disease.
Marling claimed that the 'rats and cockroaches very numerous. A large
rat got on to my bunk last night, and there were at least half a dozen
cockroaches.'[54]

If anything, the conditions and experiences on board the coastal
troopships which journeyed along the coasts of South Africa, India and
China were even worse, for many of the vessels used had been hastily
adapted and were not fit for purpose. Thus Private Collett described the
Mongolian – in which he travelled from Cape Town to Durban in 1899
– as a 'proper stinking old tub, the rations were quite as bad as the boat
I reckon both had attained a great age.'[55] Private Joseph Hewitt, of the
94th Regiment, wrote of a particularly appalling voyage along the Indian
coast in 1846 on board the *Loujee*. Hewitt claimed that the boat was

> ... that crowded it was hard to get a place to lie down at night. Undressing
> and getting into bed was out of the question altogether. The women
> managed the best way they could for themselves and children among
> the crowd on the under deck. The upper deck was crowded as the under
> one. The sailors could not move about by night when necessary without
> treading on the men, we were so wedged together. All men were ordered
> from the lower deck every morning, for two or three hours, to let the
> women wash and attend to themselves and the children, and that was all
> the privacy they had on the voyage of not less than 800 miles.[56]

With the risk of disease from the conditions onboard the troopships
there was a need for both officers and men to take an active interest in
their own health. Whilst Captain Knox refrained from drinking alcohol
and ensured that he bathed regularly during his voyage to China, he
described how the regimental vet did little but 'drink gin and water
and sleep all day'. Furthermore, Knox claimed that this man was 'the
only one on board who has not made any change in his style of living
– he is visibly going down hill, and the doctor expects he will soon
have a very serious attack of some sort.'[57]

With so many risks to health it is not surprising that soldiers recorded
deaths on board the troopships. Travelling to South Africa in 1846,

Lieutenant Jary described the conditions on board the *Charlotte* as murderous and noted that three men were lost during the transit.[58] As late as 1899, Private Collett recorded that one man died during the voyage to South Africa. Private Grant wrote movingly of the loss of two men during his voyage to India in 1887, and of the measures taken to reduce the risk of further illness.

> … it is with great sorrow that I have to record the Death of one of the Manchester men who died last night at about 11 pm. He died of fever. The Funeral took place at about 12 am the men of the regiment carried him to the entry of the starboard side here the Minister read the funeral service which was very solemn and impressive and our brother was committed to the deep and many a sad face was seen as they stood around the Minister, the ship was stopped whilst the service was performed.

The following day, Grant wrote

> I am very sorry to record the second Death which makes some of our chaps think that we are going to have a few more deaths. So the Captain ordered that the decks of the main and lower troops deck shall not be scrubbed out with water but only twice a week as the Doctor thinks that the poor fellows Death occurred from a severe cold there is no doubt that too much water thrown on to the lower deck is injurious to health as I noticed that at 6 o'clock in the morning the lower decks have not been dry and one could see with one's own eyes that troops were constantly laying down in the damp decks. The poor fellow belonged to the North Lancaster the funeral took place this afternoon and it was a very solemn sight it seems more solemn on board a ship than on shore.[59]

The journey to war of the nineteenth-century colonial soldier was thus long and tedious, fraught with danger, and with a substantial risk of illness or death. Yet this was only the beginning of an adventure which was to see the troops serve their Queen in colonial garrisons. Again, the Victorian soldier was to be at risk from illness and disease, which would claim more lives than those lost to conflict, and once more they would experience prolonged periods of boredom and inactivity before they would face the hardships and dangers of campaigning. As Kipling recognised in Lahore, they would face all that confronted them with a high degree of stoicism, and even humour.

Notes

1. Cost of Principal British Wars, 1857–1899, REF: WO33/256.
2. B. Farwell, *Queen Victoria's Little Wars*, (Allan Lane, London, 1973), p.191.
3. E. Wood, *From Midshipman to Field Marshal*, Vol.I, (Methuen, London, 1906), p.257.
4. H. Brackenbury, *The Ashanti War of 1873–4*, Vol.I, (Frank Cass, New Impression, London, 1968), p.144.
5. E. Wood, *From Midshipman to Field Marshal*, Vol.II (Methuen, London, 1906), p. 233.
6. Cost of Principal British Wars, 1857–1899, REF: WO33/256.
7. PRO, MT 23/15, T3504 and 3351–52.
8. R. Holmes, *Dusty Warriors*, (Harper Collins, London, 2007), pp.106–7.
9. Ibid, p.109.
10. H. Rogers, *Troopships and their History*, (Seeley Service & Co., London, 1963), p.85.
11. Ibid, p.131.
12. J. Duncan & J. Walton, *Heroes for Victoria*, (Spellmount, Tunbridge Wells, 1991), p.46.
13. H. Rogers, p.107.
14. Ibid, p. 115.
15. S. David, *Victoria's Wars: The Rise of Empire*, (Viking, London, 2006), p.248.
16. H. Rogers, p.115.
17. Ibid, pp.134–5.
18. J. Bowie, *The Empire at War*, (Batsford, London, 1989), p.84.
19. G. Blake, *B.I. Centenary 1856–1956*, (Collins, London, 1956), p.63.
20. H. Rogers, p.132.
21. M. Murray, *Union-Castle Chronicle*, (Longmans, London, 1953), p.95
22. Unpublished PhD, University of Exeter, 2005, S. Manning, 'Foreign News Gathering and Reporting in the London and Devon Press: The Anglo-Zulu War, 1879, A Case Study', p.63.
23. H. Rogers, p. 148.
24. G. Blake, p.179.
25. H. Rogers, p.160.
26. J. Duncan & J. Walton, p.47.
27. H. Rogers, p.163.
28. *Dartmouth Chronicle* 30 May 1879.

29. Diary of Bandsman Barwood, REF: BWRA 0203/1, p.87, From E. Spiers, *The Scottish Soldier and Empire, 1854–1902*, (Edinburgh University Press, 2006), p.67.

30. Diary of Pvt. E. Grant, REF: NAM 2001-07-233-1.

31. Diary of Lance-Corp. Rose, Duke of Cornwall's Light Infantry Museum, Bodmin.

32. Diary of Pvt.E. Stanton, REF: SRO DD/SLI 17/1/32.

33. Diary of Private J. Lasby, 19 October 1899, REF: DRM Acc 2029.

34. P. Stewart, *The History of the XII Royal Lancers*, (Oxford University Press, 1950), p.115.

35. Pvt. John Pine, letter to father, 20 April 1852, REF: NAM 1996-05-4-3.

36. F. Tucker (ed.), *The Chronicle of Private Henry Metcalfe, H.M. 32nd Regiment of Foot*, (Cassell, London, 1953), p.16.

37. H. Rogers, p.131.

38. Diary of Captain Thomas Knox, RA, REF RAM MD 2943.

39. Diary of Colour Sergeant John McGrath, 33rd Regiment, REF: Bankfield Museum RMDWR.

40. J. Duncan & J. Walton, p.46.

41. Diary of an unknown private of the 2nd Devons, REF: DRM Acc No.5.

42. Diary of Lance-Corporal A.W. Rose, 2nd Battalion, Duke of Cornwall's Light Infantry, REF: DCLIM.

43. Diary of Pvt. Charles Gibson, 2nd Devons, REF: DRM Acc 1323.

44. Diary of Colour Sergeant John McGrath, 33rd Regiment, REF: Bankfield Museum RMDWR.

45. Recollections of a Life in India, 1858–1868, REF: ASHM N-C91 GRA.

46. Diary of Captain Thomas Knox, RA, REF RAM MD 2943.

47. Diary Pvt. W.E. Milton, REF: NAM 2006-04-09.

48. Diary of Pvt. E. Grant, REF: NAM 2001-07-233-1.

49. Diary of Captain Thomas Knox, RA, REF RAM MD 2943.

50. Diary of Pvt. E. Grant, REF: NAM 2001-07-233-1.

51. Colonel Sir Percival Marling, V.C., *Rifleman and Hussar*, (John Murray, London, 1931), p.69.

52. Diary Pvt. W.E. Milton, REF: NAM 2006-04-09.

53. Diary of Pvt. Collett, REF: NAM 9403-106.

54. Colonel Sir Percival Marling, V.C., pp.26 & 66.

55. Diary of Pvt. Collett, REF: NAM 9403-106.

56. The Journal of Joseph Hewitt A Soldier in India 1834–1863, REF: NAM 2005-12-24.

57. Diary of Captain Thomas Knox, RA, REF RAM MD 2943.

58. P. Stewart, p.115.

59. Diary of Pvt. E. Grant, REF: NAM 2001-07-233-1.

CHAPTER THREE

COLONIAL POSTINGS

Following all the hardship that the Victorian soldier suffered whilst on board a troopship, he could hope for a little comfort once he arrived at his colonial barracks. It should be remembered that the Victorian army was designed for 'imperial policing' and not simply for conquest, and this meant that the troops would, more than likely, be found in garrisons in countries as diverse as Canada, Egypt, India and New Zealand. Here the soldiers experienced the daily activity of repetitious drill and the soul-destroying boredom that typified life in an overseas garrison. The troops also had to cope with the ever-present threat of tropical diseases that were to claim the lives of many thousands of British troops during the nineteenth century. Their lives would be plagued by tropical pests, bugs and vermin. Thus it is not surprising that many longed to return to Britain, or even the activity of a campaign, to relieve the tedium of colonial service.

Many recruits must have initially viewed an overseas posting – away from the urban squalor and greyness of barrack life in Britain – as exotic and exciting. Some of this early excitement can be seen in a letter written from India by Lance-Corporal William Eaton to his brother in 1880.

When I came first I could not sleep for the wolves and jackals shouting at night but I have got use to them now I have not seen a tiger yet, but we have passed through the jungle, I have seen plenty of monkeys, leopards, stags, snakes, wolves, jackals, and several wild beasts I do not know the name of.[1]

Within just a matter of weeks, Eaton was to write again to his brother and the wonders of Indian fauna no longer feature.

> We had a few cases of sunstroke, and since we came here we have buried a lot who have died of fever and sunstroke. It is hard to see the poor fellows dieing in the morning and buried at night in a country like this, away from home and friends with no one to care for you unless it be a comrade. There is 170 in hospital and there is plenty men here that was stout strong men a year ago and they are like skeletons now, with the hardships and the heat it would knock any men up if he were as strong as a horse, you could not believe how hot it is in the middle of the day we can hardly breathe.[2]

Likewise, Private John Moloney of the 2nd Battalion the Royal Inniskilling Fusiliers, soon came to dislike his posting to Meean Meer, India in 1899. He wrote in a letter to a friend.

> I do not like India, it was horrible hot in this place, I was often on Guard and I was hardly able to hold the rifle. I was in Peshawar for about 6 months it was very dangerous place for you never knew when you might get stabbed.[3]

There were some significant improvements in the conditions of the barracks in which troops were housed – both in Britain and her colonies – during the nineteenth century. However, it should be stressed that any improvements were from a very low base, and the living conditions themselves were directly responsible for the higher than average mortality rates amongst the troops, as compared to the civilian population. Furthermore, any changes to barrack construction, layout or sanitation facilities were first orchestrated in Britain and it often took several years, if not decades, before these alterations were seen in the overseas garrisons.

In 1857, a Royal Commission was appointed to examine the health of the Army and to make a valid comparison with illness and mortality rates in the civilian population. The commission reported that the mortality rate in the army was significantly greater than that of the civilian male population of the same age and even higher than that found amongst the most dangerous civilian occupations, such as mining. In addition, the commission discovered that within the same urban area of London, detachments of the army had a much higher death rate than that of the surrounding population.[4] The commission claimed that the Army, comprising as it did a group of young men, should have had a significantly lower mortality rate than the civilian population, and concluded that the higher mortality rate had to be directly linked to the conditions of military service. There is no doubt that it was the soldier's living conditions which, more than anything, contributed to the excessive amounts of sickness and early mortality in the Army. Tuberculosis, respiratory ailments and fevers, all of which were directly connected to the poor barrack conditions, were responsible for hospitalising 37% of the rank and file in 1860 alone. By the 1850s, poor barrack room design, faulty and negligent construction 'coupled with overcrowding, inadequate ventilation and sewage disposal, neglected sanitation, and faulty lighting and heating contributed to a rate of illness which yearly sapped the army of much of its strength.'[5]

Although medical science was aware that there was a general correlation between contaminated drinking water, hygiene, ventilation and the health of the troops, the exact links were not fully understood until almost the end of Victoria's reign. In 1853, the *Lancet* told the truth.

> All is darkness and confusion, vague theory and speculation. What is cholera? Is it a fungus, an insect, a miasm, an electric disturbance, a deficiency of ozone, a morbid off-scouring of the intestinal canal? We know nothing; we are at sea in a whirlpool of conjecture.[6]

It was common until the 1850s, for a wooden urine tub to stand open for use in a barrack room overnight. The tubs would then be lightly rinsed in the morning and might even be used to store rations during the day. Soldiers often blocked up the doors and windows of the barracks to keep out draughts, and the stench of urine and body odour pervaded the barrack rooms. This was a major contributory factor to the high rates of respiratory diseases, such as tuberculosis.[7]

With the lack of medical knowledge as to the spread of diseases, and the ignorance in both the civilian and military population of basic levels of hygiene and sanitation, it is perhaps surprising that so many concrete measures were taken to improve the living conditions in barracks from the late 1850s onwards. Spurred by the Royal Commission and the Barrack Accommodation Committee of 1856, influential reformers such as Florence Nightingale and Sidney Herbert campaigned for improvements in the construction of barracks, with an awareness of how living conditions could improve the welfare of the troops. Their initial efforts bore fruit with the appointment of the Army Sanitary Commission in 1857, whose first recommendation called for a minimum living space of 600 cubic feet per man, as well as separate and adequate toilet facilities, provision of running water and better heating and ventilation. Although the Commission was able to report in 1859 that the newly built barracks were indeed meeting these new minimum requirements, little or no improvement was evident in old, existing barracks. It would take both the commitment of a series of governments, as well as the determination of more enlightened army commanders, such as Evelyn Wood, for conditions in barracks to become uniform throughout mainland Britain. Improvements in the health of the Army were evident, although it could be argued that the reduction in disease and mortality in the forces mirrored developments in the health of the civilian population, and was due also in part to better medical understanding of diseases. By 1860 the mortality rates of civilians and of soldiers aged between 20 and 24 were equal; by 1899 that of the soldier was significantly less.[8]

Such improvements in the health of the Army at home and in the conditions of home barracks took longer to be seen in the overseas garrisons of the Empire. Private Mark Gray, of the 72nd Highlanders, recalled that his barracks at Mhow, India were 'nothing to brag of. Tin bedstands we slept on were old and infested with bed bugs. The floor was bad and the sheds [lavatories] not any of the best. A great many of the men were in hospital suffering from malaria fever, dysentery. Nearly every man had an attack of malaria, some very bad.'[9] Similarly, Private Waterfield, of the 32nd Foot, who served in India in the early 1850s, described his barracks in the Punjab as 'very poor ones and infested with rats, mice, bugs and millions of fleas.'[10] Percy Marling, on service in Egypt described in his diary of 25 July 1882 the conditions of his barracks.

We are quartered in some empty Gippy cavalry barracks … full of mosquitoes and other objectionable insects, and indescribably filthy. Bitten all over by bugs, mosquitoes, fleas, and sand-flies. They nearly pulled me out of bed.[11]

Such barrack conditions, combined with extremes of temperature and exotic pests and diseases, meant that life in a nineteenth-century colonial garrison could indeed be precarious.

Throughout the Victoria age, diseases such as cholera and typhoid killed far more British troops than enemy action. For example, in the Crimea, 3,845 men died in action, whilst 15,724 succumbed to disease, mainly cholera; in the Ashanti War, of 1873–4, the sickness rate was in excess of 70%, whilst even as late as the Boer War (1899–1902), over 7,500 men were killed in action, yet over 13,000 died of disease.[12] Private Milton of the Buffs, was to record in his Boer War diary of 16 March 1900 his outrage at the loss of men to disease, which he clearly felt was avoidable. At Bloemfontein, Milton wrote

> There is an awful lot of sickness amongst soldiers, poor fellows dying in dozens daily for the want of attention, many lives I am sure could have been saved, there is no comfort for the sick. Men suffering from Enteric and Dysentery, some dying, had to lay on the bare ground with but one blanket to cover them, tormented by flies and other insects. When on active service one must make allowances as to the treatment of sick soldiers. I will only say something of their diet for it was impossible to get anything in the shape of food such as eggs, milk etc, such as wanted for the sick.[13]

The early ignorance of the risks of cholera and how it was transmitted is clearly reflected in a letter written by Lieutenant-Colonel Thomas Stephens of the 49th Regiment, to his wife Eleanor after the Battle of Ching Kung Foo (21 July 1842), which led to the surrender of China and the Treaty of Nanking.

> Part of the reg't going on board this evening – this I suppose in consequence of cholera having broken out. Poor Weir the Lieutenant died yesterday morning close beside where I was lying, and where I am now writing a sergeant died this morning – we have four cases in hospital.[14]

Stephens died of cholera a few days later.

The loss of men to disease whilst on campaign, was expected, for it was often difficult to find an uncontaminated water supply.

The presence of dead animals, human and animal waste and the very presence of a large force meant that the polluting of water supplies in the immediate vicinity was nearly always inevitable. Major Woods of the 9th Lancers, who served in Afghanistan in 1879, wrote to his wife of the difficulties of removing dead carcasses from the vicinity of the camp.

> There are considerably over a hundred dead camels in all stages of decomposition round the camp and the smell from them is something too distasteful. They cannot be moved as there are no elephants to drag them away. We shall have an outbreak of sickness if something is not soon done.[15]

Habit was a factor. During the Zulu campaign of 1879, Evelyn Wood constructed a British camp at Kambula that included separate latrines for his Boer and Native allies. However, he was unable to convince either group to use them, and he was forced to move the site of the camp to avoid an outbreak of illness.[16]

Disease and death became so linked with colonial garrisons that it was viewed as commonplace. Rudyard Kipling captured the horror and inevitability of cholera in his poem *Cholera Camp (Infantry in India)*.

> We've got the cholerer in camp – it's worse than forty fights;
> We're dyin' in the wilderness the same as Isrulites.
> It's before us, an' behind us, an' we cannot get away,
> An' the doctor's just reported we've ten more to-day!
>
> Oh, strike your camp an' go, the bugle's callin',
> The Rains are fallin'
> The dead are bushed an' stoned to keep 'em safe below.
> The Band's a-doin' all she knows to cheer us;
> The Chaplain's gone and prayed to Gawd to 'ear us –
> To 'ear us –
> O Lord, for it's a-killin' of us so!

Troops sent to India found the oppressive heat and sickness almost unbearable and some even committed suicide. John Ryder recalled his first experience of cholera in India.

Great numbers began to die very suddenly … The regiment not being used to the like of this, the whole began to look melancholy, and fear was seen on every face, as much as to say, 'it will be my turn next.' Some gave themselves up to utter despair and died … It was dreadful to see fine, stout, healthy young fellows, well and dead in a few hours … Not a day passed but we had someone to put in his last resting place. [17]

Similarly, Private Samuel Clunie wrote to his sister from Sebathoo, India, in 1843 and told her that 'there is scarcely a day passes but we lose one or two men and there is nothing day after day but funeral parties.'[18]

The strain that such experiences of death and illness placed upon the troops was immense, as illustrated in the reminiscences of Colonel George Jerome Kellie of the Indian Medical Service, India 1879.

Morar was a very melancholy place. The C.O. and the Adjutant of the 62nd had died in one day from cholera and everyone was in a funk. There had been so many deaths that the bands did not play at funerals on account of the depressing effect on the men. When I got back to Morar I found that cholera had broken out among the British troops and they were all out in camp. One young officer in the Gunners shot himself in camp either from funk or worry. Our Subaltern had got into such a funk over the cholera that he went into such a state of collapse and had been carried to Bromes' quarters more dead than alive. He is now a D.S.O. [Distinguished Service Order] which he got for gallant behaviour on service. This will give you an idea how a big strong man will give in from fear of cholera. [19]

Some postings were considered more unhealthy than others and certainly Dacca, a station in east Bengal, was notorious for its high death rate, particularly from sunstroke and cholera. Colour Sergeant John McGrath, of the 33rd Regiment:

During our stay in Dessa − 3 years − we lost 90 men, 8 women and I cannot say how many children; the greater number of those died of cholera, the others chiefly from heat apoplexy. It was a common thing for a man to be jolly going to bed at the usual hour, but the poor fellow would be silent enough in the morning. Very few of those attacked ever recovered. There were two cholera outbreaks during the above period, the 1st a very mild one, the last pretty severe. I remember having been at a funeral of one of our company (Chadwick); that afternoon 6 men, 2 women and 3 children were put away. I need not say that such sudden deaths makes the strongest men feel down, no matter what their outward show may be. Far better face bullets than such a thing; there is something manly about the latter, but to be attacked by this fell disease when in full vigour and carried off as it were in a few hours after great agony, one can hardly describe it. I may add here that the heat at this station reached 150 in the shade one season.[20]

It took only a few months from the arrival of the 38th Regiment in Dacca in April 1852 for its men to be virtually annihilated by the extreme heat and disease. Of the 600 men who were first stationed there, only three were fit enough to stand at muster six months later; the rest were either dead or in hospital.[21]

Hong Kong was considered an unhealthy posting. Major Macleod of the Royal Artillery recalled in his memoirs that a monument was erected in memory of all the men in one particular barracks who were discovered dead in their beds one morning. All had died of cholera.[22]

Whilst the risk of cholera was high in the tropics, it also struck down large numbers of troops elsewhere. The Crimean War was not simply remembered for feats of arms or the logistical problems of the Army, but also for the large number of Allied soldiers who died of the disease. The Medical Officer (MO) of the 4th South Devonshire Regiment recorded in his report of the Crimean campaign that 304 men of the Regiment were treated for cholera between 1 October 1855 and 31 March 1856 and of that number 113 died. During the same period, a further 379 men suffered from diarrhoea, of whom 42 died. The MO also left a vivid description of the last days of one of the victims of cholera, Private Patrick Shields, who was aged 20. Shields was admitted to hospital on 28 March 1856 'with aggravated symptoms of common continued fever which gradually increased and on the 3rd of April he was seized with collapse – his lips, face and hands became purple and he expired.'[23]

Commissionary-General A.W. Downes recorded in his diary the sobering site of a mass burial of victims of cholera in the Crimea.

I went across to Makrikioi and walked afterwards down to Scutari to the
wharf. As we passed the Hospital I saw Rocke of the 49th commanding
a burial party and I afterwards heard he was burying a doctor who had
attended him when ill with fever. There was a melancholy sight to be
seen. One grave in which 41 Protestants and 20 Catholic soldiers were
laid merely sewn-up in blankets, poor fellows they looked not bigger
than children, so wasted away they appeared from cholera.[24]

Captain Charles Ramsden, in his Crimea diary, wrote of the suddenness of death by cholera.

> The amount of sickness and death here is most shocking, 10 last night and 2
> or 3 some nights ago, it is so awfully sudden in most cases. Men are carried
> off in a surprisingly short time. Strong healthy men go down as if shot.[25]

In his journal, John Everett of the 13th Somerset Light Infantry told
again of the fear of disease that surrounded the men, and records that it
was not just cholera that caused concern.

> We found this morning that two more men had died during the night,
> and the hospitals were filling very fast with men suffering from diar-
> rhoea, and most of the officers were attacked by the same complaint.
> Fuller was rather ill of it, and many others. I got rather nervous about
> myself; and all our spirits being very low, I thought I had better satisfy
> my conscience with a dose of castor oil.[26]

Although cholera was a significant killer of troops serving overseas
throughout the Victorian period, it was just one of several complaints
that could result in death or debilitation. Malaria, typhoid and dysentery
all claimed lives. In a letter to his mother from Amritsar in September
1878, Lieutenant J. Campbell of the 72nd Regiment wrote of the effects
of malaria upon the troops stationed there.

> Fever here is raging and we have to parade every morning for Quinne,
> other parades are out of the Question as the men fall out one after
> another. On Tuesday I had a parade of 20 minutes. There were 30 men
> present when they fell in and only 14 when I dismissed as all the rest had
> to fall out with fever.[27]

With the ever present chance of drinking contaminated water, typhoid was another serious danger. Captain Charles Egerton, of the Bengal Staff Corps, wrote to his mother from Camp Jampur in Afghanistan, in November 1880.

> We lost our adjutant poor Mardall on the 9th from typhoid fever. Poor young chap he never had a chance what with the incessant jolting day after day in the dooly and the utter absence of proper food for him; milk, eggs fowls etc, being quite unprocurable and though he never lost heart we all felt somehow that it would be a miracle if he pulled round. I was sitting up with him when he died, which he did quite suddenly.[28]

Sergeant Hooper, of the 2nd Battalion of the Buffs, kept a journal of his experiences while his regiment was besieged at Eshowe during the Zulu War of 1879. He wrote of his frustration at seeing men die of illnesses, simply for the want of food or medicines, and he recorded the deaths of many of his comrades from dysentery. One such man was Private McLoud, who died 'about 5.30 this morning and buried at 11 am. No coffin simply the blanket round him which he was carried and used as a bed during the campaign, no firing partys at grave as we cannot afford the ammunition.'[29]

It was not just diseases with which the Victorian soldier had to contend, but also a vast array of pests and vermin, many of them exotic, which at the very least made their existence even more uncomfortable, and at worst threatened their lives. In his diary of the Crimea, Captain Richard Nugent Clayton of the 13th Regiment of Foot wrote of the creatures that shared his sleeping quarters. 'I managed to get into a hut by myself this time which is perhaps better on the whole than a tent, though the insects bite me shockingly, there are also lots of mice in my personal abode.'[30] Private Clunie wrote in despair to his sister that

> Here [India] we have nothing to do but lie upon our beds all day and to be eat alive by fleas all night. It is no matter what part of India we go to we are sure to be tormented by some sort of vermin. Mosquitoes, bugs or fleas.[31]

Frederick Anley of the Essex Regiment served in Egypt in 1885 and wrote home to inform his family that 'the fleas and the gnats don't give one a moment's peace; there are the most persistent brutes and continued wearing of handkerchiefs round ones head does not keep them off.'[32] Private Thomas Lloyd of the 7th Royal Fusiliers served in Afghanistan in 1880 and from there he described the flies as 'a complete plague' and that, when eating, the flies would swarm around the soldiers' faces. Lloyd even went so far as to say he would prefer to take to the field 'again and again', so as to get away from the 'cursed desert'.[33]

The mosquitoes were a particular torment to the Victorian soldier. Private Appleby of the 51st Regiment was probably not exaggerating when he declared in a letter sent to his brother from Burma in 1853, during the Second Burma War

> they [mosquitoes] are very troublesome and they kept up a constant war with us biting through our clothes in such a manner that not one of us could get any sleep during the night. I leave you to judge when I tell you that the lamp was three inches deep with mosquitos that had been killed in the oil – had we to stop here long I think I should have gone mad.[34]

Corporal Sandford of the 2nd Battalion the Buffs expressed a perverse delight in the suffering mosquitoes would inflict on his new comrades in his diary from Singapore in 1880.

> We have just landed a draft of recruits here to join us … they came straight from Canterbury; won't the mosquitos have a fine feed tonight? Tomorrow morning they'll [the recruits] have Black eyes and heads swollen up as Big as bushel baskets, unless they can afford a mosquito curtain to put round the bed.[35]

Although uncomfortable, the insect life did, on rare occasions, offer a moment of humour, as Colonel Kellie recorded in his reminiscences of his time in Hyderabad in 1897.

> A dinner was given in the mess in honour of Captain G.E. who was going to Moninabad, and all the cadres were invited. Just as the wine was put on the table a swarm of white ants came out of a small hole in the wall. They soon filled the room, and as is their habit crawled about getting rid of their wings as fast as possible. They got on the bare necks of the ladies and down their backs, and made them most

unhappy. There was a regular rout, and in a few minutes all the ladies bolted home.[36]

Of greater danger to the life of the British soldier were snakes and scorpions. Sergeant Henry Williams served as a non-commissioned British soldier in Evelyn Wood's newly reformed Egyptian Army between 1883–85, and took part in the unsuccessful attempts to relieve Gordon in Khartoum. In his reminiscences, Williams recalled that he was stung by a scorpion whilst looking through some papers in a chest. Fortunately, he reacted quickly.

> I went and got my razor and made several cuts in my hand, on, and near the place stung. I then sucked as much of the poison out as I could, but the sting caused me great pain for sometime. I had to lie down, the pain eventually passed off, but a few days after my right elbow became stiff and sore, a very bad abscess formed right on the point of the elbow, a lump formed under my arm, to my idea as large as a fair sized apple, the abscess eventually broke and a large open and deep sore about the size of a crown piece, which appeared to go into the bone was the result. I was compelled to carry my arm in a sling for sometime, but it eventually healed.[37]

Even more horrific was the experience of Private Mark Gray of the 72nd Regiment, who served in India between 1858–68.

> Another man and myself were not long here until we had to go to hospital with a worm that had laid an egg in one of our toes. After being hatched it worked its way up until it formed an abscess at the calf of the leg, which finally burst and came out as a worm. My leg got terribly inflamed and swollen, and as the doctor had not seen any cases before this he did not know what to do for the best. But he lanced it twice and applied linseed meal poultices to it. I got hold of it again and got most if not all of it out. It was over two feet and quite a thickness. We got it while in bathing at Poona. I was in hospital 3 weeks and got the best of treatment and found no bad effects from it afterwards. The other man's case proved fatal but they did not tell me about it until I got out.[38]

Whilst Gray's terrible experience was fortunately rare, everyone had to bear the excessive, inescapable heat, which was often the defining characteristic of overseas service. Private Clunie, who served in Afghanistan in 1840, wrote to his brother that 'the weather is dreadful hot the glass very often rising to 120 which I dare say the people in England will not believe.'[39] Also writing from Afghanistan in 1880, Private Lloyd recorded in his diary,' As for the heat it must be felt to be credited, I am sure there is no one in England can form any idea of 115 in the shade.'[40] Similarly, Frederick Anley suffered from the heat in Egypt and he wrote of 27 March 1885 that it was 'an awfully hot day; the thermometer in a tent went up to 115; the hospital one went up to 121; we feel awful having no method of cooling our water, which gets quite lukewarm passing through a filter.'[41] Soldiers in India were more resourceful in being able to cool their water supply. Mark Gray described how 'The water for drinking was brought by the bhistis (water carriers) and filtered through three or four large crocks of sand which made it cooler and better.'[42] Private Clunie also described how life was made bearable in the heat of Afghanistan by the daily sale of limes and 'refreshing snow'.

Colonial service was not only about avoiding the worst of the day's heat, tropical illnesses and pests; the troops also had to escape from the drudgery and boredom. For the illiterate, the hours could not be whiled away by reading. For those that could read, the choice of reading material was severely limited. In the first half of the nineteenth century, the only books allowed in barracks were those included on a prescribed list of 28 volumes that had been approved by a bench of bishops, intent on preventing subversive literature reaching the lower orders.[43] Officers, too, suffered from want of accessible reading material, as Ensign C. Bourne described in a letter to his mother from Hong Kong, written in 1845.

> You asked me in your last letter if I was reading any interesting books. I answer NO but I am reading uninteresting ones, namely all the books I can lay hold of concerning drill or military evolutions, as these are all that is available to me.[44]

Overseas, the one common factor of all foreign garrisons was cheap liquor, whether it brought profit to the government by being sold in the canteens, or was native-brewed using wood-alcohol that could cause blindness or a painful death. Troops could be most resourceful in obtaining drink. Private Robert Waterfield of the 32nd Foot served in India in 1848 and described an incident in which the troops gained an extra ration of grog.

> In consequence of several men having been confined for drunkenness the Colonel issued an order for every man to drink his grog at the tub where it is served out, thinking by this means to put a stop to the men getting drunk. They might as well try to stop the wind, for the men get false bottoms fixed in their tin pots, and when they go for their grog it is measured into these. Those who want to carry grog away will take a small portion of bread with them, which will be eaten, so as to allow the grog sufficient time to run through a small hole which is in the false bottom. They can raise the pot nearly upside down without spilling the liquor; this enables them to carry it away and if they don't want to drink it, they can always get plenty of men who will purchase it at four times its first cost. By this means are the Colonel's wishes baffled![45]

Many soldiers sought to escape the boredom of colonial barrack life by resorting to the oblivion offered by this readily available drink and this is reflected in regimental disciplinary records. For example, the Casualty Book of the 1st Battalion, the Buffs from 1884–1892, when the regiment served in India, records many occasions when soldiers received punishment for drink-related incidents. Private G. Smith was convicted for being drunk on duty on 17 September 1891, and was sentenced to 21 days imprisonment and fined £1. Similarly, Private F. Stalls was found guilty of being drunk on duty on 6 June 1892 and received 21 days imprisonment and forfeited his 1d per day G.C.P., or Good Conduct Pay. This Casualty Book also records trials in which drink undoubtedly played a significant role in the commission of the misdemeanour. So, Private Barry was imprisoned for 56 days, on 9 June 1891, for 'using threatening language to an officer', and, later the same month, Lance Corporal W. Furrent was jailed for 49 days for 'striking his superior officer.'[46]

Captain Clayton recorded in his diary of the Crimea:

> Had 5 men drunk on my Guard – the sentry having opened a rum cask helped himself, when 4 others got into the same delightful state of

inebriation, and so I must quietly confine them all, as there is no choice in the matter, and they will all be C.M.[47]

Bandsman Barwood of the Black Watch, wrote in his diary of service in Egypt in 1884, that the regiment had left Cairo in a 'disgraceful state', with some men too drunk to stand in the ranks and another twenty so 'riotous' that they swore at bystanders and had to be detained in the guard room.[48]

Drink, or the desire to get it, was certainly central to the lives of the majority of Victorian soldiers. At any celebration, such as Christmas, the presence of drink was considered vital. Private Lloyd described a less than alcoholic Christmas Day 1880 in his diary from Afghanistan; 'No Porter and rather difficult to get spirits. Great crushing to get a bottle of fire water, which turned out a failure'. Similarly, Lloyd recorded a rather disappointing St Patrick's Day at which 'We made an attempt to keep up the old day but it was a failure as you may suppose with the thermometre at 115 in the shade and not a drop of the creator [whisky] within a thousand miles of us.'[49] The desire to acquire drink was not just limited to those in the ranks, for it is clear that officers too partook of a drop to relieve the boredom of garrison duty. In a letter to his mother from Ali Kheyl, Afghanistan, in 1879, Lieutenant J. Campbell of the 72nd Regiment wrote 'we are in clover now having got 7 barrels of beer up and though it is all turned quite black and sow, yet we drink it with great gusto, stirring up soda and sugar in it to make it drinkable.'[50] In contrast, Captain Egerton wrote to his brother in September 1880, in disgust at General Primrose's decision to abandon 1,200 dozen bottles of beer to the enemy in Afghanistan.

> I believe fellows in their innermost hearts berate the loss of the beer more than any other of the General's shortcomings and it might easily have been saved. He will never be forgiven for this as long as he lives.[51]

In the first half of Victoria's reign, punishment for drink-related offences was not restricted to imprisonment or fines, and a sentence of corporal punishment was not uncommon. Private Robert Waterfield served throughout the Second Sikh War, and in his memoirs he recalled that a parade of the whole regiment was called on 6 December 1848 to 'witness the infliction of 50 lashes each on two of our men, for being

drunk on the line of march'. Waterfield had no sympathy for the predicament of his comrades for he wrote, 'Such characters ought to be
discharged with ignominy from the service.'[52]

Even in later years, being drunk on sentry duty was considered a very
serious offence for which a flogging could be administered. Private
Lloyd wrote in his 1880 diary from Afghanistan that a court martial was
summoned during the Commanding Officer's Parade, at which one
soldier was found guilty of being drunk on sentry duty and was sentenced to 25 lashes.[53] During the Zulu War of 1879, over 500 soldiers
were flogged for a range of offences, and this large number caused a
public outcry, which led to this form of punishment being abolished in
1881. Other possible sentences included periods of 'pack drill', in which
the offender would be forced to march or run in full kit. This was often
so prolonged that in the heat of the desert or tropics the troops were
reduced to a state of complete exhaustion. Flogging was replaced by
'Field Punishment No. 1', in which offenders were tied to the wheel of
a gun carriage for a specified period. Extreme crimes, such as murder
or rape, could warrant execution, although only 37 men suffered this
fate between 1865 and 1898.[54]

The other serious offence which merited grave punishment was that
of desertion. There can be little doubt that some individuals used overseas service as an opportunity to escape the drudgery and squalor of
urban Britain for a new life in the colonies, with the Army paying
their shipping fee. Desertion was a serious problem in English-speaking
colonies such as Canada and South Africa, in which employment for
white men, and the opportunity to acquire land was a real possibility. With its proximity to America, desertion from Canadian barracks
was rife, and even in India soldiers deserted to seek new opportunities or to form a lasting relationship with a local girl. In the Transvaal
during 1880, over 250 troops out of a total of 3,000 men deserted; 70
in one month alone.[55] Until 1871, deserters who were apprehended
were flogged, then branded on the upper arm with a needle-device,
gunpowder being rubbed in to make the letter 'D' permanent. The fear
of such punishment does not seem to have deterred the deserters, but if
apprehended the likelihood of such punishment drove some to extreme
action. Private Gray recalled one deserter of the 72nd Regiment who
fired a bullet through the palm of his hand so as to be taken to hospital,
thus avoiding the flogging punishment.[56] In later years, apprehended

deserters were usually imprisoned, fined and reduced to the ranks. However, the chances of evading arrest were high. For example, in the period of May 1884 to August 1885, three soldiers of the Buffs, serving in India, deserted. It appears that both Private Fullford and Private N. Smith were not recaptured, but Sergeant Lowe was apprehended. He was imprisoned and reduced to the ranks.[57]

If drunkenness in the Victorian soldier was officially frowned upon and could result in harsh punishments, the Army held no such strictures when it came to prostitution. For the British soldier overseas, service allowed for a degree of sexual adventure not so readily available at home. The majority of colonial garrisons supported brothels. For troops stationed in India, these were officially sanctioned, and, between 1860 and 1890, 75 official brothels were actually built within regimental cantonments.[58] Such brothels first appeared in the years after the Indian Mutiny and were cheap, with the official rate being set at about one rupee.[59]

Despite the fact that the brothels were regularly inspected by the regimental medical officers to check on the health of the prostitutes, such inspections certainly seemed to have failed to check the spread of venereal disease amongst British troops. Sexually transmitted diseases were a constant problem among the troops in India, and in the early 1860s a serious outbreak occurred in the home army as troops returned from overseas. In 1860 the incidence of disease reached its highest level across the Army at 369 cases per 1,000 men, as compared to 78 cases per 1,000 men in the Navy. This figure probably reflected the ease of access to brothels for British soldiers, particularly those serving abroad.[60]

Whilst E. Sellon wrote adoringly of the mixed-blood women of the West Indies that they 'understand in perfection all the arts and wiles of love, are capable of gratifying any tastes, and in face and figure they are unsurpassed by any women in the world', Trooper Charles Quevillart was not so complementary of the women to be found in a Karachi brothel.

> The sight of the older women was simply disgusting for they were one and all deplorably ugly and little was left for the imagination as a yard of calico would have furnished a dozen of them with a full dress. Some had breasts hanging as low as their waists.[61]

In Egypt, which from 1882 had a British garrison of at least 4,000, prostitutes were abundant. Although descriptions of visits to brothels by Victorian troops, or the services offered there, are very rare, Lieutenant L. Perry of the Royal Artillery has left us with a description of an Egyptian brothel. In a letter of October 1882, Perry wrote to his friend Peter that 'such fellies you never saw, all strip stark naked and dance in the middle of a big room and then want you to "compete" afterwards (which they call out her "gig a gig") but they are too dangerous and rather over worked for my liking.'[62] In South Africa, brothels could be found in all the towns that supported garrisons, as well as in boom-towns like Johannesburg. During the Boer War, Lord Roberts took steps to inspect and license some of these premises. Prostitutes in Cape Town were quick to adapt to the growing market created by the war, and when troopships docked, soldiers were showered with yellow discs, like sovereigns, each with the name and address of a local prostitute. Boer women of the bywoner class also appear to have been willing to offer sex to soldiers, one of whom commented that 'They don't wear drawers'. He was presumably speaking from experience. The desperate Boer women in refugee camps also offered opportunities, and a corporal in the King's Own Lancashire Regiment was reduced to the ranks for twice entering a refugee camp for indecent behaviour with one of the inmates, during which payment was made.[63]

The British Victorian soldier was able, to quote Ian Hernon, to 'rampage sexually across the world'.[64] Overseas, the troops discovered that there were far fewer sexual taboos or restraints as there were in Britain. Their meagre pay, once it had been used to supplement their poor diet and pay for tobacco and drink, could be spent in the nearby brothel. It seems clear that the local delights offered by the prostitutes of India, Egypt, West Africa and the Chinese women of Malaya and Hong Kong brightened the drudgery of colonial garrison life for a very significant number of British troops.

For those soldiers who did not take part in such activities, some other limited leisure pursuits were available. Garrisons in or near the urban centres of Egypt and South Africa at least provided the troops with an occasional opportunity to visit the music halls. Those found in Pietermaritzburg was considered particularly good.[65] Otherwise, while the officers amused themselves by hunting, the troops could take part in sport. Both India and South Africa offered plenty of hunting opportunities, which could at least incorporate some military skills. In India, the hunting of wild boar on horseback with a lance – known as pig-sticking – was popular, as was hunting jackals with hounds. In Africa, hunting the local wildlife seriously reduced its population, as it did in India to the Indian tiger. Polo was also played by the officer class.

For the ranks, cricket was the main sporting pastime. In his recollections, Private Gray wrote that cricket was a very common pursuit, with every company having its own team, which played against the others.[66] It was also one of the few activities in which both officers and men could equally take part. Running races amongst the men were also popular. At other times, the endless hours were filled by pipe-smoking, playing cards, grumbling and writing home.

For all the leisure pursuits, and for the hours consumed by drunkenness and whoring, the overseas garrison life of the Victorian soldier was primarily one of boredom, interrupted by the extreme dangers of illness and disease, which meant many longed for home or military action. This is spelt out in a letter written by Captain Egerton, serving in Afghanistan, to his brother in England.

> I can't tell you how I am longing and wearying for 2 years rest at home. I shall feel a new man after it, at least I feel as if I should. I'm afraid you will think this a very grumbling growling letter but up here one has nothing else to do but grumble and growl.[67]

Egerton's desire to return home is again seen in a letter written two months later.

> Major Vivian started off for England today. Jealousy is not as a rule a part of my nature but I feel uncommonly envious of him when I said goodbye to him this morning.[68]

For those left at home, news from their loved ones must have been anxiously awaited. For most parents and wives, their biggest concern was probably the fear that their loved one would be killed or wounded in battle, but, as has been shown, the greatest risk to the Victorian soldier on overseas service was not the enemy's spears, swords or bullets, but disease. Whatever the cause of the loss, all those worrying at home must have dreaded receiving the letter that Mrs Oakes received from Private

J. Wilkins, of the 9th Lancers, who served in Afghanistan in 1879. Wilkins wrote to offer his condolences to Mrs Oakes on the death of her son.

> May our Heavenly father give you strength and comfort to bear this great loss for your dear son died after a short illness on the 25th of December. During his short illness we done all that we could to alleviate his suffering and his thoughts were of the bright land above and those he loved so far away.[69]

Private Wilkins' thoughts and words summed up the grim reality of overseas service.

Notes

1. Letter L/Corp. W. Eaton to brother, 10 April 1880, REF:NAM 1992-04-115.
2. Letter L/Corp. W. Eaton to brother, 25 June 1880, REF:NAM 1992-04-115.
3. Pvt. Molony, letter to friend, 25 October 1899, REF:NAM 9306-150-7.
4. *Report of the Army Sanitary Commission* (1857–8), pp.vii–xi, xxx, From A. Skelley, *The Victorian Army at Home: The Recruitment and Terms and Conditions of the British Regular, 1859–1899*, (Croom Helm, London, 1977), p. 22.
5. A. Skelley, pp.27–8.
6. *The Lancet*, II (1853), p.393.
7. I. Knight, *Go to Your God Like a Soldier: The British Soldier Fighting for Empire, 1837–1902*, (Greenhill, London, 1996), p.16.
8. A. Skelley, p.25.
9. M. Gray, *Recollections of a Life in India 1858–68*, p.34. REF: ASHM N-C91 GRA.
10. A. Swanson & D. Scott, (eds.), *The Memoirs of Private Waterfield*, (Cassell, London, 1968), p.148.
11. Colonel Sir Percival Marling, V.C., *Rifleman and Hussar*, (John Murray, London, 1931), p.74.
12. I. Knight, p.220.
13. Diary of Pvt. Milton, 16 March 1900, REF:NAM 2006-04-09.
14. Lt. Col. T. Stephens, letter to his wife, 23 July 1842, REF:NAM 2004-03-37.
15. Major Woods, letter to wife, 24 March 1879, REF:NAM 7205-80-1.

16. S. Manning, *Evelyn Wood: Pillar of Empire*, (Pen and Sword, Barnsley, 2007), p.107.

17. J. Ryder, *Four Year's Service in India*, (Leicester, 1853), p.199.

18. Pvt. Samuel Clunie, letter to sister, 1 August 1843, REF: NAM 2002-07-12-3.

19. Reminiscences of Col. Kellie, REF:NAM 7507-56.

20. Journal of CSM J. McGrath, 33rd Regiment, REF: Bankfield Museum RMDWR.

21. S. David, *Victoria's Wars: The Rise of Empire*, (Viking, London, 2006), p. 161.

22. *The Memoirs of Major Macleod referring to service in the Crimean War 1854–6 and the China War 1857–60,* p.61, REF:RAM MD/2410.

23. Medical Report of the 4th South Devonshire Regiment, 1845–1857, REF: NAM 9409-34.

24. Diary of Commissionary-General A.W. Downes, 28 January 1855, REF: NAM 9802-198.

25. Capt. J. Ramsden, *Diary of Service in the Crimea and India 1855–1857*, 22 May 1855 REF: RAM D 1185/1.

26. Journal of John Everett, 13th Reg., 4 July 1855, REF: SRO DD/SLI 17/1/3.

27. Lt. J. Campbell, letter to mother, 22 September 1878, REF:NAM 9006-220-1.

28. Capt. Egerton, letter to mother, 16 November1880, REF:NAM 2000-06-129-2.

29. Sgt. Hooper, *My Diary in Zululand*, 13 February 1879, REF:NAM 2001-03-73.

30. Diary of Capt. R. Clayton, REF:SRO DD/SLI 17/1/4.

31. Pvt. Samuel Clunie, letter to sister, 1 August 1843, REF: NAM 2002-07-12-3.

32. Frederick Anley, Essex Reg., 27 March 1885, REF:NAM 1984-12-50.

33. Diary of Pvt. T. Lloyd, 17 Mar,1880, REF:NAM 9404-86.

34. Pvt. Appleby, letter to brother, 29 January 1853, REF:NAM 9308-89-1.

35. Diary Corp. Sandford, 5 February 1880, REF:NAM 2001-08-588-1.

36. Reminiscences of Col. Kellie, REF:NAM 7507-56.

37. Sgt. H. Williams, *Reminiscences of a Soldier*, REF:NAM 9208-372.

38. M. Gray, *Recollections of a Life in India 1858–68*, p.95. REF: ASHM N-C91 GRA.

39. Pvt. Clunie, letter to brother, 28 July 1840, REF: NAM 2002-07-12-2.

40. Diary of Pvt. T. Lloyd, 17 Mar,1880, REF:NAM 9404-86.

41. Frederick Anley, Essex Reg., 27 March 1885, REF:NAM 1984-12-50.

42. M. Gray, *Recollections of a Life in India 1858–68*, p.44. REF: ASHM N-C91 GRA.

43. D. Featherstone, *Khaki and Red-Soldiers of the Queen in India and Africa*, (Arms & Armour Press, London, 1995), p.21.

44. Ensign C. Bourne, letter to mother, 8 September 1845, REF:NAM 2004-10-81.

45. A. Swanson & D. Scott, (eds.), p.37.

46. The Casualty Book, The Buffs, 1884–1892, REF:NAM 2001-02-452-1.

47. Diary of Capt. R. Clayton, 29 July 1855, REF:SRO DD/SLI 17/1/4.

48. E. Spiers, *The Scottish Regiments and Empire*, (Edinburgh University Press, 2006) p.97.

49. Diary of Pvt. Lloyd, 17 March & 25 December 1880, REF:NAM 9404-86.

50. Lt. J. Campbell, letter to mother, 25 June 1879, REF: NAM 9006-220-23.

51. Capt. Egerton, letter to brother, 12 September 1880, REF:NAM 2000-06-129-1.

52. A. Swanson & D. Scott, (eds.), p. 71.

53. Diary of Pvt. T. Lloyd, 12 April 1880, REF:NAM 9404-86.

54. I. Knight, p.226.

55. Ibid, p.16.

56. M. Gray, *Recollections of a Life in India 1858–68*, p.3. REF: ASHM N-C91 GRA.

57. The Casualty Book, The Buffs, 1884–1892, REF:NAM 2001-02-452-1.

58. I. Hernon, *Britain's Forgotten Wars: Colonial Campaigns of the 19th Century*, (Alan Sutton, Stroud, 2003), p.18

59. I. Knight, p.224.

60. A. Skelley, pp. 53–4.

61. I.Hernon, p.17.

62. Lt. Perry, 22 October 1882, REF: RAM: MD22.

63. J. Lawrence, *The Savage Wars: British Campaigns in Africa, 1870–1920*, (Robert Hale, London, 1985), p.236.

64. I. Hernon, p.17

65. Ibid, p.235.

66. M. Gray, *Recollections of a Life in India 1858–68*, p.3. REF: ASHM N-C91 GRA.

67. Capt. Egerton, letter to brother, 12 September 1880, REF:NAM 2000-06-129-1.

68. Capt. Egerton, letter to brother, 16 November1880, REF:NAM 2000-06-129-1.

69. Pvt. Wilkens, letter to Mrs Oakes, undated, REF:NAM 8101-18-2.

CHAPTER FOUR

THE MARCH TO WAR

I can assure you we feel more dead than alive, when we got to Lucknow we had 4 days rest ... the only rest have I had in a bed since we left England. We are in tents, and there is 24 men in a tent, we have one blanket to lie on and a rug to put over us, when I get up in a morning my back and sides are very sore with the stones under us, I have seen more life and hardship since I came here than ever I thought I should see, no one knows but themselves what a soldier has to go through, it is all very well when you are in England but come out on an expedition like this and they will soon find out what soldiering is.

(Lance Corporal William Eaton, letter to his brother, April 1880)

The Soldiers of the Queen were to be found in some of the most inhospitable regions of the world. Whether it was in the mountains and valleys of Afghanistan, the scorching plains of India, the deserts of Egypt and the Sudan, or the South African veldt, the Victorian British soldier had to cope with extremes of temperature, rough terrain and the depredations of disease. All this often had to be endured on an empty stomach and with clothing and equipment unsuited to such conditions.

As the century progressed the British soldier found himself spending less and less time in Britain. His entitlement to five years at home for every ten years spent overseas could only be fulfilled by steadily reducing overseas garrisons, so that any threatening situation in Africa or India cut into already curtailed periods of home service. In addition, crises would impose additional foreign service. The crushing of the Indian Mutiny eventually required the presence in the subcontinent of 50% of all British cavalry and infantry; the deployment there for the first time in the nineteenth century of the Royal Artillery; and the raising of 26 new infantry battalions at home and one in Canada. Indeed, the Mutiny so stretched British military resources that only fourteen battalions remained for Home defence. The Second Afghan War involved six cavalry regiments, 38 batteries and 24 battalions of the British Army, and 29 regiments, seven batteries and 71 battalions of the reformed Indian Army.[1]

In the early part of Victoria's reign, and until the Cardwell Reforms of the 1870s, soldiers enlisted for long periods of up to 25 years. Within this period they could expect to spend years at a stretch in remote imperial garrisons or on campaign, which often so exhausted them that they were fit for nothing else upon their discharge. With such lengthy foreign service, it is not surprising that their language became littered with Hindustani and Arabic expressions, so that bread was always '*roti*', water '*pani*' and beer '*pongelow*'; food was '*skof*' and the cook the '*bobbajee*'. The recruit was a 'rooky', the veteran 'an old sweat' and the soldier always spoke of himself as a 'swaddy'; his lady-friend or whore was a 'pusher' with whom he 'square-pushed'; the teetotaller was a 'bun strangler' or 'pop-wallah'. His bed his 'kip', his helmet his 'topee' and uniform 'clobber', working clothes were 'fatigues'; boots were 'daisy-roots'; to be under arrest was to be 'on the peg' and prison was 'college'. Work was 'graft' and the 'grouser' groused about it; arguing made him a 'barrack room lawyer' or he might be a 'Queen's bad bargain' who, turning over a new leaf, was said to be 'on the cot'. His breakfast, if he had any, of bread and coffee was always known as 'slingers'.[2] For a new recruit, recently arrived in India, the language of the veterans must have seemed as foreign as the country he had just entered.

On arrival, after weeks at sea, the British soldier could expect to march not only to his new barracks, but then further into the interior, if there was a campaign or a lesson to be taught to the locals. The distances involved could be immense. This was particularly true of India. Sergeant Ford of the 61st Regiment, who served during the Sikh wars of the 1840s, claimed that in the five years between November 1845 and November 1850 he marched 5,295 miles, often covering 40 miles a day. In September 1858, the 33rd Regiment marched from Deesa in India to Coromo al Cast, a distance of 500 miles, which was achieved

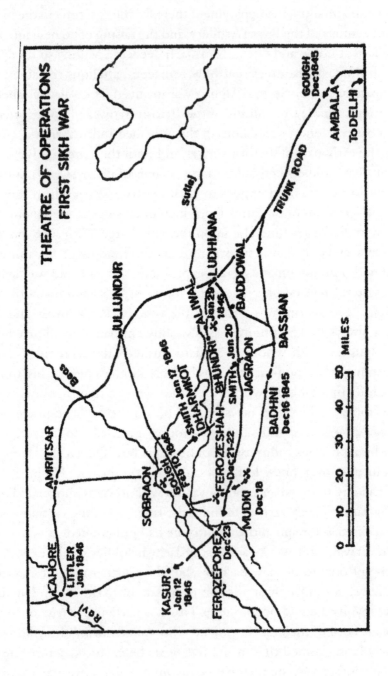

in 30 days, despite being hindered by the monsoon season. The requirement for a rapid movement of troops in times of crisis would impose
huge demands on the British soldier. The need to march to the relief of
Kandahar from Kabul in August 1880 saw General Roberts march his
10,000 troops (and all their supplies) the 280 miles in just twenty days.[3]

Although the utilisation of the railways in India to move troops
became commonplace from the 1880s onwards, the situation in Africa
was very different. At the beginning of the 1870s the railway age had
hardly begun on that continent. There existed only two short rail lines
in Egypt, and, with the exception of 152 miles in the Cape and Natal,
there were no tracks in all of Africa south of the Sahara.[4] Thus, the
24th Regiment of Foot arrived in Cape Town on New Year's Day
1875, and their journey ended in disaster at the hands of the Zulus
at the Battle of Isandlwana on 22 January 1879, the whole journey
being undertaken on foot. By the time of the Boer War (1899–1902),
rail lines were in place to transfer troops, horses and stores from Cape
Town, but more specifically from the port of Durban, into Natal and
the Transvaal. Certainly the Boers understood the importance of the
railway and both trains and lines were targeted by them. For the British
ranker the railways did not offer much comfort, as is illustrated in
the following anonymous account from a private in the 1st Battalion
Devonshire Regiment.

> Landed in Durban from Bombay and once disembarked – About 6 o'clock
> in the evening we were packed like sardines in open cattle trucks which
> were in a very wet condition. We had several loaves of bread, and fruit,
> etc, given to us by the civilians. We eventually moved off amidst great
> cheering … we almost cheered ourselves hoarse going through Durban
> and the outskirts. About midnight there came on a drizzling rain, and the
> wind blew very cold, and it was by far the coldest time I had ever expe-
> rienced up to that date. We could hardly move a hand, or foot, and being
> wet through, we looked rather dejected objects.[5]

However, the British of all ranks came to appreciate the railways, not
just for their own transportation, but for the supplies that they brought.
This can be seen from the entry for 26 March 1900 of the diary of the
9th Earl of Airlie.

I think I have been cured of my dislike of railways. *I love them* now and look upon them and the snorting engine as the treasured links between the dear Homeland and ourselves – to say nothing of them as conveyors of food for ourselves and horses!'[6]

However, the benefits of railway transport were to be only enjoyed towards the end of the nineteenth century. For most of Victoria's reign, warfare moved at the speed of an ox wagon, and few ever covered more than twelve miles a day. A flooded river or soft ground could bring a column to a halt and a smashed wheel or broken axle could take up to a week to repair. Private J. Davies of the Duke of Edinburgh Own Volunteers fought in the Basuto War in South Africa during 1880, and in a letter to his mother he described how his marching column took five hours to cover one mile due to the fact that their wagons had become stuck in a drift.[7] British and native infantry, cavalry and artillery snaked slowly through the dust of India and Africa, often accompanied by a menagerie of animals: mules, bullocks, elephants, camels and even yaks. The camels, in particular, could be tiresome as Major Carr of the Devonshire Regiment recorded in Afghanistan in 1880.

Our camels were very troublesome – they had never before seen a European and bolted at the first opportunity. Kits, cooking utensils, light baggage, etc. were lost for ever, nothing of value was recovered.[8]

The climate did not seriously affect the health of the British soldier only in the tropics. The Crimean War was noted for the high number of troops who fell to disease, and the understanding of how much the climate of the area affected the men's health was recognised by the Medical Officer of the 4th South Devonshire Regiment when he wrote his official report.

The climate of the Crimea is exceedingly capricious – the changes from Heat to Cold, from Rain to Sleet and snow have at times been so random and rapid that we might say that in 24 or 36 hours we have felt the influence of all the seasons. These alterations of temperature had a very serious effect in producing disease.[9]

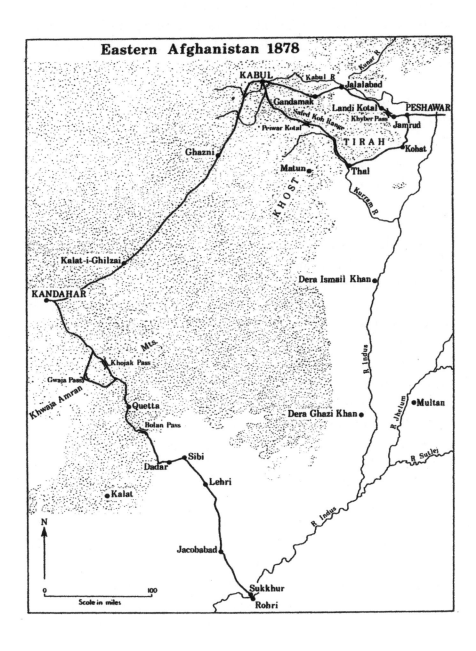

Eastern Afghanistan 1878

Kunar R.

KABUL

Kabul R.

Jalalabad

Gandamak

Landi Kotal

PESHAWAR

Safed Koh Range

Khyber Pass

Peiwar Kotal

Jamrud

TIRAH

Kohat

Ghazni

Matun

Thal

KHOST

Kurram R.

Kalat-i-Ghilzai

Dera Ismail Khan

KANDAHAR

Mts.

Khojak Pass

R. Indus

Gwaja Pass

Khwaja Amran

Quetta

Dera Ghazi Khan

Multan

Bolan Pass

R. Jhelum

Sibi

Dadar

Lehri

R. Sutlej

Kalat

N

R. Indus

Jacobabad

Sukkhur

0   100

Scale in miles

Rohri

Along with the physical hardship of long marches over inhospitable terrain, often in conditions of appalling heat, was the ever present risk of
sunstroke, which claimed the lives of many a British soldier. Rudyard
Kipling pointed up the risks of sunstroke in his poem *The Young British
Soldier*.

> But the worst o' your foes is the sun over 'ead:
> You *must* wear your 'elmet for all that is said:
> If 'e finds you uncovered 'e'll knock you down dead,
> An; you'll die like a fool of a soldier.
> Fool, fool, fool of a soldier ...

Private Waterfield, a soldier of the 32nd Foot during the Sikh wars,
recorded that he had to march with the accoutrements of the infantry which included leather belt and braces, with two pouches on the
front, each containing some fifty rounds of ammunition, bayonet, rifle,
entrenching tool, together with knapsack.[10] The British soldier in
the Crimean War, when fully laden with uniform, shako cap, musket,
ammunition pouches, water bottle, bayonet and haversack, would have
carried a burden in excess of 70 pounds when on the march.[11] Such
loads, combined with the harsh conditions in which the men had to
march, naturally took their toll.

The conditions experienced by British troops on the march during
the Sikh wars were particularly gruelling, whilst the care for the sick
was basic in the extreme, as described by Private Waterfield in his diary
on 21 August 1848.

> 14 miles 2 furlongs – we had more than 200 men taken sick on the road
> this morning, and after we got to camp the dhooly bearers were car-
> rying men to hospital tents all day. As soon as a man was brought into
> hospital he was laid on the ground underneath a tent, when an apoth-
> ecary would make his appearance, instantly bleed the patient and leave
> him lying there, until he fainted then they would bind his arm, and go
> to attend to some other poor fellow. Thermometer 123 degrees in the
> tents, sixteen men died this morning and the poor fellows were laid in
> one grave in the evening.[12]

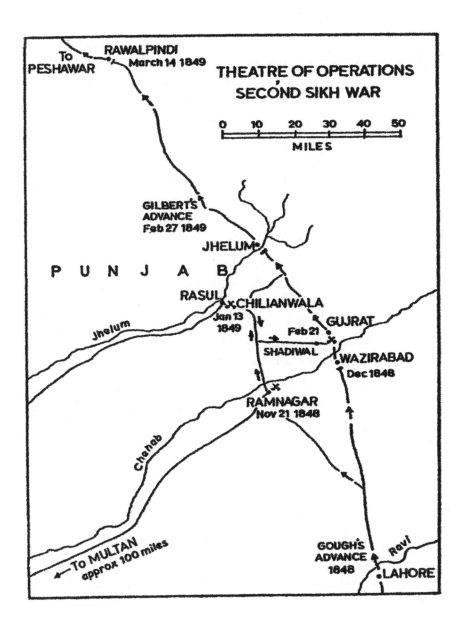

To PESHAWAR

RAWALPINDI
March 14 1849

THEATRE OF OPERATIONS
SECOND SIKH WAR

0   10   20   30   40   50
MILES

GILBERT'S
ADVANCE
Feb 27 1849

JHELUM

P U N J A B

RASUL

x CHILIANWALA
Jan 13
1849

Jhelum

Feb 21

GUJRAT
x

SHADIWAL

WAZIRABAD
Dec 1848

x

RAMNAGAR
Nov 21 1848

Chenab

TO MULTAN
approx 100 miles

GOUGH'S
ADVANCE
1848

Ravi

LAHORE

Two days later, Waterfield recorded an even more arduous and traumatic march of eleven miles and six furlongs:

> A great number fell out sick this morning. My Company was more than a hundred strong, but only 13 men out of the whole Company marched into camp with the column; the remainder were taken ill on the road. Poor John Buxton died a few hours after leaving camp. It was only yesterday when the poor fellow was singing songs on the road to cheer up the men, for wherever poor 'Buxton' was, mirth and jollity there existed. He was deeply regretted by all ... Many there who shed a tear at the loss of poor 'Buxton', he was interred this evening in the one grave with Sergeant Creah, who enlisted me, and was always my sincere friend. [13]

The dangers of sunstroke were not limited to small numbers of men for large numbers of troops, newly arrived from Britain and not yet acclimatised to the harsh climate, fell to the effects of sunstroke during the Indian Mutiny of 1857–9. Over 1,000 men died of sunstroke, fatigue and disease in May 1858 alone. [14]

Major Carr, of the Devonshire Regiment, described the effects of sunstroke in Afghanistan in 1880:

> Marching in a country without roads, in stifling heat and dust, tired all ranks, but they were cheerful withal. The men bathed in the Bolan river at Pirchowki in the early morning and tried to rest in the landys (mud sheds) during the day, but the intense heat began to take toll, Sergeant Downs and Private Longshaw died of heat apoplexy. We entered the pass that night for a 21 miles march to Mach, and for most of the way, only the sky over head could be seen. The pass is very narrow and the rocks retaining the heat during the night made it very trying. The river crossed and recrossed the road track many times, and while struggling with the bullocks and carts at the fords, many of the men stripped to the waists and bathed their heads and bodies. We arrived at Mach in the early morning, but it was late ere the last cart came in. We had a rest camp of double Fly tents (Indian E.P.) but the heat was awful, two more men died, one on the march (Sturmey) and one in camp (Timpson) – good hardy old soldiers. [15]

The effects of sunstroke during a battle could be of course just as fatal, as Lieutenant Meiklejohn witnessed as the Battle of Omdurman on 2 September 1898.

> Everybody pretty weary. Two or three deaths from sunstroke, and one of our men suddenly started singing, went raving mad and died with five or six men holding him down.[16]

For those that collapsed and died while on the march, only a shallow grave, at best, could be expected. Joseph Hewitt, a soldier in 62nd Wiltshire Regiment, recalled, in his journal of service in India in the 1840s, the horror of marching back over the same ground that his regiment had covered only two months before.

> … we encamped at the same places that we did on coming up, and in every place where we had buried a comrade, found that they had been torn out of their graves by jackals or some other uncultivated beasts and eaten.

Such grisly discoveries must have reminded Hewitt and his comrades of their possible fate if they did not take care to avoid sunstroke. Yet, despite all their best efforts, their lives depended on the provision of water, which was not always available. During the pursuit of the Sikh army in 1845, Hewitt described how both the officers and men of the 62nd Regiment suffered terribly from thirst and dust and that not a drop of water was to be had.

> An officer held up a purse. He said there were fifty rupees in it and he would give it to anyone for a dram of water. If it had been five hundred he could not have got it.[17]

It was in the deserts of Egypt and the Sudan that the supply of water became so vital. This was recognised by the War Office for it was able to issue, in July 1882, what it described as a *Distance Map of Upper Egypt*. This provided senior officers with approximate distances in miles and furlongs between towns and watering holes, and, crucially for journeys over the desert, it gave times, in days and hours, between such holes. For example, the time distance between Kosseir and

Edfu was shown as being two days, whilst that between Abydos and El Khargeh was 38 to 40 hours. The War Office also issued a similar map that indicated where the telegraph stations could be found throughout the country.[18]

Despite such information, the desert environment was always exhausting and if, for example, troops were required to cover larger distances or march hastily, as in the British attempts to relieve Khartoum in 1884–5, then the men's suffering increased. In his memoirs, Lord Charles Beresford described the march to Metemmeh – where steamers sent from Khartoum were to rendezvous with the British column – as one in which the 'soldiers suffered dreadfully from thirst; their tongues were so swollen as to cause intense pain, their lips black, their mouths covered with white mucus. Several men fainted.' When water was reached, even though it was yellow and creamy, it tasted 'cool, sweet and delicious' to such men.[19] Similarly, Percy Marling, who was present on the same march, described the wells of Abu Klea as 'just a collection of about 20 holes in the sand, from about 8 to 20 feet deep, with about a foot of the dirtiest, filthiest water at the bottom. I should think I drank a bucket of it all the same.'[20] During this campaign water was rationed to a mere quart per day for each man and since it was carried in iron tanks, mounted on transport camels, it was often heated to boiling point by the desert sun and would often scald the dry and blistered lips of the troops.[21]

When British troops again returned to the Sudan in 1898 to march on Khartoum, the desert environment once more took a toll on the soldiers. Private Teigh of the Lincolnshire Regiment recorded that

We had taken the wrong way and had got too far from the Nile and we ran short of water. There were about 500 men of the Brigade fell out and we marched 32 miles. As soon as I saw the Nile I made for it, for I felt very faint, but how much water I drank I cannot say. When the men saw the water there was no such thing as keeping them in the ranks. They strolled all over the shore, so you can bet how they felt. We stopped here for an hour and then marched another 5 miles in the heat of the sun. Officers and everyone were falling out. I stopped and made a drink of tea and had some cold meat. When we got there I was pleased to have a rest.[22]

One of Teigh's officers, Lieutenant Meiklejohn wrote of the same scene.

> A scorching hot day [27 February 1898]: very heavy going in patches
> of deep sand: boots wearing out on the flinty desert: no water and eve-
> rybody suffering from thirst: all very exhausted and the men falling out
> in scores. These were brought on by camel. When at last we sighted the
> Nile again about 11 am there was a regular stampede for the water and
> we all waded in and drank, not caring whether it was pure or not.[23]

The risk of illness from drinking polluted water was very real, particularly after a battle. Lieutenant Kirby wrote in his journal, of the First
Sikh War, that after the Battle of Ferozeshah (21 December 1845) water
had to be obtained from a well close to the battlefield. Kirby described
the water as

> … very bad – indeed afterwards it was said that there were dead bodies
> of the enemy thrown into it, and it has always since gone by the name of
> 'Sikh Soup', however, it was drunk with great avidity and for two days
> we had no other water.[24]

After the Battle of Kassassin on 28 August 1882, the British troops, following the lead of the Duke of Connaught, drunk from the nearby
Sweetwater Canal. The Duke who had pronounced the water safe
was later taken ill with diarrhoea, as were scores of British soldiers, for
Egyptian dead were later found floating in the canal.[25] Percy Marling
was ordered to remain as part of the garrison of Kassassin, as the rest of
the British force advanced on Tel-el-Kebir. He wrote in his diary on
29 August 1882.

> The place smells frightfully and the water is dreadful, as the Canal is
> full of dead Arabs, camels and horses. Within 50 yards of where we were
> drinking we pulled out 2 dead Arabs, 1 camel, and a horse.[26]

In Afghanistan in 1880 the 2nd Battalion of the Devonshire Regiment
suffered terribly during its forced march to attempt the relief of
Kandahar. Already exhausted men fell to polluted water, as Major Carr
told in his diary of the march.

Our hopes of remaining at Kandahar were dashed – orders were received for the Battalion to proceed up the Arghandab Valley to facilitate the getting in of supplies ... we made the best of things, rigged up field ovens, baked bread, and caught fish – a great treat. Alas it was found that the water was slightly charged with sulphur and aggravated the illness from which the men were already suffering, and what can only be described as an epidemic of Dysentery broke out – convoy after convoy was sent to the Base Hospital at Kandahar. The only means of transport being camel Kajawahs, and unhappily several men died on the way. The M.O. and his Staff were greatly concerned about our men and although every attention was given, the death roll increased. Many of the men were incurable, their intestines being worn out, and more than 100 found their last resting place round an Obelisk, which we erected in the small British Cemetery at Kandahar.[27]

In South Africa, on 12 May 1900, officers of the 12th Lancers discovered that the only water to be found was from a pool in which a dead horse was seen under the surface. The Regimental history confirmed that 'Three officers could not curb their impatience to drink before the water was boiled and took it with a liberal dash of whisky. All three contracted enteric fever and only one, Lieutenant Grant, survived. The other two, Ralli and Hamilton, succumbed.'[28] Although medical science advanced at a rapid pace during the nineteenth century, it was not until its end that the link between typhoid and cholera and polluted water was understood. Contaminated water could be more catastrophic than enemy action.

Whilst the desert environment could be tortuous, the conditions, and distances, to be found on the South African veldt also imposed huge demands upon the British soldier. Writing to his parents in 1880 of his experiences during the Basuto War, Private J. Davies wrote

Yesterday we arrived here on the Banks of the Orange River and we were nearly all ready to drop for want of water and fatigue. Our lips were cracked and our faces peeled with the heat. We get up every morning at 4 o'clock when the Bugle sounds, and do as much marching as we can before the heat comes on. Some days we march a long distance before the wagons and we have to wait for them to come up before we can have food. Some nights we had to sleep in the open air as the wagons were a long way behind us and in the morning the dew was so thick on the blankets that we could wring it out. The water here is not good and brings on dysentery.[29]

Ensign William Fleming of the 45th Regiment of Foot recorded his experiences of marching across Africa during the Kaffir War of 1847.

It was very pleasant when we first started but soon the sun got up and the heat became frightful. Our 22 carts kicked up a most fearful dust the road being simply sand and hands, faces and clothes soon became covered with a sort of mud … Each cart had a man driving it and another with a long whip about 10 feet long walking by the side to keep the mules going but with all our endeavours we could not manage more than three miles an hour the road soon became fearfully steep and the whole journey was simply a continual climb round and round hills … in the mornings there is a beastly mist which wets everything through and through and the ticks and the flies are awful. I am a mass of bites and the ticks stick into you and have to be pulled out.[30]

Private M.M. Tuck, a bandsman in the 58th (Rutlandshire) Regiment, described in his diary a march of 72 kilometres from Dundee in Natal to Utrecht in the Transvaal, which began on 18 October 1879.

On we trudged … up one hill and down another one again, only to see another appear. No regular roads, only a beaten track. No vegetation, nothing but … ant hills … We have now travelled 17 African miles and the heat commenced to tell its tale. A few men fell out, some because their soles refused to carry them further, others from fatigue. No joking now, no singing, every man's shoulder to the wheel … no water to be got anywhere, nothing but stagnant pools. On we go over one hill to find another in front of us, no signs of a Camp, more falling out for the want of shoe-leather. Heels left here, soles left there, tips all over the place till at last after marching from sunrise till long after sunset, we espy the camp having marched 29 African miles in the heat of the day, on about two or three ounces of dry bread and half boiled coffee.[31]

Twenty years later, despite some of the journey being undertaken on the railways, troops were still forced to march many hundreds of miles during the Boer War. Lance-Corporal A. Rose recorded in his diary a march of 14 February 1900.

> ... left camp early this morning for Riet River. Today's march was awful, no water on the way and the sun very hot and the dust very thick. My chum was properly done up. I carried his rifle for him which enabled him to get along a little better. We got to the River at last and after helping to pull the Naval Guns across the Drift went and had a good drink and a rest then went into camp having marched 16 miles today.[32]

If the troops were to be engaged in battle, forced marches were regularly undertaken so as to surprise the enemy, no easy task against the guerrilla tactics of the Boers. Private Wilton of 'The Buffs' recorded such a march in his diary of 7 March 1900.

> a very hard and trying day marching from 3 am until 9 pm. Made a long and trying flank march so as to get around enemy's left ... very tired and thirsty ... all we had in the shape of food was 2 dry biscuits and contents of our water bottles, the latter lasting but a very short time.[33]

Lance-Corporal William Fitzwilliams of the Argyll and Sutherland Highlanders wrote to his parents from the Boer War as he journeyed with Lord Roberts on the forced march to Pretoria. Fitzwilliam told of very severe marching and of one week in which his Regiment covered 17 to 20 miles each day, on half rations. He described how the days were mostly scorching and that he and his comrades felt

> ... the heat of the sun notably on knees and noses ... the best protection against noses and knees is to let them get dirty and on no account wash your nose. The company is getting most disreputable. No-one has shaved for 10 days and do not intend to do so until we get to Pretoria.[34]

Africa is a continent of extremes, and these were certainly experienced by the Soldiers of the Queen. When the British, commanded by Colonel Evelyn Wood, advanced on the Ashanti positions in the

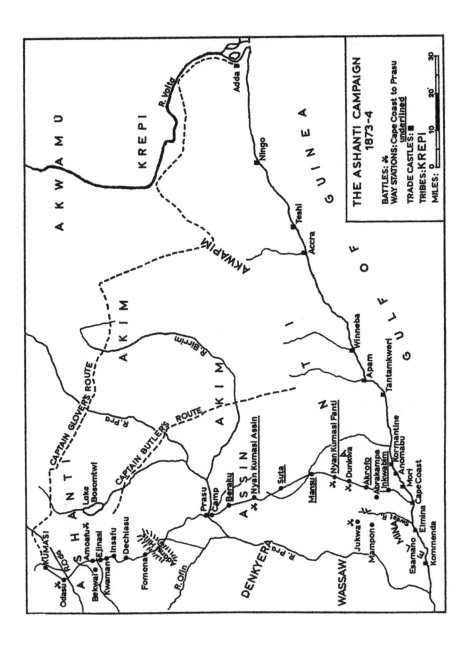

THE ASHANTI CAMPAIGN
1873-4

BATTLES: ✗
WAY STATIONS: Cape Coast to Prasu underlined
TRADE CASTLES: ■
TRIBES: KREPI
MILES: 0 10 20´ 30

jungles of West Africa on 14 October 1873, the temperatures and humidity experienced, along with the harsh terrain, made covering the 22 miles on this first expedition extremely difficult. At one point, Wood's column could only achieve four miles in nearly three hours. Lieutenant Eyre dropped from exhaustion and although the men had carried as much water as possible, this had been insufficient and some were without any liquid for the last six hours of the march.[35]

In contrast, when Napier led a British force into Abyssinia in 1867 he and his men suffered from the extreme cold. Captain Francis Barker of the Royal Artillery, who accompanied the march to King Tewodros' capital at Magdala, wrote to his father on 29 March 1868.

> For the last week we have been flying through the mountains of Abyssinia – one day encamping at seven thousand feet above the sea – and perhaps the next day at over twelve thousand: and I can tell you that the cold has at times been something tremendous. We all sleep on the ground now and no beds or baggage are we permitted to take. Yesterday it was very hot in the valley in which we encamped and tonight we have ice in the tent.[36]

Ensign W. Wynter of the 33rd Regiment also fought in the Abyssinian campaign and in his journal described the climate, with sang froid, as 'trying'. Wynter stated that whilst there was six or seven degrees of frost at night, the midday temperatures rose to 90 degrees. In such conditions, Wynter saw that 'the faces of those who couldn't grow beards or moustaches were covered with blisters!'[37]

It was not only extremes of temperature and endless miles of deserts that the Victorian soldier had to contend with, but also torrents of rain and rivers that had to be forded. Sergeant McMilan (Light Division) landed onshore at Calamita Bay 14 September 1854 with the first of the landing forces. He described in his diary the subsequent day march towards Sebastopol.

> It was dark when we halted last night and the rain came down in torrents. We got a few dead weeds to lay on and we lay all night exposed to the pelting storm … We kept our belts on all the time and our flintlocks piled near us. When I got up in the morning I was that stiff I scarce could stand, the men got together some of the weed we had to lay on

and made fires. I managed to boil about half a pint of water ... and made some tea.[38]

Colour Sergeant John McGrath of the 33rd Regiment told of a march he undertook in September 1858 between Deesa and Coromo al Cast in India, a distance of 500 miles.

Getting to this place was very difficult, the month of September being the close of the monsoon season, the country we had to travel over being flat. Scarcely a day past without our wading through water 3 or 4 times during our days march. This had to be done with boots on, and my readers can imagine what an unpleasant thing it is to walk or march in wet socks and boots.[39]

During the campaign to relieve Khartoum in 1884–5, those assigned to the Nile route not only experienced great physical tests, but were also repeatedly soaked. Men had to row or pull their boats over the rapids, try to keep the boats of each company together, and periodically unload, carry and then reload their cargo of 70 boxes (some of which weighed as much as 65 pounds). Bandsman Barwood of the Black Watch recalled how he was at times 'quite exhausted, my hands cut and blistered, wet through all day, scarcely any clothes whole, and my feet and legs also cut'. As boats floundered occasionally on the rocks or capsized or broke their rudders, Barwood found himself 'up to the waist in water every day and at all times of the day'.[40]

Lance-Corporal A. Rose of the Duke of Cornwall Light Infantry fought during the Boer War, yet much of his diary records the times he was either marching or on outpost duty, when he experienced the rains of Africa. On 20 February 1900 Rose wrote

We received orders to go on outpost about 4 miles on the other side of the river. Of course we got another wetting and to make matters worse it began raining and came down in torrents and having no change of clothing we have to wait until the sun comes out before we can dry ourselves – oh it is lovely![41]

For all the hardship of marching in Africa, it was probably in Afghanistan that the British soldier faced his greatest physical challenge. Lieutenant

Thomas Gaisford of the 1st Battalion Horse Artillery wrote to his brother from Kabul in 1839 and described to him the hardship of the Battalion's march to the city.

> The Gun horses of the Bombay forces performed 220 miles over mountains and desert with often no forage and sometimes no water on 7 days half rations of grain – followers of the camp, fighting men being reduced to half rations were to be seen gorging carrion and picking grains of corn from the excrements of animals! Never was such an advance seen – I saw one day the body of a man who had died by the wayside in the act of gnawing the gristle from the carcass of a dead bullock![42]

Although Gaisford's experience was particularly horrific, the topography of Afghanistan, as well as extremes of temperature, inflicted constant hardship. In his papers concerning Royal Artillery operations in and around Kabul in 1879–80, Lieutenant-Colonel Gordon of the Royal Artillery graphically described the manhandling of six guns and six wagons up and over the 10,500 feet of Shutargarden Mountain on 22 September 1879.

> This Kotal is very steep, having an average slope from base to summit of 1 in 9, and here and there turns so sharp, that the guns and wagons had to be unlimbered and run–up by hard labour ... we at length succeeded in getting all the carriages to the summit, the ascent of 1,100 yards having taken 3½ hours ... The steepness of the road too rendered driving the more difficult, and by far the worst part of the whole road was the short decline just at the bottom of the slope, so that it was almost impossible for the drivers to see where they were going. We could only drag one wheel, as the steepness of the inside bank prevented our using hand–spikes for the limber wheels, but with the gunners holding on to drag ropes behind, the descent was safely accomplished.[43]

Despite, the difficulties imposed by the terrain, Private Lloyd, at least, clearly found the countryside captivating. In his diary of 18 April 1880, Lloyd wrote

> Our march today laid through Khojak Pass. This the hardest march we have seen especially for the poor camels. The Pass is so steep in some

places nearly perpendicular, at length we reach the top and the sight that presented itself I am afraid to attempt a description – it was near midday, the sun which we had not seen all the time we were labouring up the pass was glazing down in all its glory. The path we had to descend was almost perpendicular. The ascend had been 5 miles, while the descend was only two miles laid at our feet, beyond laid the plain of Chamon which in the suns powerful rays had more the appearance of a sea of molten silver than a parch sandy plain as we found it to be. After a short halt we commenced the descend and after a good deal of rolling and tumbling we got safely to the bottom and glad we were to be on the level once more.[44]

Major Carr left a less romantic account of the reality of marching through Afghanistan as he journeyed with the Devonshire Regiment to Kandahar in 1880.

The Division crossed the Khojak on the morning of the 30th August and we followed the same night, half a day's march behind. We had nominally half rations (really much less), no bread or biscuits, only flour to be made into Chuppaties without Ghee, or fat of any kind; salt and sugar gave out quickly and later tea. Meat was provided by killing the starving bullocks, as their loads were used up – and the carts were broken up for firewood. We arrived at Chaman as the Division left and after resting started off again for Gatai, 19½ miles across sand through the Registan Desert (called by the men, Chaman Plain). This march was very trying, the men suffering from lack of food, were now short of water for the very small quantity carried in their water bottles (soda water bottles covered with leather) and by the few Bhistis, soon gave out and it was a jaded, thirsty and absolutely worn out body that reached the wells of Gatai that night. Officers and men simply threw themselves on the ground and slept.[45]

For the officers of the British Army, the march to war was not always about privation and hardship. There was some enjoyment to be had. Ensign Wynter had, whilst serving on the Abyssinian Campaign of 1867, the surprisingly agreeable responsibility of supplying meat for the officers' table.

[He] had an enjoyable time as every evening he went out shooting 'for the pot'. There were great quantities of guinea fowl and pigeons. His supply of cartridges for a 'pinfire gun' by Reilly was limited, and he used to creep up on his stomach, and get half a dozen birds in line on the ground before firing! He was very successful, and consequently very popular with his friends.[46]

Captain Barker also had the role of meat provider during the same campaign and recorded in his diary of 25 February that with his rifle he shot an elephant, but he did not record how the beast tasted, nor how it was butchered and cooked.

Similarly, Captain H. Austin of the Royal Engineers was able to enjoy moments of safari and big game hunting whilst campaigning in Uganda in 1897. On 25 August, Austin recorded that

Tracey and I had a long but fruitless hunt after four lions that we detected out on the plains. They were as cunning as foxes in the way they doubled back on their tracks, and it was some time before either of us could get a shot at them. Eventually I let drive at one with my .303, to which he answered with an angry snarl, showing his teeth and lashing his tail. It was only for a moment, though, and before I could get another shot he was gone. Then the other three jumped up out of a nullah one after the other, and Tracy and I both fired, but we failed to bag any of them, and they went off. We hunted them for a long time, but never came across them again. The main body enjoyed considerable sport before we reached the Athi, and Major Macdonald and Kirkpatrick had an exciting beat after lions quite close to the camp; but they met with no better luck then we had, and it was not until we reached Lake Nakuru that the first lion was bagged by the expedition. This was secured by Kirkpatrick, who dropped one stone dead with a snap shot, the bullet entering the animal's brain and killing it instantaneously.

As the campaign progressed opportunities for hunting became fewer, but by November 1897 Austin entered an area in which

Game was very abundant, but we had little leisure now for shooting, and we saw many hartebeeste and a fine herd of about twenty giraffes.

Osborn and I were both fortunate enough to shoot a hartebeeste each, so the men had plenty of meat that day.[47]

The journey in 1898 along the Nile to Omdurman also offered opportunities to bag food for the pot, as shown by the 15 February diary entry of Lieutenant S. FitzGibbon Cox of the Royal Lincolnshire Regiment.

Went out with my rifle and Barlow this afternoon up the river, with gun, got a dove and a quail, I got a goose, shot him on the water about 60 yards off and sent a native in to fetch him – also winged another – a very good long shot, but couldn't get him as he got into the cataract.

Two days later, he wrote

Got leave and up early to shoot with Barlow, started at 4.30 am and walked up the river, and shoot another goose, an eagle and two other furry black birds, all with rifle, which shoots very straight. One wants a boat to do it properly, as you have to send a native to fetch birds.

Not all animals that were seen were eaten. Lieutenant S. FitzGibbon Cox, who fought in Sudan in 1898, wrote in his diary of 15 August that he 'saw three hippopotamuses swimming about close to us in the evening, caused great excitement and nearly capsized one of the barges by men running to the side.' The following day he recorded that he saw 'three more in the evening. We thought they were going to ram us but they turned off when close. I shan't think much of a salmon rise after a hippo one!'[48] Of course, some of the larger animals, as well as the insects and poisonous snakes, presented a real threat to the British soldier on the march, as was recorded by Lance-Corporal William Eaton in a letter to his brother in 1880.

We have only lost one man of our draft since leaving Bradford ... one day we got to a place called Jubebad, there was a river at this place, and as soon as we got an opportunity, a lot of us went to bathe, this man they called him Moore he was a Bradford man, he was hurrying to get in first, as soon as he got in some alligators sprung up and took him down and we never saw him after.[49]

In addition to such large beasts, the British soldier had to contend with smaller but equally unwelcome pests, as described by Sergeant Spratt in a letter to his mother during the Boer War.

Cannot get any soap to wash with so you can tell we have some live-stock about us. It seems amazing to see us all sitting on the ground, or on ant-hills picking them out – looks like a lot of monkeys at the zoo. I shall miss them when they are all gone for I think they helps to keep one warm of a night.[50]

Likewise, an unidentified soldier from the South Staffordshire Regiment wrote home from the Boer War, on 27 May 1900.

I think it was the 8th of April when I last changed my shirt and we sleep in all our clothes, you can judge how we are for being (nitty) we pull our things off every time we have a chance and have a pick at the livestock, it is enough to make anyone sick who have been used to being clean.[51]

Food, or the lack of it, was a natural preoccupation for the Victorian soldier on the march. When serving in Britain, food was plain and monotonous. The ration was fixed in 1813 at three-quarters of a pound of meat and one pound of bread per day. It remained at that level to the end of the Boer War. When serving overseas most troops received an extra allowance of a quarter of a pound of meat on the grounds that foreign meat was inferior to that produced in England, and the same addition was granted to troops at camp. The disparity between the meat ration at home and overseas stations was made greater for married men by the fact that their ration in Britain had to suffice for both the soldier and his family, while in India in 1876, for example, the ration for a married soldier was two pounds of meat and bread.

The daily ration was divided between two meals, breakfast at 0730 hrs or 0800 hrs and dinner at 1230 hrs or 1300 hrs – the former usually consisting of bread and a basin of tea or coffee and the latter beef and potatoes. All food in excess of the official ration had to be purchased regimentally using money deducted from a soldier's pay, or by the soldiers individually from local tradesmen. The only cooking utensils were two coppers, one for potatoes and the other for meat, which meant that the principal fare for the day was invariably boiled beef, as there was no equipment available for baking or roasting. During the 19-hour gap between dinner at 1230 hrs and breakfast at 0730 hrs the soldier went hungry, filled his stomach with beer or bought extra food. Some commanding officers introduced, on their own initiative, a third daily meal paid for by stoppage of pay agreed to by the men. In 1840 a third meal, consisting of 'tea or coffee, with a portion of bread', was sanctioned by Horse Guards and it was usually served at 1600 hrs or 1630 hrs. Until 1873, deductions were made from each man's pay to cover the cost of rations: the soldier provided his own plate and basin, used for soup, tea, coffee, beer and shaving-water.[52]

On campaign much of the sickness that affected troops could be blamed on the abominable food provided by the Army and purchased from dubious private sources. Outdoors, over smokey fires amid dust and flies, unwashed native cooks transformed half-rotten food into unpalatable, sickness-producing meals. If this was not bad enough, the alternatives supplied from Britain could be just as dangerous. 'Bully Beef' was a staple, but if exposed to the sun too long the contents of the tin would emerge as a 'loathsome greasy mess'. Yet, faced with no alternative, the desperate would somehow force it down, only to later pay the price. Nine men from a machine-gun detachment were invalided home from the Sudan in 1898 as a result of eating contaminated bully beef. The monotony of this diet was sometimes broken by another form of canned meat known by the maker's name of 'Maconochie', a preserved meat and vegetable stew whose taste was frequently tainted by the flavours of the chemical preservatives and the can.[53] The tins also had the disquieting habit of exploding when pierced. General Fuller's memory of Maconochie was that it was 'dog's vomit'.[54]

Despite official pronouncements as to the rations that British troops should receive whilst on the march and on campaign, the reality, judging by the letters and the diaries of the men that served, was very different. Even on the rare occasion when the officially sanctioned ration was supplied, its nutritional value was limited. The Crimean Commissioners – called upon to investigate the failings of the Crimean

War – requested Dr Robert Christison of Edinburgh University to compare the nutritive principle of the British soldier's ration in the Crimea (i.e. one pound salt meat, one pound biscuit, two ounces sugar) with similar diets. Christison concluded that the diet of Scottish prisoners was more nutritious than that of the British soldier fighting in the Crimea.[55] This supported the view of the medical officer of the 4th South Devonshire Regiment expressed in his report of the campaign.

> The Rations do not appear to have been sufficiently nutritious – the quantity might have been generally enough but to men who had to perform duties of such severity a more nourishing diet i.e. a greater proportion of fresh meat and vegetables would have been to say the least of it highly judicious.[56]

When food was issued the quality was often substandard. The three-day meat ration issued to all troops on landing in Calamita Bay on 14 September 1854 was found to be rancid by the second day and the advancing troops were unable to eat it.[57]

The nature of campaigning meant that the supply of food and water to the troops could be often erratic, limited, and poor quality. Private James Oates fought in New Zealand in 1863 and, in a letter home, wrote of the food made available on the line of march.

> On the morning of the 20th [November] we marched from an old native position called Mere-Mese with 1 blanket rolled on our shoulders and 2 days provisions of salt pork and biscuit, the pork had been in salt about 10 years and the biscuit as hard as a ram rod – nice food to fight on.[58]

Captain Barker, in letters to his father from the Abyssinian Campaign, told of the hardships and the difficulty of receiving adequate food and how the lack of it affected morale. On the 17 April 1868, Barker wrote

> Sleepless nights, nothing to eat, less to drink, no beds and lots of hard work – will make us truly value the comforts of home life. A day's ration (when you get it) consists of half an ounce of vegetables, 12 ounces of flour, 1lb of meat (or rather leather) half an ounce of potatoes and a little

tea. The day before yesterday I was bursting and destroying Theodores guns and got nothing but one handful of roasted grain and some water spooned out of the hoof marks of a horse in mud, from 7 am to 8 pm. Little jokes of this kind, and sleeping under the dew harden, and stiffen – but do not strengthen a fellow much.[59]

Likewise, Percy Marling recorded the hardship of the attempted relief of Khartoum in his journal.

For the whole of last week I have felt as empty as possible, as there was literally not enough to eat. In England people can have no idea of what an awfully hard time we have had up here. In our march from Gakdul which took eight days we did not get 16 hours sleep, 3 pints of water per day, and for the last four days next to nothing to eat.'[60]

Earlier, during the Boer War of 1881, Marling wrote in his diary of the rations then available on campaign.

All our bread is finished. We now have biscuit so hard it has to be soaked first. Some of the biscuit is rotten and full of weevils. Yesterday Ryder broke a tooth in one.[61]

Captain Harry Earle of the 1st Yorkshire Regiment recorded some of the deprivations he and his men faced during the Boer War in a letter to his wife.

Hardly any water here – men had one little cup last night – I have not washed for about a week and have not had my clothes off for days ... shall probably get water tomorrow if we can force on to Modder River – my hair is matted! What odd details I tell you.[62]

It appears that supplying the men with both food and clothing during the Boer War was a major problem. Roberts' rapid march to outflank the Boer positions at Magersfontein and capture Pretoria in 1900 placed huge demands on the new centrally controlled Army Service Corps. The previous British commander, Redvers Buller, had placed great store in ensuring that each battalion had its own transport to facilitate the supply of food and stores to the men on the march and in the line. Roberts considered such a system costly and, far worse in his eyes, slow, cumbersome and wasteful. Roberts' plans for a rapid advance meant that an alternative central pool of supply wagons was adopted. However, these were extremely vulnerable to attack, as demonstrated on 15 February 1900 when the Boer commander, De Wet, caught one of these long columns at Riet Drift where he captured or destroyed nearly 2,000 oxen and 170 wagons. This action forced Roberts to abandon rations for his entire advancing force.

Thus, Lance Corporal Fitzwilliams was forced to write to his parents that

> Yesterday we started on one cup of coffee and then went 20 miles without a bite … the first food we got was some mutton at 7 pm and no biscuits or bread. Today we got 4 biscuits per man and were told they would have to do us for 3 days – a fine prospect![63]

Lance-Corporal Rose wrote in his diary entry for 21 February 1900 that he was 'starving having nothing whatever to eat. The Boers having captured our convey at Reit River.' Two days later Rose pleaded 'I wish they would give us something to eat. If they keep us like this much longer I shall be dropping through my clothes.' The following month the supply problems had still to be rectified and he noted that he was 'getting as weak as a kitten, but still smiling'.[64] Even Kitchener was to later admit that although Buller had had his failings as a commander, at least he kept his men fed. Private Henry Saunders of the West Riding Regiment recorded in a letter to his wife that even when food was available it could sometimes have unwelcome additional ingredients; 'we often find a few dozen ants and beetles stewed up in our dinner, don't laugh its a fact.'[65]

As the supply of food was often chaotic and unreliable during the Boer War, the Victorian soldier became used to an empty stomach and unsatisfied thirst when on the march. While some enterprising commanders like Buller tried to ensure regular supplies and some, such as Evelyn Wood, placed great store in establishing mobile field bakeries, generally the men had to survive on hard army biscuits, often for days at a time. When Wood entrenched his camp site at Kambula in March 1879, one of his first tasks was to make sure a bakery was set up and the men received a daily ration of fresh bread. However, the quality of the bread was not high and Private Alfred Davies claimed that it was made of Indian corn and mealies and that half of it was sand![66] Even when a meat ration was issued it was often from the carcasses of dead transport animals – oxen, horses, mules and camels – and the tough meat could be unappetising, to say the least. Yet the men themselves could be enterprising in their search for food. During the Battle of the Alma on 20 September 1854, Highland troops took refuge in a vineyard as they advanced and satisfied their thirst with grapes. Generally, foraging was not permitted, although during the Crimean War the French frequently had to complain to the British commander, Lord Raglan, that their horses were prone to disappearing overnight![67] Private soldiers relied heavily on regimental canteens, which were managed by NCOs and were established near regimental lines. The Scots Guards set up one in Cairo in 1882, which offered such luxuries as tinned jam, salmon and potted lobster, although the main selling line came from seven barrels of Younger's Edinburgh Ale. On the first day of opening the takings were over £50.[68]

On rare occasions the officers took matters into their own hands to provide the men with luxuries. Vincent Kennett-Barrington, who was Medical Officer to General Graham's force during the Suakin Campaign of 1885, distributed large numbers of medical comforts, oranges, tobacco etc. to the soldiers through their officers. In a letter to his wife of 7 April 1885 Kennett-Barrington wrote

During the last four days we have given out 3,000 oranges and 4 cwt of tobacco! The tired and worn out men are so grateful for their presents. Perhaps I may be criticised for this in the press but I consider that what I am doing carries out the spirit of adding to the comfort of our forces in the field. The poor fellows come in *loaded* with dust and so thirsty, so parched. An orange is indeed a blessing to them. The limes which I sent out on the Tamai march were greedily sought after …[69]

On joining the ranks, troops were issued with two uniforms – 'full dress' – a smart uniform to be worn on all important occasions, and 'undress' – a more informal dress for working. When on campaign both would be seen, although the 'undress' would be most commonly worn. The huge variety of environments in which the Victorian soldier found himself meant that uniforms were adapted to to them. During the Second Maori War (1863–4) in New Zealand the fighting uniform was a blue version of the standard scarlet jackets as it was considered more suitable to the fighting in the dense fern-bush that characterised the terrain, and on the Indian frontier most troops fought in smocks.[70]

Whatever the local variation, all campaigns were characterised by the fact that the public's image of the British soldier, smartly dressed in his scarlet or khaki uniform, was not the reality. Hard marching and campaigning across the plains of India or the veldt of South Africa took a heavy toll on the uniform. For troops campaigning in remote areas the annual replacement of uniforms could take a great deal longer to arrive. The pristine, parade-ground uniforms as depicted in the illustrated press were more likely to be patched and worn out. The men of the 24th Regiment who fought and died on the slopes of Isandlwana were dressed in rags. After a long campaign against the Gaika tribes the year before and the arduous march from Cape Town, many of the soldiers' uniforms were held together by patches. Percy Marling recorded, in his journal of the attempted relief of Khartoum in 1884–5, that by the end of the campaign the soldiers were 'literally in rags, both officers and men, and the latter's boots are in the most shameful state'.[71] Earlier, during the Crimean War, British troops were forced to resort to taking the boots and heavy coats from their dead comrades, or Russians, to supplement their disintegrating uniforms.

On 4 September 1882, Hay, the officer commanding the 1st Division of the Royal Artillery at Kassassin during the Egypt campaign of that year, was obliged to write to his District Command that

> I have the honour to bring to your notice seriously the state of the clothes and boots of the N.C.Os. and men under my command. There is something in the extreme degrees of the climate which causes the threads in boots and clothes to wear out and fray; and the sand and stones are hugely destructive to boots. Unless some steps be taken in the direction in which I point (e.g. repair materials) we shall march into Cairo in rags and tatters and without soles to our men's boots.

The men of the Royal Artillery were fortunate on this particular occasion, for three weeks later an additional pair of trousers was issued to them.[72] The extended lines in the Boer War meant that the men received scant re-supply of uniforms or boots. The sartorial mess Sergeant William Spratt described to his mother in a letter from Balmoral in South Africa on 17 September 1900 is typical of the condition in which many of the British troops found themselves: 'I want a pair of trousers and a pair of boots – the seat and knees are out of our trousers and I have had to do my boots up with wire to keep the sides from falling off.'[73] Even Spratt was lucky for Lance-Corporal Rose was to record, on 9 March 1900, that his boots had simply disintegrated and that he marched that day 'without any boots on doing the distance of 18 miles in stocking feet. Oh it is lovely!'[74] By the conclusion of the Boer War many British troops were dressed like their enemy, wearing dusty patched uniforms and weathered and battered slouch hats.[75]

The Soldiers of the Queen marched many hundreds, and even thousands of miles, as they campaigned in some of the most inhospitable environments on earth. They did so, often thirsty, hungry, dressed in rags. Although men succumbed and fell by the wayside, many achieved feats, in appalling conditions, of physical endurance that we can only gasp at and admire today.

There is no better way to describe their achievements than to quote Winston Churchill, who in 1899 and 1900, shared their hardships in South Africa.

All through the morning and on into the afternoon the long stream of men and guns flowed through the streets of Ladysmith, and all marvelled to see what manner of men these were – dirty, war-worn, travel-stained, tanned, their uniforms in tatters, their boots falling to pieces, their helmets dinted and broken, but nevertheless magnificent soldiers, striding along, deep-chested and broad-shouldered, with the light of triumph in their eyes and the blood of fighting ancestors in their veins. It was a procession of lions.[76]

Notes

1. M. Barthorp, *The British Army on Campaign 1856–1881*, (Osprey, London, 1988), p.4.

2. D. Featherstone, *Khaki and Red: Soldiers of the Queen in India and Africa*, (Arms and Armour Press, London, 1995), p.19.

3. I. Knight, *Marching to the Drums: From the Kabul Massacre to the Siege of Mafikeng*, (Greenhill Books, London, 1999), p.141.

4. L.H. Gann & P. Duignan, *The Rulers of British Africa, 1870–1914*, (Croom Helm, London, 1978), p.77.

5. Anon. Diary, 1st Devons, REF:DRM Acc No.810.

6. D.W. Stanley, *The Happy Warrior: A Short Account of the Life of David, 9th Earl of Airlie*, (Winchester, 1901).

7. Pvt. J. Davies, letter to mother, 17 October 1880, REF NAM 9309-98-3.

8. Diary of Major Carr, REF: DRM Box PO3 7.

9. Medical Report of the 4th South Devonshire Regiment, 1 October 1854 to 31 March 1855, REF: NAM 9409-34.

10. A. Swanson & D. Scott, (eds.), *The Memoirs of Private Waterfield*, (Cassell, London, 1968), p.159.

11. S. David, *Victoria's Wars: The Rise of Empire*, (Viking, London, 2006), p.23.

12. A. Swanson & D. Scott, p.50.

13. Ibid, p.51.

14. S. David, p.349.

15. Diary of Major Carr, REF: DRM Box PO3 7.

16. J. Meredith (ed.), *Omdurman Diaries 1898: Eye Witness Accounts of the legendary campaign*, (Leo Cooper, Barnsley, 1998), p.185.

17. Journal of Jospeh Hewitt, 62nd Regiment, p.10, REF: NAM 2005-12-24.

18. RAM MD/2510/1.

19. Lord Charles Beresford, *Memoirs*, (Methuen, London, 1914), p.269.

20. F. Emery, *Marching Over Africa: Letters from Victorian Soldiers*, (Hodder and Stoughton, London, 1986), p.144.

21. J. Lawrence, *The Savage Wars: British Campaigns in Africa, 1870–1920*, (Robert Hale, London, 1985), p.217.

22. J. Meredith (ed.), p.50.

23. Ibid, p.51.

24. Journal of Lt. Kirby, REF:NAM 1999-05-31.

25. J. Lawrence, p.217.

26. Colonel Sir Percival Marling, V.C., *Rifleman and Hussar*, (John Murray, London, 1931), p.80.

27. Diary of Major Carr, REF: DRM Box PO3 7.

28. P.F. Stewart, *The History of XII Lancer*, (Oxford University Press, 1950), p.209.

29. Pvt. J. Davies, letter to parents, 9 October 1880, REF: NAM 9309-98-3.

30. Ensign William Fleming, letter home, 8 January 1847, REF: NAM 1972-02-36-3.

31. Diary of Pvt. M. Tuck, REF:NAM 1970-05-21.
32. Diary of Lance-Corp. Rose, 14 February 1900, Duke of Cornwall's Light Infantry Museum, Bodmin.
33. Diary of Pvt. W. Milton, 7 March 1900, REF:NAM 2006-04-09.
34. L/C Fitzwilliam, letter to parents, 13 May 1900, REF: ASHM N-DI.FIT.
35. L. Maxwell, *The Ashanti Ring: Sir Garnet Wolseley's Campaigns 1870–1882*, (Leo Cooper, London, 1985) p.29.
36. Capt. F. Barker, letter to father, 29 March 1868, REF: RAM MD/1615.
37. Journal of Ensign W.A. Wynter, 33rd Regiment, REF: Bankfield Museum RMDWR.
38. J. Duncan & J. Walton, *Heroes for Victoria*, (Spellmount, Tunbridge Wells, 1991), p.52.
39. Journal of CSM J. McGrath, 33rd Regiment, REF: Bankfield Museum RMDWR.
40. E. Spiers, *The Scottish Regiments and Empire*, (Edinburgh University Press, 2006) pp.97–8.
41. Diary of Lance-Corp. Rose, 20 February 1900, Duke of Cornwall's Light Infantry Museum, Bodmin.
42. Lt. T. Gaisford, letter to brother, 20 August 1839, REF:NAM 1983-11-28.
43. Papers concerning Operations around Kabul 1879-1883, REF: RAM MD/942/1.
44. Diary of Pvt. Lloyd, 18 April 1880, REF:NAM 9404-86.
45. Diary of Major Carr, REF: DRM Box PO37.
46. Journal of Ensign W.A. Wynter, 33rd Regiment, REF: Bankfield Museum RMDWR.
47. Captain H. Austin, *With Macdonald in Uganda*, (Dawsons, London, reissue 1973), pp.22 and 81.
48. J. Meredith (ed), p.168.
49. Letter L/Corp. W. Eaton to brother, 10 April 1880, REF:NAM 1992-04-115.
50. Sgt. Spratt, letter to mother, 17 September 1900, REF: NAM 1985-07-75-1.
51. Letter from Unidentified solider, 1st Bn., South Staffordshire Regiment, Senekal, 27 May 1900, REF: NAM 1980-03-17-1.
52. Captain H. Austin, p.75.
53. J. Lawrence, p.217.
54. J. Fuller, *The Last of the Gentleman's Wars*, (Faber and Faber, London, 1937), p.44.

55. M. Harding (ed.), *The Victorian Soldier: Studies in the History of the British Army 1816–1914*, (National Army Museum, London, 1993), p.80.

56. Medical Report of the 4th South Devonshire Regiment, 1845–1857, REF: NAM 9409-34.

57. J. Duncan & J. Walton, p.52.

58. Pvt. J. Oats, 11th Regiment, letter to parents, 25 November 1863, REF: NAM 1984-01-98.

59. Capt. F. Barker, letter to father, 17 April 1868, REF: RAM MD/1615.

60. Colonel Sir Percival Marling, V.C., p.149.

61. Ibid, p.41.

62. Capt. H. Earle, letter to wife, 26 November 1899, REF:NAM 9611-60-189.

63. L/C Fitzwilliam, ;etter to parents, 13 May 1900, REF: ASHM N-DI.FIT.

64. Diary of Lance-Corp. Rose, 21 February, 23 February and 11 March 1900, Duke of Cornwall's Light Infantry Museum, Bodmin.

65. Pvt. H. Saunders, letter to wife, 2 November 1900, REF: Bankfield Museum RMDWR.

66. F. Emery, *The Red Soldier*, (Hodder & Stoughton, London, 1977) p.155.

67. S. Manning, *Evelyn Wood,* p.21.

68. J. Lawrence, p.224.

69. P. Morris (ed.), *First Aid to the Battlefront: Life and Letters of Sir Vincent Kennett-Barrington,* (Alan Sutton, Stroud, 1992), p.80.

70. I. Knight, *Go to Your God Like a Soldier: The British Soldier Fighting for Empire, 1837–1902,* (Greenhill, London, 1996) pp.139–140.

71. F. Emery, *Marching Over Africa*, p.150.

72. Letter from O/C 1st Div R.A. to D/C RA, 4 September 1882, REF: RAM MD/2510/3.

73. Sgt. Spratt, letter to mother, 17 September 1900, REF: NAM 1985-07-75-1.

74. Diary of Lance-Corp. Rose, 9 March 1900, Duke of Cornwall's Light Infantry Museum, Bodmin.

75. I. Knight, p.153.

76. W.S. Churchill, *London to Ladysmith via Pretoria and Ian Hamilton's March*, (Pimlico Edition, London, 2002), p.214.

CHAPTER FIVE

CONFLICT AND ITS AFTERMATH

Then, with a shout, such as only angry demons could give and which is still ringing in my ears, they made a rush for our guns. In ten minutes it was all over; they leapt into the deep ditch or moat in our front, soon filling it, and then swarmed up the opposite side on the shoulders of their comrades, dashed for the guns, which were still bravely defended by a strong body of our infantry, who fought bravely. But who could withstand such fierce demons, with those awful bayonets … and then, with a ringing cheer, which was heard for miles, they announced their victory. *(Hookhum Singh, a Sikh gunner manning an artillery piece, who faced the charge of the 10th Foot at the Battle of Sobraon, 10 February 1846)*

The 'fierce demons' that terrorised Hookhum Singh were to fight Victoria's wars throughout her long reign of 64 years. During this period, the British soldier's experience of conflict and battle was of course to change considerably and the terrain over which he fought was extremely varied. From the veldt of South Africa to the mountainous regions of the Northwest Frontier, the British soldier had to adapt to fighting in different conditions, and his tactics and training evolved accordingly.

Similarly, the enemies he faced in battle presented different challenges. Apart from Canadian Fenians and South African Boers, the only white opponents to confront the British Army were, in 1854, rebellious Australian miners and Russians in the Crimean War. The Victorian soldier faced huge Sikh armies, trained and organised by veterans of

Napoleon's Grande Armée; he fought scores of native forces, some, such as the Ashantis and the Zulus, who attacked in an organised fashion, whilst others, such as the Burmese and Maoris, preferred hit and run guerrilla warfare tactics. The 1857 Indian Mutiny found British Regulars and loyal native units faced by field armies in superior numbers, composed of experienced and competent Sepoys trained along British lines. They faced Afghan and Egyptian forces, equipped with the latest artillery pieces, and Boers who fired superior rifles to their own, yet, despite the occasional battlefield reversal, the Victorian British soldier prevailed.

It is not the purpose of this chapter to look at the 'whys and wherefores' of each campaign. This is not a book about politicians or commanders, so I have avoided the temptation to become too engrossed in long descriptions of the numerous conflicts, for the histories the soldiers tell in their letters and diaries, of their own experiences of the battles in which they were engaged, form the bedrock of this book However, I do on occasion supply some details of specific campaigns and battles so as to give the reader the context of the soldier's role in that particular fight.

Much to my regret, whilst correspondence has been included from the majority of the nineteenth century campaigns throughout the book as a whole, it has not been possible to include worthwhile letters and diary records of actual combat from every campaign. This is simply because surviving firsthand records from many of the smaller conflicts are extremely rare. The geographical spread of regimental archives also placed a constraint on research. However, despite this, archival research has been undertaken in such diverse locations as Bodmin and Stirling, through which I hope that the reader will gain a new insight into the combat experiences of Victoria's soldiers.

At the start of Victoria's reign, the tactics, uniforms and weapons used were reminiscent of the Duke of Wellington's army at Waterloo (18 June 1815) and indeed, during the Sikh wars of the 1840s as well as the Crimean War of 1854–6, Napoleonic tactics and troop dispositions could still be seen on the battlefield. At the Battle of Mudki (18 December 1845), the rather unimaginative British commander – General Gough, who was a veteran of the Peninsular War – formed his men into order of battle using the same formations which had been used against Napoleon 30 years earlier. The troops' uniforms –

their shakos, scarlet coatees and white cross belts – had changed little since Waterloo.

Ranjit Singh, the first leader of a unified Sikh state, created a formidable fighting machine, which was furnished with the most modern equipment and guided by foreign expertise. French Napoleonic veterans, such as Avitabille, Allard and Ventura, trained the Sikh Army to European standards of discipline and skill. The latter two had both been colonels in Napoleon's army and they introduced the French drill book, which resulted in the Sikh Army adopting the standard Napoleonic forms of column formation, deployed order and skirmishers. Another Frenchman, Henri Court, trained the Sikh artillery men to a high level of professionalism and they became very skilful at their task. By the time of Ranjit Singh's death in 1839, his army presented a real threat to British supremacy and, although few of the foreign officers were still serving by the time of the First Sikh War (1843–5), their influence lived on. Massed cannonade, the deployment of square formation to deter charging cavalry and the heavy use of both the bayonet and the frontal charge, were all seen on the battlefields of the Sikh wars.

At the Battle of the Alma (20 September 1854), General Buller deployed the 88th Regiment from line formation – as they advanced to support the Light Division in its attack upon the Russian Redoubt – into a square formation at the sight of Russian cavalry on their left flank. The Russians understood the message this deployment sent and were deterred from an attack upon the 88th. However, later in the conflict, at the Battle of Balaclava (25 October 1854) a single line of infantry, the 93rd Highland Regiment, halted a mass attack of Russian cavalry by firing a mere two volleys. This British success, and such an obvious departure from Napoleonic tactics, can be considered as achieved both through the courage and steadfastness of the British soldier, as well as the superior firepower possessed by the British in the new Minie rifle. During the Sikh wars British troops had been issued with standard flintlock muskets, which were similar in many respects to the 'Brown Bess' muskets used by Wellington's troops, although in 1830 muskets were converted to percussion cap ignition, which had the effect of reducing misfiring. Even so, such weapons were slow to load and had a limited effective killing-range, limitations which resulted in the tactic of closing on the enemy, to use the bayonet against them.

Patented by Captain Claude-Etienne Minie in 1849, the Minie
bullet was a lead cylindro-conoidal design that expanded when fired,
thus creating a tight seal within the rifle and therefore a higher muzzle
velocity than other contemporary rifles. The bullet, when fitted in the
muzzle, slid easily down the bore, which significantly improved loading times. When the gun was fired, 'the charge pushed the iron plug
into the base of the bullet, causing it to expand and grip the rifling
of the bore. Thus it was fired on an accurate trajectory.'[1] Improved
accuracy and the new ease of loading considerably altered the British
soldiers' experience of battle.

In 1851 the Minie rifle was introduced into the British Army, with
a new improved 1853 Pattern version first seeing active service in the
Crimean War. It was sighted to 1,000 yards and was accurate to 800.
At that range 77 out of 100 hits were registered on a target eight foot
square. At ranges between 300 and 600 yards it was calculated that
150 men armed with Minies could equal the devastation achieved by
525 equipped with muskets.[2] Its effective range of more than a quarter
of a mile dramatically changed the nature of engagements.

Not only did this weapon halt the Russian cavalry at Balaclava, but it
was also a major factor in the Allied victory at the Battle of Inkerman
(5 November 1854). Here the attacking Russian infantry columns
sought to close to bayonet point, but the accuracy and range of the
new technology inflicted major casualties on them. Earlier, at the Battle
of the Alma, the Minie first demonstrated its enhanced killing ability
when the British infantry were able to stop a Russian infantry counter-
attack. Captain Wilson of the Coldstream Guards described the effects
of the Minie upon the advancing Russians.

> A thick wedge of grey-coated helmeted foot shows on the slope to the
> right of the grand battery; it waits an opportunity of hurling an over-
> whelming mass upon our thin line. Another round of deafening cheers,
> and file firing is commenced right into that close-grained column. Every
> soldier takes deliberate aim; the distance does not exceed sixty paces;
> hence the Minie has easy game and works miracles.[3]

The example of the Minie rifle serves to illustrate how the British soldier's experience of war would have constantly evolved as Victoria's
reign progressed and her troops were called upon to fight in numerous

wars, whether they were one of her 'Little Wars', or more substantial conflicts. In the latter, the British suffered from long-range smoke-less fire from the Boers' Mauser magazine rifles and, once again, the British adapted their tactics against their unseen foe. An appropriate use of cover, creeping barrages of continuous artillery fire, and infan-try advances in rushes, with co-ordinated artillery support, transformed the British soldier's experience of combat and brought him rapidly into the twentieth century. Such changes in the tactics and experi-ences on the battlefield – whether initiated by technological advances or by the dangers presented by their foes – is reflected in the letters and diaries of the Victorian soldier that are quoted in this chapter.

Part One 1837–1870

According to Byron Farwell, 'There were more wars during Victoria's reign than there had been in the previous two centuries', and in this proc-ess the size of the British Empire quadrupled.[4] In the period 1837–1870, the British soldier fought in Afghanistan (1838–42), India (Conquest of Sind 1843, Gwalior Campaign 1843, First Sikh War 1843–5, Second Sikh War 1848–9, Indian Mutiny 1857–9), China (First China War 1839–42, Second China War 1857–60), Burma (Second Burma War 1851–3), South Africa (Seventh Cape Frontier War 1846–7, Eighth Cape Frontier War 1850–3), Persia (1856–7), New Zealand (First Maori War 1845–7, Second Maori War 1860–1, Third Maori War 1863–6), Canada (Canadian Rebellion 1837–8, Fenian Raids 1866, Red River Expedition 1870), the Crimea (1854–6) and Abyssinia (1867). While some expeditions – such as the Red River Canadian Expedition of 1870 – involved no loss of life, campaigns such as the Crimea saw the deaths of thousands of British troops on the battlefield.

A number of factors combine to make the number of surviving let-ters from these early campaigns of Victoria's reign less common than those that remain from, say, the Boer War, or the numerous expeditions into Egypt and the Sudan. At one very basic level, campaigns such as the First Afghan War saw few British survivors, at least from those that first entered Kabul and then retreated from it. Baggage too was lost, and presumably with it so were letters and diaries. The brutal Sikh wars afforded little time for letter writing, and both the climate and distance from England would have taken a toll on surviving correspondence. The same can also be said of the China wars and conflict in Burma. This – and the fact that literacy improved only slowly through the nineteenth century – means that surviving letters are more common towards the end of the period. The majority of letters, diaries and memoirs that are quoted in this chapter appear in print for the very first time.

As numerous as the campaigns and military expeditions in Victoria's reign were the reasons why such conflicts began. It was easy enough to find excuses for all; to repel a provoked attack, to save Europeans held hostage by savages, to suppress a rebellion, to extend a boundary or prevent another empire from expanding.

Whatever the reasons, or thinking, behind each campaign, and this thinking was to alter as the century progressed, one factor was common to all conflicts and that was that Britain had the ability, or power, to prosecute its claim or will. As Byron Farwell has stated, 'the simple possession of power, and the ability to use it, always provides a powerful temptation to exercise it', and exercise it the British most certainly did. Thus wars of aggression or pre-emptive conflicts were far more common than is perhaps realised. Britain had the power, both militarily and economically, and its leaders were prepared to use it to further Britain's and the imperial cause. Whether the cause or threat was real or perceived scarcely mattered.

The first major conflict of Victoria's reign occurred in Afghanistan with the First Afghan War (1838–42). The war can be said to have begun as a result of British worries of undue Russian influence in Afghanistan, for the British perceived the Russians as a long-term threat to security in both Afghanistan and its crucial neighbour – the gem of the British Empire – India.

The Russians supported the pro-Russian Shah of Persia in his claim to the western Afghan city of Herat and it seemed that the then Afghan ruler, Dost Muhammad, was incapable of halting the advance of Russian influence. Both Britain and Russia sent envoys to Kabul in an attempt to extend their own influence over the court, but it became clear to the British that a more radical approach was required. Thus Britain decided upon military force to support the former Amir, Shah Shuja, in his claims to the Afghan throne. The 'Army of the Indus' was assembled, comprised of 39,000 troops, and in February 1839 it began the 1,200-mile march to Kabul. Dost Muhammed was taken by surprise both by the direction of the march and the size of the British force, and the cities of Quetta and Kandahar were taken with relative ease. However, the Afghans were more prepared at the city of Ghazni, which was vigorously defended. When an Afghan deserter brought the British news that one of the city's great gateways, the Kabul Gate, had been simply barricaded and not bricked-up as was the usual practice, the besiegers knew that it was vulnerable to an explosive charge. In the early hours of 23 July, sappers were able to place and explode a charge against the weak gate and British troops successfully entered and captured the city.

Major Thomas Gaisford of the Royal Artillery described the British attack, under the cover of darkness, on the Afghan fortress of Ghazni. Gaisford described how the Royal Engineers advanced, under enemy fire, to place a 300lb charge against the gate. When this exploded the advance was sounded and columns of men stumbled through the ruins of the gate. The British had divested themselves of all white clothing and, in the darkness, the enemy 'could not see us at all, and always fired over our heads'. Once inside the gates, after a deadly struggle during which repeated volleys were fired at the garrison troops, the British gained a foothold and the city was taken.[5] Over 600 Afghans were killed, with the loss of only eighteen British dead.

With the capture of Ghazni the Afghan resistance collapsed and, on 7 August, an Anglo-Indian Army entered Kabul and placed their puppet-king on the throne. The British built a camp outside the city and offered their military support to an apparently unwelcome king, for Dost Muhammed had evaded capture and still maintained support amongst the population at large. Resentment grew against British rule throughout 1840 and into 1841. A British force, under Sir Robert Sale, was besieged in Gandamak by Afghan forces in September 1841, and in November violence spread to Kabul itself, when a large mob succeeded in breaking into the British envoy's residence and murdering him and his associates. The elderly commander of British forces, Major-General Elphinstone, hesitated to take action against the mob and this British inaction only seemed to embolden the Afghans. Ordered to return to Kabul, Sale was able to extricate his force from Gandamak but only managed to reach Jellalabad. The increasingly threatening Afghans now occupied a ridge overlooking the poorly sited British military cantonment at Kabul and fired down into it. At the end of November,

even Elphinstone realised the seriousness of the situation and he
ordered a British sortie to drive the Afghans from the ridge, but this
ended in failure.

By the middle of December it was clear to all that the British position was now untenable and the senior political officer, Sir William
MacNaughton, began negotiations with Muhammed Akbar Khan, the
son of Dost Muhammed, for a British withdrawal. Fatally, MacNaughton
attempted to play off the Afghan chiefs one against another and Akbar
had him brutally murdered. The indecisive Elphinstone now received
an offer from Akbar of safe passage for the British garrison, which he
accepted. The British left Kabul on 6 January 1842, with 4,500 troops,
including the Queen's Regiment, the 44th Foot, and around 12,000
camp followers, including women and children.

No sooner had the British left the city than the Afghans – probably
in defiance of Akbar's orders – began to attack the column. Stragglers
were the first to be murdered and then hundreds began to fall to both
Afghan bullets and the terrible cold. On the second day, as many as
3,000 were slaughtered in the narrow Khurd Kabul Pass. The nightmare lasted for a week as the Afghans continued to inflict a heavy toll
upon the weakening force. The last resistance occurred on 13 January,
when the survivors of the 44th managed to make a last stand on the
hill above Gandamak. The only European to escape capture or death
was Doctor Brydon who, on an exhausted pony, was able to reach
Jellalabad the same day.

Once Brydon had reached safety he left an account of the retreat,
which included many close escapes.

> We had not gone far in the dark before I found myself surrounded …
> I was pulled off my horse and knocked down by a blow on the head by
> an Afghan knife, which must have killed me had I not had a portion of a
> *Blackwood's Magazine* in my forage cap. As it was a piece of bone the size
> of a wafer was cut from my skull, and I was nearly stunned … those who
> had been with me I never saw again.[6]

The remaining British forces at Jellalabad and Kandahar were besieged
by the Afghans, but both garrisons were able to hold out, and even
managed to launch the occasional sortie to surprise their foes. Help was
sent in the form of a strong Anglo-Indian force, under the command of

Major-General Pollock. In April 1842, Pollock led a surprise advance along the Khyber Pass and was able to relieve Jellalabad on 16 April, and in July Pollock and Nott, leading a force from Kandahar, marched on Kabul. The avenging British were forced to march along the same route the refugees from Kabul had taken six months earlier and thus the troops were able to view the skeletons of the dead, still piled in heaps. Retribution, when it came to Kabul on 12 September, was sweet for the British troops.

For the loss of 32 men, Pollock's force drove off the Afghan cavalry, bayoneted the enemy infantry and inflicted over a thousand fatalities. The British re-entered the city four days later and remained for one month, during which European prisoners were freed and the Kabul bazaar and some surrounding villages torched.

Lieutenant Dennys of the 11th Bengal Native Infantry was part of General Pollock's army of retribution. Dennys described one action in the Baba-Wallee Valley in which the force under his command was engaged. He captures the sudden and confused nature of this particular engagement.

> Some 500 Afghan Horse emerged from a part of the nullah and came straight down upon our cavalry and followed them as they rushed helter-skelter back. All that I could possibly do was to sound the bugle for my men to close on the centre and some twenty file had time to do it and to open a volley as the main body of the Afghans came on us. The rest of the men in extended order behaved splendidly. All knelt down as steady as rocks and commenced file firing, whilst numbers of the Afghans actually followed through their extended places in pursuit of our cavalry; but the main body was checked by my volley and made off under an evident impression that a whole regiment was opposed to them.

Dennys had no illusions as to his own involvement in the successful repulse of the enemy's cavalry.

> I can truly say … I had personally done nothing whatever. It was a man of the name of Nelson of the 40th Foot, who was by an accident near me at the moment and saw what was happening, who ran up to me saying 'sound on the centre close'. I am not able to say that but for him I should have done this, it was all so sudden; but I do think that the fact

of having got a few files together to open a volley was probably the means of saving us all.[7]

Despite the British gaining some revenge, the First Afghan War must be considered a failure, for the British were unable to establish a regime which they favoured. At the same time the war created further suspicion of the British and reduced their influence still further. The British decided upon a fresh course and concentrated instead on a less forward policy, which focused on the need to secure their North West frontier from within the boundaries of India. This too, would see British troops engaged in conflict.

As the Afghan conflict drew to a close, Britain was again involved in a war of its own making. The First China War or Opium War (1839–42) began because the Chinese authorities attempted to restrict British traders from selling opium to the thousands of addicted Chinese, of course to the detriment of their health and well-being. The war was a trade dispute, one in which the British could hardly claim the moral high ground. This first war established the course of future conflicts between Britain and China, in that fighting was not continuous, with intense negotiations interspersed with outbursts of violence.

The most intense fighting occurred in 1840 and into the summer of 1841, when British soldiers, under the command of Sir Hugh Gough, claimed the high ground above Canton and took a number of towns in the vicinity of Nankin. Although the Chinese fought bravely, they did so with primarily medieval weapons of swords, spears and bows, and were no match for disciplined British firepower. Before Gough could capture Nankin, the Chinese sued for peace. Under the terms of peace, the British were allowed trading access to four Chinese ports and their opium trade was allowed to continue unmolested. The Chinese, however, still refused to allow foreign representatives to the Imperial Court and this issue was to be at the heart of future conflict.

Lt. Colonel Thomas Stephens wrote to his wife Eleanor to describe the Battle of Ching Kung Foo (21 July 1842). War in China was a fight as much against the heat and disease as the enemy, and in his letter Stephens writes of the rudimentary medical facilities that were a feature of early colonial campaigns. In describing the battle, Stephens told how his force had to advance by a narrow bridleway, choked with wood, until the British began to be involved in some skirmishing outside the town. He then described how his brigade managed to blow open one of the gates and entered the city. Once on the ramparts the British came under heavy enemy fire and Stephens described how the Chinese

> … pitched into us at a furious rate, and many were killed and wounded – I thank God, who spared my life through the fight – poor Gibbons was shot dead near me and a very nice fellow, Baddely, had his thigh broken and Grant was slightly wounded – Baddely won't suffer his leg to be amputated, and there is little hope for him.[8]

The agreement reached to settle the war and secure the opium trade for the British was due for revision in 1854, with the Chinese authorities still reluctant to allow a continuation of the trade. Negotiations and arguments rumbled onto until October 1856, when the Chinese arrested the British captain and crew of the *Arrow* under the pretext that they were trading illegally. The British demanded an apology, which was not forthcoming, and fighting broke out (The Second China War 1857–60). The French took the opportunity presented by the renewed conflict to air their own trading grievances, and French troops joined the British to capture Canton in December 1857. In May of the following year, the allies launched an attack upon the Taku forts, sited at the mouth of the strategically important Peiho River, only 100 miles from Peking. A bombardment of the forts by the Anglo-French flotilla forced the Emperor to accept foreign representatives at his court.

However, when in June 1859 both French and British troops arrived once more at the forts to escort their representatives to Peking, they were fired upon. Attempts to storm the forts failed. Reinforced with troops from Britain, France and India, the allies again attacked the forts in August 1860. This time, the Allied forces landed eight miles up the coast from the mouth of the Peiho, so as to attack the forts from the rear. A large Imperial force was defeated on 12 August and on 21 August the smallest of the forts was attacked. Despite stubborn Chinese resistance, the British and French storming parties succeeded. With the fall of the smaller fort, the others surrendered. The allies now marched on Peking and, within weeks, heavy guns including the new Armstrong breech-loading 12 pounder surrounded the city and, with just minutes to go before the order was given to open fire, the Chinese capitulated. French forces stormed and looted the beautiful Summer

Palace and, in revenge for the ill-treatment the Chinese had inflicted upon their envoy, the British burnt it to the ground. This act of vandalism was universally condemned. A formal peace treaty was signed in October, which met all of Britain's demands, and the inclusion of Kowloon and Teintsen as treaty ports. China was now devastated by the Taiping Rebellion throughout much of the next decade, and although British officers such as Charles 'Chinese' Gordon were to later take commissions in the Imperial Army, the influence and interference of foreign powers was not to be seen again in China until the 1880s.

The failure of Britain to secure a favourable position in Afghanistan meant that security concerns over possible Russian interference in India still dominated British thinking. In an attempt to impose a buffer between India and Afghanistan, the East India Company tasked General Sir Charles Napier with the annexation of the province of Sind in 1843. A war was provoked by Napier when he presented a treaty to the amirs of Sind, the terms of which Napier knew to be unacceptable. As a result of the anti-British feeling caused by the treaty, a British resident was attacked at Haiderabad, and, seizing the opportunity this presented, Napier quickly launched an advance into Sind in February 1843. Napier's army of only 2,600 men was opposed by the Amir's 20,000 troops at Miani.

Despite the odds against the British, Napier attacked the position on 17 February, and the disciplined volley fire of his troops drove the Amir's force from the field. The battle was a bloody one in which no quarter was given by the British troops; only three prisoners were taken and Napier himself was unable to stop his men from killing the captured and wounded enemy. The British lost twenty officers and 250 men, the Amir in excess of 6,000. Napier described the aftermath of the battle: 'God knows I was very miserable when I rode over the fields, and saw the heaps of the slain: and then all my own soldiers stark and stiff as we laid them in a row for burial the next day.'[9] The only other major battle of the campaign was at Dubba, which was again a bloody British victory. The Amir was forced to accept the British terms and the Sind was occupied, although the border regions continued to be troublesome.

The year 1843 also saw the East India Company (EIC) involved in a campaign against the Maratha state of Gwalior, which had long been suspicious of the EIC and was opposed to the company's rule. Whilst the company was engaged in troubles in the west of India, the Maratha princes began to build up their own military forces east of Delhi, at Gwalior, apparently seeking an opportune moment to strike. The company decided to launch a pre-emptive strike and General Sir Hugh Gough, at the head of a 12,000 strong force, was sent to annex Gwalior in December 1843. On 29 December, the British force was opposed by a strong enemy force at Maharajpore and Gough resorted to a frontal attack. This unimaginative approach, although ultimately successful, cost the lives of 800 troops of the British force and over 3,000 of the enemy. A further British victory at Punniar saw the collapse of Maratha resistance and another region was annexed by the British.

The British success in Sind meant that it was only the Punjab that remained out of the EIC's control, along the region of the Afghan foothills. This territory of the Sikhs had been formed into the Kingdom of Lahore in the early nineteenth century by the militaristic ruler, Ranjit Singh. Although he had been an ally of the EIC, his death in 1839 left something of a power vacuum in which the formidable Sikh Army, the Khalsa, became dominant. The mood shifted against the Company, fuelled by suspicion and emboldened by its apparent weakness after the failure in Afghanistan. Tensions grew, and by 1845 the Sikh military leadership decided upon a strike, moved into Company territory and attacked the town of Ferozepore.

The response of the EIC was immediate and Gough was sent to halt the Sikh advance. Gough shunned the use of scouts and was thus surprised by a large Sikh force at Mudki on 18 December 1845. Again, Gough resorted to a costly frontal assault in which the Sikh artillery wrought havoc through the lines of advancing British infantry. Only through the skill of the British cavalry units was the Sikh position outflanked and their withdrawal from the field under cover of darkness enforced.

Three days later Gough once more engaged the Sikh Army in another bloody tussle, this time at Ferozeshah. The Sikh artillery repeatedly tore holes through the British line, but the infantry maintained their advance into the Sikh entrenchments and a horrific close quarter battle resulted. Lieutenant Walter Kirby, of the 29th, fought at the Battle of Ferozeshah and described the bloody action in his journal.

After drawing in our skirmishers we wheeled from open column into line, fronting the enemy, and then advanced covered by our Artillery, The artillery was immediately answered by the enemy, who had very heavy metal, our own being light Horse Artillery guns. After some time, as we began to see the enemy had the advantage of us at long shots we advanced in front of the Artillery for about half a mile and then charged forwards, pouring in a heavy fire of musketery ... we gave a loud cheer and charged up to the guns, crossing the enemy's entrenchment. When advancing upon the guns, a fearful discharge of grape was poured into our ranks, and one entire section of a company was swept away at once. The enemy's artillery was very true when at some distance and before our regiment fired a shot, a round shot struck two men next to me, and sprinkled my sword with their blood.[10]

Similarly, Private Joseph Hewitt recorded in his journal that the Sikh artillery at Ferozeshah was particularly devastating; as his regiment moved forward to engage the Sikh guns, they were met by round shot from the enemy. Hewitt and his comrades were then ordered to charge, and 'soon had grape shot and musket balls flying about us (a grape shot struck my left arm and took a piece of my coat, shirt and skin away just above the elbow)'. Hewitt then described the close fighting that was typical of battles during the Sikh wars, once the British had reached the Sikh guns.

Away we ran shouting, and when up to their earthworks discharged our muskets point blank at them. The enemy were in overwhelming numbers. We passed many lying on the ground, as I thought dead, that jumped up behind us. Our bugles were sounding 'the retire' as Lieut. Gubbins, I and four other men were rushing towards a gun a short distance in front of us. We were completely cut off from the remainder and surrounded. The officer and four men were soon on the ground, and I pulling my bayonet out of a Sikh, swung myself round to bolt, when I found a Sikh behind me with his *tulwar* [sabre] up going to cut me down. I drew my musket to my chest and shot it out at him. With the whole weight of my body, I caught him just under the chin and toppled him over like a nine pin. [11]

Somehow Hewitt managed to extract himself from the melee and retreat over the bodies of his comrades, to find the remainder of his regiment in a square formation, ready to meet the charge of the Sikh cavalry. The battle lasted until nightfall and the following day the British renewed their attack and retook the Sikh artillery position. Despite the arrival of Sikh reinforcements who threatened the British position, indecision amongst the Sikh commanders allowed the British to remain on the field. Gough was able to claim a victory, but at the cost of over 2,400 men. The aftermath of the battle was described by Hewitt in his journal.

> When the morning came it was a heartrending sight to see so many wounded and so many that had died at night, all mixed together outside the tent, there being no room inside. A large pit was dug outside the gate, all the dead were put in it and covered up making one huge grave.

Writing the day after the battle, Lieutenant Kirby wrote that, in his regiment alone, three officers had been killed, three wounded and 250 men were killed or wounded out of 750. On 23 December his journal recorded the disposal of the officers' bodies.

> This afternoon we had the melancholy duty of burying three of our officers, killed on the 21st. A grave was dug and they were laid in it with their clothes on, without any funeral honours, these not being possible on active service.

The devastating nature of the battles of the Sikh wars was witnessed by Private Richard Perkes of the 1st European Bengal Fusiliers, who was present at both the battles of Ferozeshah and Sobraon (10 February 1846). This latter battle began with a two-hour artillery duel, after which the British guns ran out of ammunition. When this was reported to General Gough, he is reported to have said 'Thank God! Then I'll be at them with the bayonet!'[12] This, of course, resulted in a further slaughter of British troops. In a letter to his brother, Perkes described his sense of loss at the death of a comrade, as well as the actions in which he was engaged.

> My best friend was killed in the first action [Ferozeshah] which I am very sorry for, for we was together more than three years and agreed like two brothers. He must abeen blown to pieces for I never could get any account off him.

Of the action at Sobraon, Perkes wrote

> I ham verry sorry to say that the regiment I belong to suffered greately the
> company I belong to thirty off us marched that morning to the enemys
> battery hand only eight off us returned In our Camp safe without being
> wounded ... it was a miracle how any off us escaped for the balls had to
> come has thick as a shower of hail the same I never wish to see again the
> roar off the guns was heard more than eighty miles away at Simla.[13]

Further carnage was to be seen at the Battle of Aliwal (28 January 1846),
although on this occasion the British cavalry relieved some of the pressure on the battle-scarred infantry. Private John Pearman of the 3rd
Light Dragoons described the action.

> Our army came into line as steady as a field day. I sat on my horse and
> looked at our two armies. It was a lovely sight ... At about 700 yards
> from the enemy, the Colonel shouted: 'Action! Front! Unlimber and
> prepare for action!' ... We all dismounted and held the horses, when
> 'bang' went our guns. About the third shot I saw was making holes in the
> ranks in the front of us ... At this time the firing was terrific, and look-
> ing back, the plain was covered with wounded and dead men, and horses
> and pieces of broken guns ... We were in a cross fire from the enemy's
> guns and we had seven horses down at once in my guns out of the eight
> horses. We now galloped close to the enemy, about three hundred yards,
> and 'Bang! Bang! went our guns to a good tune and they had something
> to think about. At this time I looked to the left and saw the 16th Lancers
> coming on to a trot, then a gallop. I took off my cap and hollered out:
> 'The First charge of the British Lancers!' The enemy formed square, but
> the 16th Lancers went right on and broke it. Such cutting and stabbing I
> never saw before or since.[14]

A succession of bloody British victories brought the First Sikh War to
an unsatisfactory conclusion in March 1846. The Sikh kingdom was
declared a Protectorate of the EIC and the Sikh Army was dissolved.
Tensions remained, however, and in April 1848 two officials of the EIC
were murdered in a popular uprising in the city of Multan. Troops of
the EIC left garrisons across the country to convene at Multan, and
former members of the Sikh Army, or Khalsa, joined the rebellion, to

clash once again with British and native troops of the EIC. Gough was again given command of the Army. His tactics remained depressingly familiar and the Second Sikh War was even more brutal and devastating than the first. Furthermore, hardened by their experiences of the First Sikh War, both the Sikh and British troops showed little mercy for each other and atrocities by both sides were not uncommon. A series of bloody British victories, such as Chillianwallah (13 January 1849), Goojerat (21 February 1849) and finally the retaking of Multan, saw the Sikh rebellion collapse in March 1849. This time there would be no renewed conflict, for the Sikh kingdom was annexed outright and the army dispersed for ever.

Private Waterfield was present when the British troops retook the city of Multan and he recorded in his memoirs the bloody conclusion to the siege.

> We dashed on to a large house. This building was entrenched and enclosed on all sides by loop holed walls some 10 or 12 feet high. From this place the enemy peppered us in a grand style when advancing. We were not long in bursting open the door of this refuge place, and the massacre which took place in it was frightful, our Grenadiers soon had the place covered with the dead and dying. In the interior of the building was a narrow staircase. The enemy rushed up there followed by the Grenadiers, and in the gallery we had to close upon them, and the struggle for life and death was desperate. We hurled them over the bannisters where they were dashed to pieces on the marble floor beneath.

The furious nature of the fighting is evident from Waterfield's description of one of his friends: 'My comrade received nine sabre cuts on the head and arms and his neck half severed from his body. He lingered until about 10 o'clock the next day.'[15] Waterfield also fought at the Battle of Goojerat and he left a vivid description of the aftermath of the battle.

> I only saw one European amongst the dead, at least part of one. He was a sergeant of the 2nd Europeans; his cap, his grog bottle and his head was all we saw. There was a letter in the cap, but I could not make any of it out, for it was saturated with blood.[16]

Private John Ryder was also present at both Multan and Goojerat and in the latter battle he wrote of how the British artillery had swept away whole battalions of the enemy. He also recorded that when he and his infantry comrades closed on the Sikh artillery men they defended their guns to the last and that the enemy would spit at the British troops even when they were bayoneted, as a last act of defiance. Ryder also wrote poignantly of the aftermath of Multan, in which both his regiment's colonel and quartermaster were slain. Ryder described the last moments of his quartermaster.

> A musket ball had passed through his body, he was in great agony before he died, for about half an hour he bit the ground and tore-up the sand with his hands. His last words were, 'Oh, my dear wife, tell her all I have is hers; tell her my last words were for her.'

Finally, Ryder told of the horrific scenes as the enemy dead were set on fire.

> It was a shocking sight to see the flesh burning and all in flames, whilst the blood and other matter was running along the ground, but cruel as this may appear it is nothing more than the custom of this country calls for.[17]

From the brutality of the Sikh wars, British troops were next engaged in conflict in South Africa. In the years 1846–7, British forces fought in the Seventh Cape Frontier War, which was soon followed by the Eighth Cape Frontier War of 1850–3. During this conflict the 12th Lancers were heavily engaged and suffered some casualties in the bush warfare to which they, and their mounts and lancers, were unsuited. For example, on 20 March 1853, Basuto tribesmen managed to lure a company of Lancers into a trap in which four NCOs and 23 men of the 12th Lancers were butchered. This disaster saw the remaining Lancers rapidly switch to the use of sidearms rather than the lance. Elsewhere in South Africa, the British had an early clash with the Boers in numerous small expeditions in both 1845 and 1848. In the Boomplaats Campaign, Lieutenant Dyneley of the Royal Artillery first experienced the satisfaction of a victory over the Boers when, on 27 August 1848, he responded to a Boer attack by firing at the advancing enemy. Dyneley

1. The Cape of Good Hope – A brig-rigged steamship of 500 gross tons. It was chartered by Her Majesty's Government in 1857 and brought the first British reinforcements to India.

2. RMS Windsor Castle – 2,672 gross tons. A Castle-Line record-breaking vessel, 1873. From a watercolour by John W. Juritz.

3. H.M. Troopship Orontes in Table Bay *c*.1881.

4. H.M. Troopship *Jumna* at Suakin, 1885.

5. The 2nd Battalion The Devonshire Regiment parading for embarkation to South Africa, Southampton, 21 October 1899.

6. Officers of the 99th Regiment on board the troopship *Mars* en route from Calcutta to China, 1860.

7. Communal bath time on board a troopship heading for India *c.*1890.

8. Exercising on board a troopship heading for Cape Town *circa* 1900.

9. The West Yorkshire Regiment disembarking at Durban from the Roslin Castle, 1899.

10. Soldier's barracks, India *c.*1870. Note the high ceilings to aid ventilation.

11. Cricket Match, Kohat, India, 1873. The Garrison's church is in the background.

12. The British garrison on parade at Grahamstown, South Africa *c.*1875.

13. Liquor Bar,
65th Battery Royal
Artillery, Madras,
1895.

14. Camp of
the 97th Earl of
Ulster's Regiment,
Crimean War, 1855.

15. Abyssinian
Campaign, 1868. Base
Camp at Annersley Bay.

16. British tents
erected in the
captured Pehtang
Fort at the mouth of
the Pehtang River,
China, 1860.

17. Camp of the
Peshawar Valley
Field Force,
Afghanistan, 1878.

18. Seaforth
Highlanders
on the march.
Black Mountain
Expedition, 1888.

19. Elephant Field
Battery, Tirah
Campaign, 1897.

20. Ammunition
Column, Boer War,
1900.

21. The Royal
Artillery crossing
a drift over the
Valsch River, South
Africa, 1900.

22. The 2nd Battalion The Devonshire Regiment Crossing the Modder River, South Africa, February 1900.

23. Officers of the Grenadier Guards on board a train heading for the front, Sudan, 1898.

24. Troops and wagons loaded on board a train, South Africa, 1900.

25. Boarding an armoured train, South Africa, 1900.

26. The luxury of a bath whilst on Campaign, Sudan, 1898.

27. Officers' Mess, Boer War, 1900.

28. Lunch on the veldt, South Africa, 1900.

29. Men of the 2nd Battalion Somerset Light Infantry, newly arrived in South Africa, November 1899.

30. The 2nd Battalion Somerset Light Infantry, South Africa, 1900.

31. Crimean War – soldiers and an officer wearing winter fur coats, known as 'bunnies', sent out from England during the winter of 1854.

32. Lieutenant C.H. Meecham and Assistant Surgeon T. Anderson serving during the Indian Mutiny, 1858. Note the laxity in dress.

33. Commissariat Officers, Kabul, Afghanistan, 1880. Note the great variety of 'uniforms'.

34. Officers of the 2nd Battalion Somerset Light Infantry during the Third Burmese War c.1886; again, with unorthodox uniforms.

35. Dead Chinese lying upon the ramparts of the North Taku Fort, China, 1860.

36. British Graveyard, Chitral Campaign, 1895.

37. Kings' Own Scottish Borderers in action in the Arhanga Pass during the Tirah Campaign, 1897.

38. Battle of Atbara, 1898. The British troops are in square formation awaiting the attack.

39. Atbara – the aftermath – Dervish dead upon the battlefield.

40. The Battle of Omdurman, September 1898. MacDonald's Brigade in action.

41. Dervishes lying dead on the battlefield of Omdurman, Sudan, September 1898.

42. The aftermath of Spion Kop, South Africa, 1900; medical orderlies search for the living.

43. British troops firing at Boers near Colesburg, 1900.

44. The Royal Artillery firing at Boer positions across the Modder River, January 1900.

45. The 2nd Battalion
The Devonshire
Regiment firing
at retreating Boers,
27 February 1900.

46. The hanging of
mutineers, Indian
Mutiny, 1858.

47. *A Gentleman in Khaki* by
R. Caton Woodville.

wrote 'You cannot think of the great pleasure we had in seeing the Boers drop off their horses!'[18] His second contact with the enemy was less successful and, from the tone of Dyneley's writing, it is clear that this action was more sobering.

> On the 29th we came up with the Boers and had an action with them. We kept up a fire for about two hours and then they were all off. We lost, I am sorry to say, altogether 12 or 14 men and 42 wounded, 7 officers one since dead. Poor Captain Murray of the Rifle Brigade. Liversey in the arm which he must have taken off. Steel will also have his leg off if he does not die poor fellow.[19]

Burma had already engaged in conflict against the British (First Burmese War 1824–6), but during Victoria's reign it was to be involved in two major conflicts, the second of which was to rumble on for several years. The Second Burmese War (1851–3) began as little more than a trading dispute, as a truculent Governor of Rangoon harassed British merchants. The Governor-General of India, Lord Dalhousie, demanded redress from the Burmese king, Pagan Min, and, although the troublesome Governor was removed, his replacement proved to be even more officious. In response, the commodore of the nearest British Naval squadron seized a Burmese ship and blockaded the Irrawaddy Delta. On 15 March 1852, Dalhousie issued the Burmese government with an ultimatum to stop interfering with British shipping and, when this was ignored, an expeditionary force was despatched. The trade dispute had become that most dangerous of conflicts, one in which the British could not lose face; a show of force became inevitable.

The campaign involved a large contingent of troops from the EIC, along with four Queen's Regiments, the 18th, 35th, 51st and 80th, and was characterised by the use by the British of the Burmese river system, chiefly the Irrawaddy, to launch amphibious operations against Burmese positions.

On 5 April 1852, the British took the Burmese position at Martaban at the mouth of the Irrawaddy, thus allowing the British flotilla to proceed on to Rangoon. On 12 April, troops were put ashore at Rangoon and, with artillery support, the landing party advanced through the surrounding jungle towards the city. Despite formidable defences, and the tenacity of the Burmese defenders, the British were able to take the city for the loss of 22 officers and men. From their new base at Rangoon, the British launched further punitive expeditions against enemy positions at Bassein and beyond, although a Burmese acceptance of defeat was not forthcoming. Instead, the British simply annexed Lower Burma, the Irrawaddy Delta around Rangoon, placing a force to occupy the region. A military road was constructed from Calcutta to the delta, thus improving communications. Although British prestige and influence was maintained, the lack of a satisfactory peace was to have serious consequences later in Victoria's reign.

Ensign William Whitlock left a vivid account in his memoirs of the storming of Rangoon. He recalled that the British were forced to take shelter in an avenue of trees to try and escape the heavy fire which was coming from the Burmese defenders in their stockade. As the fire increased 'the leaves of the trees overhead were dropping in front of my eyes, cut off by bullets, and again and again I heard the thud of bullets striking the trunks of trees close at my side.' Whitlock then led a party to storm the Burmese defences, and wrote of his feelings during the assault.

> I remember well bracing myself up for a dash rush across the open space of 20 yards or so which separated us from the enemy, it was rather like a rush at football (barring the bullets). Away I went as hard as I could spin along and soon reached the foot of the stockade untouched by the shower of bullets whirring past me. The gallant little sappers of the Madras Army were up planting their scaling ladders against the stockade. I went up amongst the first three or four and as I ascended rung after rung of the ladder I remember anticipating seeing a crowd of savage faces belonging to men fully armed and ready to chop me to pieces on my getting to the top. I recollect during these few moments deciding to jump in amongst them and lay about me with my sword, tho' I shouldn't have lasted long in such an unequal fight for the place was crowded with the enemy; but when I reached the top of the parapet the enemy were just turning to bolt out at the opposite side to that by which we were entering so that we all at last got comfortably into the place.[20]

Throughout Victoria's reign, her soldiers were constantly engaged in warfare, yet it was only during the Crimean War (1854–6) that the

British faced a European foe. During this conflict, Britain and her allies, France, Sardinia and Turkey, battled against Russian forces around the Black Sea port of Sebastopol. The names of such battles as the Alma, Balaclava, and Inkerman are now little more than battle honours on regimental flags, but for the soldiers who fought in the Crimea, their numerous letters and memoirs tell stories of hardship, endurance and courage in the face of a determined Russian foe. Fortunately for the British soldier, the mass infantry attacks of this war against entrenched European forces were not to be repeated during Victoria's reign, although the British were to face an equally belligerent enemy during the Indian Mutiny.

The Allied landings at Calamita Bay on 14 September 1854 were unopposed by the Russians, who, under the command of Prince Menschikoff, had deployed in a strong position on the heights above the River Alma, thereby blocking the road to Sebastopol. Menschikoff believed that his forces could delay the Allied advance for at least three weeks, if not defeat it at the Alma.

The resultant battle of 20 September was, for the vast majority of the Allied troops, their first experience of combat, and for many it would be their last. Although the Russian defence of the heights was initially tenacious, the Allied forces were able to prevail, despite suffering enormous losses. The British Light Division, which bore the brunt of the fighting to capture the Russian redoubt positions, suffered nearly 900 casualties alone.

For the British troops who survived the carnage, their letters and memoirs are filled with disbelief that they had not only experienced such warfare, but had survived it. For many, the aftermath of the battle was as harrowing as the fight itself.

Private Charles Gray of the 93rd Highland Regiment advanced in support of the Light Division, which had attacked the centre of the Russian line.

We were all in three lines when we commenced the ascent of the Alma. It was hard work going up the hill. The Russians were above us, quite in sight, and as the ground was of an undulating character, spread out like waves of the sea, we could see the movements of the whole of the allied armies as we toiled upwards. Ah! It was a grand sight.

When the Highlanders were given the order to advance, Gray recalled that the pipers skirled a Highland air. It was not long before men began to fall to the Russian fire.

> The first man shot in our regiment was my left hand man, and I felt it quite possible that my turn would come next. When a soldier is doing nothing he has his natural fears about him, I can tell you and I had mine when I saw my comrade biting the dust – I mean the grass. As soon as we commenced firing at the enemy, however, the feeling of fear entirely left me and I lost self-consciousness in the excitement of actual contact with the enemy. But it is terrible work shooting down people against whom you have no animosity or particular grudge – in fact nobody can understand it who has not gone through it.[21]

Private Donald Cameron, also of the 93rd Highlanders, joined Gray in the advance. In his diary, Cameron gave an account of the storming of the heights.

> The Russian bullets coming buzzing about us, advanced through a vine-yard, I took some grapes. A thin high hedge before us. We got through a gap two abreast and into the river which came up about my henches. After crossing we sheltered beside a little knoll until the rest got through and advanced in line and extended in skirmishing order and passed the Light Division, and closed into the right again and charged up the hill … the Russians not caring for cold steel turned heel and fled…[22]

Gray too had reached the top, and, in his reminiscences, was critical of the Russian troops.

> The poor Russians on the heights of the Alma were a contemptible lot. If they had been anything like British soldiers they could have hurled three times the number of those who assailed them into the middle of next week and kept their position as impregnable as a rock.

After trying to alleviate the misery of the wounded, Gray simply collapsed with exhaustion and 'slept as soundly as heart could wish', despite the cries and groans of the injured men. William Nairn also reached the top of the heights with his comrades of the 93rd, even though he had been wounded by a Russian bullet in his left thigh. Nairn simply wrapped his wound with a cloth to stem the blood and carried on, and was even fit enough to gather the wounded and bury the dead – of which there were many – on the following day.[23] Major Macleod of the Royal Artillery carried water to both the Russian and British wounded until it was too dark to see. He recalled that the Russians, in particular, clung to the water bottles with a death grip so as to empty the contents, and that the line of the Russian retreat was marked by dead and wounded men.[24]

When the sun rose on the 21 September, the men of the 93rd, and all the surviving Allied troops, witnessed the full horror of the battlefield. Many of the living were tasked with the burial of the dead. Private Burrows served in one of the fatigue parties instructed to collect and bury the bodies.

> [It was] a very painful and awful duty. Large square pits were dug, and to those the corpses were carried and laid side by side; the officers in one, the British soldiers in others, and the Russians in others.[25]

Sergeant Gowling of the 7th Fusiliers was also on burial detail and described the duty as a 'very mournful and ghastly sight ... for many had been literally cut in pieces. It was a difficult matter really to find out what had killed some of them.'[26] In addition to the horrors of the mutilated corpses, Burrows recalled a poignant moment as the men attempted to bury some of the Russian dead.

> The corpse of one nice looking fair haired Russian youth was guarded by a big dog. This dog would allow no one to approach his master's body and it was so fierce that I am sorry to say it had to be shot before his master's body could be removed.

The Battle of Inkerman was the next major clash of arms in the Crimean conflict, and one in which the Allies were surprised by the Russians' ability to secretly bring up reserve forces and descend upon them through an early morning fog. The battle developed into a close-quarter struggle in which the effective use of the bayonet and the firepower of the minie rifle were decisive for the Allies. Major Macleod's experience at Inkerman was, perhaps, typical of the close nature of the fighting:

At daybreak on Sunday, 5th November 1854, I finished the replacing of the ammunition for day service when I heard heavy firing on the right through a thick fog and rain ... Orders came to despatch every gun got ready without waiting for the rest. So, mine being ready, I trotted off to the right and, as soon as I got into line of the Russian fire, a shot carried away a piece of my gun wheel which almost disabled it; but on I went, and when ascending the hill in a shower of shot, shell and bullets, I observed a little confusion among the men, and shouted 'Fear not; none shall fall here today without God's permission.' This had the desired effect, and we came quickly into action.

Macleod described how the weather and terrain added further to the confusion of the Battle.

The ground was covered with brushwood bushes, in some places over six feet high, so that an enemy could not be seen a few yards off. My gun and another were ordered to advance 200 yards in front of our line to take the Russian columns in flank, not knowing that one of these columns was advancing in front of us. We did so without any infantry support, and found ourselves surrounded. The other gun was taken at once, but I tried to get a canister shot into them before I fell, but found myself alone, as the last man, an English lad named Gaston, fell with three shots in his forehead. I quickly turned the empty gun upon them which threw them into momentary confusion and in this way I kept a small circle clear for a few seconds ... a Russian officer on the other side of a bush levelled his revolver at my left ear, but a private of the 57th, who was behind me, reserved his only shot for the last extremity, saw the danger, and shot the officer dead.

Macleod's story captures the confusion of Inkerman. Having survived the battle he claimed afterwards that his gun alone claimed the lives of 350 of the enemy. Macleod was also present at the Battle of Balaclava and, during an artillery duel with the Russian guns, narrowly escaped death. He recalled that 'a shot passed so close to my head that I glanced behind and saw one of the covering party cut in two by it.'

The Battle of Balaclava is known not just for the infamous charge of the Light Brigade, but also for the 93rd's stand against advancing Russian cavalry, in what became known as 'The Thin Red Line'.

Sergeant James Taylor recorded in his diary this particular action as he and his comrades faced the Russian horse. Taylor certainly did not attempt to glamourise the stand of the 93rd, and his diary is written in a matter of fact style.

> Now the Russians are advancing across the plain in grand style, no body to oppose them but a few cavalry and Sir Colin Campbell with the thin red line; the 93rd Highlanders extended on a small top of rising ground. Onward they come sweeping across the plain. They are within rifle range, the word is given to fire, and they got it round and round as fast as we could give it to them. They soon gave way.[27]

With the Russians failing to dislodge the Allies at both Inkerman and Balaclava, the war settled into a siege of Sebastopol, with the occasional probing by French and British forces of the Russian defences. Captain Mark Walker of the Buffs kept a detailed diary throughout the campaign and he was frequently involved in night sorties to look for weaknesses in the Russian line. Walker's beautiful handwriting becomes almost illegible from 10 June 1855.

> last night I went on with the reserve just as I got into our approach which joins the French on the right heavy firing commenced at the Mamalon [a Russian battery]. While I was in the act of hurrying the men up a howitzer shell dropped beside me and exploded a piece struck me on the right elbow and smashed it. I immediately tied a handkerchief above the fracture and returned to the rear until I met some of the 55th men who put me on a stretcher and carried me to camp. I was put under chloroform and on coming to consciousness I found my arm taken off above the elbow and today I suffered a good deal of pain. The loss I have experienced is very great but I am thankful that my life has been spared.

The following day's diary entry reads, 'not suffering so much, the stump was dressed today and looks well.' Three days later Walker noted that he was 'going on favourably I still feel as if I had all my fingers and they sometimes pain me very much.'[28] The bravery and resoluteness Walker displayed at the loss of his arm may seem incredible to civilians today (though not necessarily to modern-day soldiers, who suffer the same losses) but to be daily surrounded, as he and thousands of other British troops were, by death and horror must have bred a hardness verging on indifference amongst the men. As Walker wrote (with his left hand), at least his life had been spared.

The Crimean War stuttered on until February 1856, by which time both the Allies and the Russians were weary of conflict. The Allies did manage to capture Sebastopol, only for the Russians to regain it in the Peace Treaty that formally ended the conflict. Gunner John Cousins, of the Royal Artillery, was one of the first British soldiers to enter Sebastopol and he recorded in his memoirs the sights that awaited him.

> When we went into the town it baffles all description, the dead and the wounded lying about in heaps and one large shed with white flag flying was full of dead, and some still living between swollen corpses. The Russians had left their dead and wounded behind them to perish, a most dreadful sight to see. So we now had to separate the wounded from the dead, and we found it a heavy job for many hours.

Cousins described the war as one of the 'most dreadful hardship'.[29] Yet within one year of its conclusion, British troops would again be involved in a major conflict which would threaten the very existence of the Empire.

The reasons behind the Indian Mutiny of 1857 have recently been comprehensively examined by Saul David in his work, *The Indian Mutiny*, and will not be covered in any detail here. However, it can be said that this conflict, more than any other during Victoria's reign, threatened the continued existence of the Empire by jeopardising Britain's control of India.

In the early months of the Mutiny, the rebels committed numerous atrocities at such places as Delhi, Cawnpore and Lucknow, which served to further fuel British determination not only to crush the rebellion, but to do so severely. As a result, there are recorded incidences of British troop involvement in atrocities, which will be discussed in the following chapter. The number of surviving letters and memoirs is, on the face of it, remarkably small considering the length of the conflict and the number of troops involved. However, it was an extremely fluid conflict, in which British troops were forced to march hundreds of miles in severe heat to relieve besieged British residences or to bring the rebels to open battle. In such circumstances, the writing of letters and diaries would not have been a high priority.

Private Henry Metcalfe of the 32nd Regiment of Foot took part in the retreat to Lucknow, and his description gives a vivid impression of the hardship of a forced march in the heat of India, at the same time being pursued and harassed by the mutineers.

> I saw on that retreat some of our finest soldiers drop down with sunstroke, never to rise again. I saw one fine young fellow who was wounded in the leg. He coolly sat down on the road, faced the enemy, and all we could do or say to him would not urge him to try and come with us. He said – 'No you fellows push on, leave me here to blaze away at these fellows. I shan't last long and I would never be able to reach Lucknow.' He remained, and was very soon disposed of, poor fellow. Another instance of brotherly love and self sacrifice. A bonny young man, by name Jones, was being conveyed back on a gun carriage after being wounded saw his brother being struck down with a bullet from the enemy, and without the least warning he jumped off the limber on which he was riding and joined his brother to be killed with him. Another man, maddened by the heat and fatigue, charged in single-handed into the ranks of the enemy and was soon put to rest.[30]

Such sights were surely not uncommon along the lines of retreat and advance of the British troops during the Mutiny.

When the British were able to bring the mutineers to open battle, the engagements were often bloody and prolonged. Many of the rebels had been trained by the British and were familiar with British tactics and field deployments. Thus, many of the battles of 1857 were great field spectacles, although, unlike the infantry tussles of the Sikh wars, the more refined use of artillery and the mobility of the cavalry ensured that the normally numerically inferior British were victorious. Private Potiphars of the 9th Lancers was part of General Sir Colin Campbell's force, which defeated the rebel leader Tatya Tope to recapture Cawnpore on 6 December 1857. Of Campbell's deployment Potiphars wrote:

> The whole face of the town fronting the Canal and the Ganges were covered by our Infantry Brigades, one Brigade consisting of H.M. 32nd, 42nd, 93rd 53rd and 4th Punjab Infantry, and a portion of the naval

Brigade with foot artillery advanced in three lines by the right direct for the enemy camp. About 9 am operations commenced, the enemy began firing shell at us and by 10 am, every Battery of ours was opened and from the entrenchments also which made it very warm for Mr Pandy. Several of the outposts were hotly engaged by our Infantry. The enemy extreme left about this time opened a murderous fire of ball, rifles and grape, which ours replied to for nearly two hours, and as briskly as they could load and fire. About 12 o'clock they began to retreat.

Potiphars was involved in the pursuit of the fleeing rebels for around fifteen miles.

We were not long before we began to come upon them, and their guns, ammunition and stores; a great number of rebels were cut up, chiefly Infantry. We now got an order from Sir Colin who was with us watching our movements, not to proceed any further, he also remarked that we should make good Fox hunters as we bagged the game so well, meaning I suppose the 16 guns we had captured from the enemy by this pursuit.[31]

If some of the conflict could be likened to fox-hunting, this was not true of most of the bitter fighting associated with the repression of the Mutiny. Captain John Ramsden of the Royal Artillery was engaged in the pursuit of the rebel leader Tatya Tope in 1858 and recorded in his diary one of the few occasions when the British forces were able to bring the rebels to battle.

I jumped onto my horse and every man was in his proper place in a moment. The whole force changed front to rear and moved off. Gordon's guns opening on some of the enemy he could distinguish, through the trees. We now on leaving the tope saw our enemy in some 'dall' fields, extending in a long straggling line along our front. We now received the order to charge, Anderson's men formed line broke into a canter, and soon cleared the 200 yards space between us and the enemy, the latter having fired a farewell volley took to their heels.

Ramsden then described his own actions in the pursuit of the fleeing rebels.

I drew my revolver with my right hand when the pace began to increase. I was some little way ahead of the troop on first charging, when I came upon the enemy, I shot the 1st man I met, as he was throwing himself on the ground to avoid me. I then fired the remaining 4 shots, I think at random for I cannot remember to have seen any one I fired at fall. I put up my pistol and drew my sword still going at a gallop. I ran a man through as I came up to him and another I treated to a 'cut three' under the right ear which brought him on his face as I passed him, some others I have a confused remembrance of having pointed at casually as I passed.[32]

The aftermath of any battle during the Mutiny saw urgent efforts to dispose of bodies promptly in the heat of India. On returning to the Cawnpore battlefield, after his pursuit of the fleeing rebels, Private Potiphars was able to see 'heaps of the dead of the enemy being burnt, and the smell of which was odious ... the enemy's camp was strewn with all kinds of articles, clothing stores ammunition etc.' Care for the wounded was often even more basic than that given to the troops during the Crimean conflict, as Private Metcalfe recalled.

My friend was hit with a round shot which completely shattered his leg. Of course the leg had to be amputated above where it was hit so as to come at the sinews, and there being no chloroform, the poor fellow could not bear up against his sufferings and expired in great agony.

Another feature of the Mutiny was the requirement to retake garrisons and cities taken by the rebels, the most famous being that of Delhi, the recapture of which was a top military and political priority for the British. The city was again in British hands by 20 September 1857, after much furious hand-to hand fighting in its streets, lanes and buildings. Lieutenant-Colonel Gordon-Alexander recalled his involvement and that of his men in the regaining of the city and the horror and confusion that was experienced.

I formed my sections into file, and doubled up to the spot indicated by the Major, where we found the Light Company very hotly engaged with a body of some eighty of the enemy, which had retreated into a barricaded gateway built up on the outside, and were fighting like rats in

a pit. They were able to fire straight out past one of their traverses in the
gateway, and, following Major Macdonald's instructions, I unwittingly
led direct for it, losing at once poor Corporal Steel, shot through the
heart and flung a foot in the air, and the other leading man of the file.

As the attack continued, Gordon-Alexander recorded that when his
men reached the top of the stairs in the gateway they 'were able to make
very short work of its defenders, some of whom either leapt over or
were thrown down by our people, whose blood was up, for I narrowly
escaped receiving one of these gentlemen on the top of my head!'[33]

Gordon-Alexander was to recall the aftermath of the battle for
Delhi, in which he tried to offer comfort to the many wounded. He
found, amongst the 'hopeless cases' of mortally wounded that the overwhelmed doctors had no time to attend to

> … a poor fellow of the Light Company in great agony with a bullet in
> his abdomen, but clear-headed and intelligent to the last. He constantly
> cried for water, which I obtained for him at intervals throughout
> the night. He begged me continually either to shoot him, or to lend
> him my revolver to shoot himself. Towards sunrise I had fallen asleep,
> and when I awoke he was dead, after enduring quite ten hours of
> excruciating agony.

Conflicts in New Zealand (First Maori War 1845–7, Second Maori
War 1860–1, Third Maori War 1863–6) were land wars in which an
influx of settlers to Britain's new colony exacerbated tensions between
the British and the indigenous Maoris. Maori resistance, in both wars,
centred on the building and defence of strongly-held *pah*. These were
rapidly built earthwork 'forts' with interconnecting trenches and rifle-
pits, protected by palisades of timber stuffed and lined with flax to form
an elastic armour. When, at last, the British decided to storm the *pah*, it
was then usually abandoned by the Maoris who would melt into the
bush, from where they would continue a guerrilla-style war.

At Ohaeawai, in July 1845, the British attempted to storm a *pah*, held
by the rebel leader Hone Heke, but were driven back with heavy losses.
The strength and ingenuity of these Maori defences can be judged by
the fact that the British pounded the *pah* at Horokiwi for three days in
May 1846 to little effect. This was the last major battle of the First War

although conflict and disputes over land continued to flare throughout the ensuing decades.

The Second Maori War centred around the controversial 'Waitara purchase', whereby the British authorities mediated between settlers in the Taranaki district over land the ownership of which was already under dispute by two rival chiefs, the more senior of whom, Wiremu Kingi, was adamantly opposed to the land being settled. The authorities sided with the settlers and attempted to enforce the purchase of the land. Wiremu Kingi built a *pah* and took up arms. This conflict was, initially, characterised by a series of British reverses. Sergeant James Cooper of the Royal Artillery wrote in his diary of 2 May 1861 of the burial of men killed in a surprise action against the Maoris.

> The bodies layed in two half Marquees in the Burial ground, the graves were arranged in three rows officers in coffins the men in blankets, it was the most solemn sight I ever saw in my life, the Archdeacon read the Burial Service. The Band of the 68th played the death march.'[34]

Major Cyprian Bridge of the 58th Regiment wrote of an attack upon a *pah* during the Second Maori War, which was bloodily repulsed.

> When I got up close to the fence and saw the strength of it and the way it resisted the united efforts of our brave fellows … my heart sank within me lest we should be defeated … a bugle in the rear sounded our retreat … and then all that were left prepared to obey its summons carrying off the wounded with us. We had suffered very severely and many were killed or wounded whilst retiring as the enemy increased their fire upon us as they saw us in retreat. It was a heartrending sight to see the number of gallant fellows left dead upon the field and to hear the groans and cries of the wounded for us not to leave them behind. [35]

Following the British government's decision to replace the commander, Major-General Thomas Pratt arrived from England and he initiated a change in tactics. There were to be no more fruitless frontal attacks on *pahs*, but instead Pratt devised a scheme whereby saps were driven ever closer to the Maori fortifications, and from behind this cover the British ventured nearer and nearer. The Maoris seemed to find such tactics disconcerting, and the British took many *pahs* with little serious fighting. The last to be taken, Te Arei, surrendered on 19 March 1861 and the war was brought to a close.

The Third War started as a result of Maori opposition to the building of a military road through the bush towards the Waikato region. This was taken as proof by the Kingite chiefs of Britain's hostile intent and, in May 1863, fighting began again. General Sir Duncan Cameron led a British force towards the Maori fortification at Rangiriri, although his force was constantly harassed by Maori skirmishers, who would suddenly appear from their hiding places in the fern-forests to attack the British line.

Private James Oates of the 11th Regiment was present at the Battle of Rangiriri (20 November 1863) and wrote of his experiences in a letter to his brother.

> After marching for about 15 miles we were halted on the brow of the hill opposite us lay the native fortified position [*pah*]. The action commenced about half to 4 in the evening with the Big Guns shelling them and at about 4 o'clock we were ordered to charge which we did in such a manner and with three cheers that would frighten any civilisation much less a parcel of savages. We rushed down the hill on them. They fired volley after volley into ranks and twas many a gallant officer and man bit the dust but still we rushed on and with the help of scaling ladders was soon over the parapet but to our surprise they had a regular burrow of pits behind which the enemy lay concealed to the amount of 1,000 natives. We charged and charged again but of no avail, each time we had to retire with losses but they could not get out as we had them surrounded and they must fight or die.

With the failure of the frontal attack, the British commander determined on another plan of attack.

Cameron now decided to fire – as Oates described them – 'small shells' into the fortification.

> They [the Maoris] did not seem to relish [the shells] for they yelled like demons, and at the same time he ordered a lot of our men to set to work to undermine them for the purpose of blowing them up with powder – this continued all night until daylight next morning when to our great surprise they hoisted the white flag as a signal of surrender ...

And so ended a memorable a day to New Zealand as is on record in its annals.[36]

The capture of Rangiriri allowed Cameron to lead his force onto the next centre of Maori resistance at Orakau, which his men besieged from 30 March 1864. After several days of bombardment, the Maoris suddenly broke out and fled into the bush, and Orakau's capture effectively ended the Waikato campaign. However, the rising now spread along the coast to the Bay of Plenty and here resistance centred on the *pah* at Gate Pa.

The battle of 29 April became known for the ferocity of the fighting, in which the British storming party fought at close-quarters with the Maori defenders. The British suffered over 120 killed and wounded and were repulsed. However, the weight of numbers of British troops in the area finally saw the region pacified and the war formally ended. The Maoris now turned away from fixed defences to a more guerrilla-style conflict, which became well-known for its brutality. Raids and bush fighting became the norm; prisoners were rarely taken on either side and both captives and missionaries were murdered by the Maori. Captain Lloyd of the 57th Regiment was beheaded by his captors and his head was smoke-dried and passed around the various tribes as a trophy. British troops largely withdrew from the colony to leave the protection of the settlers to colonial volunteer units. Although raiding continued for several years, the Maori resistance dwindled as their numbers were reduced by clashes with the colonials.

The Abyssinian Campaign (1867–8) was one in which British forces, largely sent from India, were tasked with freeing hostages – British representatives and German missionaries – from the clutches of the Abyssinian Emperor Tewodros II. The reasons for the conflict seem rather bizarre, as was the behaviour of Tewodros. After uniting Abyssinia by a series of conflicts in the 1850s, Tewodros appeared to be keen to modernise his country in the face of internal opposition. He turned to Europe for assistance and encouraged a number of missionaries to his mountaintop court at Magdala. Unfortunately, a letter of friendship sent by Tewodros to the British government languished in the Colonial Office and no reply was sent. Thus slighted, the unstable Tewodros rashly took the Europeans hostage.

The British government took action and an expeditionary force, under the command of General Sir Robert Napier, was assembled in India. The force had to surmount the huge logistical challenge of reaching Magdala, which was over 400 miles from the Red Sea coast. The plains of Abyssinia were unbearably hot and arid, whilst in the mountains the troops would suffer downpours of rain and freezing temperatures. The expeditionary force of 13,000 troops, 19,000 supporters and 55,000 transport animals left the coast in January 1868. After three long months, Napier's army had almost reached Tewodros' capital when it was opposed by 7,000 Abyssinians on the plain of Aroge on 10 April. The battle was a one-sided affair, in which the controlled volley fire and artillery shells of the British tore into their foes. Over 700 enemy dead were found on the battlefield for the loss of two British soldiers.

Tewodros had not been present at Aroge, but remained in his mountain city. On news of his defeat, he – to the surprise of the British – released his prisoners, but refused to surrender. Napier determined to storm Magdala and, on 13 April, British troops rushed up the narrow single track approach towards the city gates. The British, despite some resistance, were able to burst through the gateway and take the city. Tewodros placed a pistol in his mouth and ended his bizarre life. Napier's engineers destroyed the city and on 16 April the British began the long march back to the sea. Strangely, the bloody nose having been meted out, the British government did not seek to impose any settlement or establish a new regime, but simply left the country to its own devices.

Captain Francis Barker of the Royal Artillery was a member of Napier's expedition to Abyssinia in 1867. He vividly described the hardship of the march to Magdala, during which the British were frequently harassed by the locals, particularly on the mountain tracks. In a letter to his father, Barker recorded one incident in which a group of fifty Gallas – a tribe of mountain people – tried to steal some of the British Army's mules. Barker's disdain for the enemy and his confidence in the superior firepower of the British is evident.

When I rode up, I got two shots at the thieves and had six of my men up, who were armed, and made the Gallas scuttle shooting two of them. There were about 50 in all, but the old story of Europeans and sniders [the regulation British rifle] against niggers and muzzle loaders, made the odds well in my favour. My six men I think were very much disappointed that the brutes would not stand.[37]

Ensign Walter Wynter of the 33rd Regiment carried the regiment's colours as he and his comrades stormed the gates at Magdala. He left an account of the incident in which Private Bergin heaved a young drummer boy up on top of the twelve-foot gatehouse, who in turn was then able to assist Bergin up. Whilst Bergin opened fire on 'every black face in sight', a comrade helped other men of the 33rd up and into the city. Wynter then describes his own ascent.

It was a tough pull up, but I was hardly ever on my feet as the men took me and the colours in their arms and passed us on to the front ... I shall never forget the exhilaration of that moment, the men firing and shouting like madmen.[38]

Whilst, during the first half of Victoria's reign, her troops had endured conflicts in which they had frequently been forced to face foes who were as well armed and drilled as themselves, this was to change in the second half of the period – though it was not made easier. The Mutiny had been repressed, the Sikhs defeated and the Russians taught a lesson. Yet as the Empire expanded, the Soldiers of the Queen were to be found fighting against new and determined foes in Africa and on the North West Frontier, the defeat of whom would require both new tactics and the better use of military technology. Once again, the British soldier rose to this new challenge.

Part Two 1871–1901

In the last thirty years of Victoria's reign, wars erupted ever more frequently. During this period the rest of Europe suddenly awoke to the benefits of empire, not just for establishing and maintaining economic vigour, but also for reasons of national prestige. Britain found itself competing with France, Germany, and even Belgium, in what has been termed the 'scramble for Africa', as the Europeans sought to add territory to their fledgling empires. To maintain the position of the British Empire – and to usurp territory before a European rival could claim it

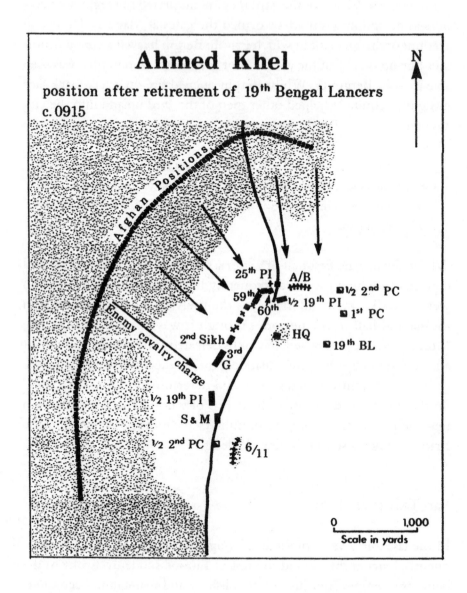

Ahmed Khel

position after retirement of 19th Bengal Lancers
c. 0915

N

Afghan Positions

Enemy cavalry charge

25th PI

A/B

½ 2nd PC

59th

½ 19th PI

60th

1st PC

2nd Sikh

HQ

19th BL

3rd
G

½ 19th PI

S & M

½ 2nd PC

6/11

0   1,000
Scale in yards

– her soldiers were involved in numerous campaigns, military expeditions and full-scale wars. So many in fact that Byron Farwell has claimed that British history books simply ignore most of them, and that, even at the time, punitive excursions, field forces and minor expeditions were so commonplace that most Britons never knew of them. Farwell states that between 1874 and 1879 in India alone, there were no fewer than fourteen military expeditions mounted against such frontier tribes as the Afridis, Utman Khels, Mohmands, Wazirs, Zaimukhts, Marris and Bhitannis.

The number of troops employed on these expeditions varied from 280 to 7,400 men, and most of them would have been of Indian origin. In 1875 British troops were brought in from Hong Kong and Calcutta to conquer the independent state of Perak in the Malay Peninsula and add it to the British Empire.[39]

During these last 30 years of the nineteenth century the British soldier campaigned extensively, and in some cases almost constantly, along the North West Frontier of India, in a major conflict in Afghanistan (the Second Afghan War 1878–1881), in Egypt (1882) and the Sudan (1884–5 and 1896–8), in Ashanti, on the West Coast of Africa (1873–4 and 1896), in South Africa (Ninth Cape Frontier War 1877–8, Zulu War 1879 and Boer Wars 1881 and 1899–1902), in Burma (Third Burma War 1885–9 and numerous expeditions between 1889–92) and in China (Boxer Rebellion 1900). In addition to these major conflicts, the British fought in such minor campaigns as the Bechuanaland Expedition of 1884 and the Matabele War of 1893, in modern-day Zimbabwe.

British troops were frequently at a numerical disadvantage against their foes, particularly during the Zulu War and the Sudanese campaigns. Tactics of entrenchment and the square formation, combined with superior firepower, usually halted charging natives or tribesmen before they could engage British soldiers in close combat. The square may have supplied all-round protection but it did not permit the maximum use of rifle-fire. This was obtained from line, and thus the square was the last resort at close quarters if the rush had not been broken up by volleys at longer ranges. On the rare occasions when the enemy was able to close-in on the deployed British troops, the outcome could be disastrous, as at Isandlwana (21 January 1879), where the Zulus overwhelmed over 1,000 British troops and their auxiliaries.

Technological advancement ensured that the British rifles would out-range and out-fire the antique flintlock muskets of the Ashantis and the Zulus. In 1866 the Snider breech-loading rifle began to be issued and was first seen in the Abyssinian campaign of 1867–8. Although still a single-shot weapon, for the first time it allowed soldiers to fire lying down from behind defensive positions, which was of particularly benefit in the jungle battles of the Ashanti War. It was during this conflict that the British first demonstrated the destructive firepower of the Gatling Gun, although the new weapon was not used operationally until the Battle of Nyezane (21 January 1879) during the Zulu War. Despite some difficulties with reliability, the Gatling and Gardner machine-guns were to prove useful in battle against both the charging Zulus and the dervishes of the Sudan. The Snider rifle was replaced by the metal-cartridged Martini-Henry during the 1870s, its range and 'stopping-power' of particular use in the Sudan. By the 1890s the Army was using the bolt-action, magazine-fed Lee Metford .303 rifle, which would remain the basic infantry weapon up to and beyond the Second World War. In 1891, smokeless powder was introduced, a vital improvement because soldiers firing from cover were not given away by a puff of white smoke, which was of particularly benefit in the hills and passes of the North West Frontier.

The types of enemies that the British fought varied enormously during the period 1870–1901. Apart from spear-wielding Zulus and dervishes, the British faced a well-armed, trained and disciplined Egyptian Army in 1882, while in 1880 an Afghan army, with Russian-trained artillery officers, inflicted a serious defeat upon Burrow's smaller Anglo-Indian force at Maiwand. The Burmese were ruthless fighters who could melt into the jungle. The Boers were superb marksmen and horsemen, who were adept at fighting from well-chosen defensive positions as well as being able to adopt guerrilla hit and run tactics when required. The various conflicts involved different levels of commitment of British forces. The second invasion of Zululand saw the despatch of more British troops than were present at the Battle of Waterloo. The Second Afghan War involved six cavalry regiments, 38 batteries and 24 battalions of the British Army, and 29 regiments, seven batteries and 71 battalions of the Indian Army. At the start of the Boer War in 1899 the initial field force, under General Redvers Buller, of 47,000 men, was a very sizeable portion of the

British Army, which then consisted of only 250,000 regulars, 70,000 of whom were in India while 60,000 were scattered across the rest of the Empire. Yet, to subdue the tough and stubborn Boers, who had under arms only between 30,000 to 45,000 men at any one time, the British were eventually forced to raise a large volunteer army of nearly 500,000 men.

The first major campaign for the British Army in the 1870s was the Ashanti Expedition of 1873–4. It was fought primarily to control the warlike and expansionist Ashantees of West Africa, who were terrorising the coastal tribes and even had the effrontery to attack the British fort at Elmina in June 1873. Commanded by Garnet Wolseley, the expedition had to deal not only with an aggressive enemy, but also the pestilential climate of the West African coast, which was known as the 'White Man's Grave'. The Ashantees were used to fighting in the jungle terrain, and were disciplined in the attack. On each occasion when the British met them in battle, the Ashantees would attempt to outflank the British and their careful use of cover, trees and jungle foliage allowed them to approach the British troops unseen. The final and decisive battle of the war was fought at Amoaful on 31 January 1874, and the conditions in which the British had to fight and win were described in a letter by Rifleman Gilham.

> We cut our way right and left into the jungle with our cutlasses, lying down in the underwood, standing behind trees for cover, pegging in where we could, and forming a semi-circle to the front; but the foliage was so dense that it was like being in a net, and the farther we went the thicker it seemed to get, so that I don't believe we advanced a hundred yards during the whole of the fight. The enemy were all armed with flintlock muskets, obtained from old Dutch settlers, and they fired at us with rough bits of lead, old nails, pebbles and rusty iron.[40]

Although these antiques weapons did cause a number of casualties, including Evelyn Wood – he was shot above the heart with a rusted nail which remained in his body for the rest of his long life – there were few British battlefield fatalities, and superior British firepower ensured that the battle was won. Wolseley advanced on the capital of Kumsai, which was duly burnt to the ground and the war was effectively brought to an end.

British troops were next engaged in Africa during the Ninth Cape Frontier War (1877–8). This was a particularly difficult war in which British soldiers of the 24th and 90th Regiments, commanded by Lord Chelmsford, were tasked with isolating rebellious Gaika tribesman in the locality of King William's Town, in the hope of either bringing them to battle or forcing their surrender. The war was very much a 'cat and mouse' game, in which the British unsuccessfully toiled for many months before deciding upon the best tactics to drive the rebels out of their bush and mountain refuges. Lieutenant Carrington of the 24th was tasked with forming a detachment of mounted infantry during the conflict, which he was later to command with distinction in the Zulu War. In a letter to his fellow officer, Nevill Coghill, Carrington wrote of his unit's first contact with the Gaika rebels and described the tactics used by the enemy to try to outflank the British.

> We were soon hotly engaged. The Kaffirs were in long grass and thorn trees and would hardly budge. I got within twenty yards frequently and got outflanked by them but by charging round on them and leading on a lot of Fingoes [tribesmen who fought for the British] we ousted them and were then hotly engaged with a lot of devils hidden by stones and small breastworks. We led our horses and fired on them up to within twenty yards and had a right hot corner. I rode my horse and four scoundrels kept potting at me and at last hit my horse in the jaw and he spun round like a top. He was only ten yards off so I potted him with my revolver. Sergeant Leslie was assegaied in the hand, but knocked the fellow over with the butt end of his gun and then shot him.[41]

Carrington and the troops who fought in Ninth Frontier War then marched to Natal, where they were to be engaged in the Zulu War of 1879. Of all the wars of Victoria's reign this was, perhaps, the most unjustified pre-emptive attack on the part of the British, in which Chelmsford and the Colonial Governor, Sir Bartle Frere, conspired to contrive a war with the Zulu kingdom. This is the most written about of Victoria's wars and also one of the most brutal. After the shock defeat at the hands of the Zulus at Isandlwana, the British sought revenge, during which Zulu villages, or kraals, were burnt and the Zulu wounded were despatched. British victories at Kambula (29 March),

Gingindlovu (1 April) and Ulundi (4 July), resulted in the destruction of the disciplined Zulu Army and the end of the kingdom.

Captain Fred Slade of the Royal Artillery was present at the Battle of Kambula and, writing the day after the fight, wrote of the jubilation after the British success. 'I shall never forget the reaction of different fellows after the battle. We all shook hands and congratulated one another on being alive and well.' This happiness and relief was tempered the day after when the butcher's bill arrived.

> Today alas! came the sad work of seeing to our dead and wounded. Poor Bright 90th died at midnight. I sat with Nicolson a long time this morning but he was in terrible pain and died at 1.00. I can't tell you how I feel the loss of one who has lived so many months in my life. We sowed him up in his blanket and with poor Bright and 2 bullock wagon loads of N.C. Officers and men we buried him in the common grave. Bigge, Bursall and Pearce and myself acted as pallbearers and I never was present at a more sad and affecting funeral. The dead march played with combined bands. Colonel Wood reading the service, the setting sun over the mountain and the march back to camp to the tune of 'Home Sweet Home', are things I shall never forget.[42]

Captain Edward Hutton fought at the Battle of Gingindlovu and, in his reminiscences, wrote of how he was forced to steady his men at the advance of the Zulu Army and how disciplined the Zulus were.

> I ordered my men to go on firing very steadily. A few men showed signs of firing wildly, but a smart rap with my stick soon helped a man to recover his self-possession. In spite of our steady fire the Zulus continued to advance nothing daunted, the force attacking our front utilising cover ... the enemy, unable to make headway against our fire, gradually withdrew, slinking off through the long grass like whipped hounds.[43]

Hutton also wrote of the pursuit of the retreating Zulus by the irregular cavalry and native allies, which became a bloody feature of all the British victories in this conflict.

An officer of the Grenadier Guards, R. Wolride Gordon, was present at the Battle of Ulundi and recorded in his diary a vivid description of the final battle of the Zulu War. This was his first experience of combat and Wolride Gordon was clearly fascinated by the actual physical effect of British firepower, and the lance, upon the Zulu.

> The battle began, and in a short time there was such a rain of bullets flying over our heads that it was, as one of the men remarked, 'for all the world like a hailstorm'. I remained standing, watching the battle through my field glasses. It was a curious sight, and one could plainly see men, when hit, throw up their arms and fall. The thud the bullet makes against a man's body is a most curious sound. At last the big guns were too much for them, and they wavered and turned. We at once sent out the cavalry; the Lancers first. They had a grand time of it; nearly all the officers killed, anyhow, one man, and all the lances were red with blood when they came back; though the Zulus dodged very well, and were difficult to catch. [44]

The British Prime Minister, Benjamin Disraeli, who by 1879 held the title of Lord Beaconsfield, was furious that Britain had been drawn into a war against the Zulus by the actions of a Colonial Governor, for Britain was already engaged in another major conflict which was stretching her forces to the limit. This was the Second Afghan War (1878–81), a conflict which had also begun because of to the unilateral actions of the Viceroy, Lord Lytton.

The Afghan king, Sher Ali, had refused a British mission entry to the Afghan capital, Kabul, although a Russian mission was permitted. Incensed, the Viceroy issued Sher Ali with an ultimatum to accept a British mission. When the ultimatum expired, the British invaded the country in three columns. Troops under Sir Donald Stewart marched on Kandahar, Sir Sam Browne struck at the capital and Frederick Roberts advanced up the Kurram valley. Stewart's force was largely unopposed, although Browne's troops fought and won a sharp action at Ali Masjid (21 November 1878).

Roberts' force was blocked at Peiwar Kotal by a strong force of Afghans on the heights above. Roberts devised a brilliant night march which outflanked the Afghans, and a dawn attack (2 December 1878) by the British on the flank and centre saw the collapse of the Afghan position. Sher Ali fled Kabul, and the throne was handed to his son, Yakub Khan. The British were able to place a British representative, Major Sir Louis Cavagnari, in Kabul.

The year 1879 was to see a reversal for British fortunes when, in September, mutinous elements of the Afghan Army murdered Cavagnari and the small British force in Kabul. Roberts was sent on a mission of revenge, in which he defeated an Afghan force outside the capital at Charasiab (5 October 1879) and entered the city. Here Roberts soon found himself besieged, but, after repeated Afghan attacks, the British beat back the enemy.

Stewart marched from Kandahar to relieve Roberts, but his force was surprised at Ahmed Khel (19 April 1880) by a large Afghan army, and only after a stubborn and bloody resistance were the British able to proceed.

Later in the year, an Afghan force assembled to attack Kandahar and General Burrows was sent from the city to attack the enemy. Burrows stumbled across them at Maiwand. His force was heavily outnumbered and outgunned and the British line collapsed, with over 1,000 soldiers lost. The survivors fled back to Kandahar where they were besieged. Roberts was forced to assemble a force from the Kabul garrison and marched to the relief of Kandahar. The epic march became part of Victorian folklore and Roberts' force defeated the Afghans outside Kandahar (1 September 1880) in what was to be the last military operation of the war. The new Liberal government, with Gladstone as Prime Minster, was keen to extract Britain from the costly war and the last British troops marched out of Afghanistan in May 1881. It was not until 1919 that Britain intervened in Afghan affairs again.

For the British soldier this conflict involved the hardship of long marches and periods of intense boredom, interspersed with violent conflict. All this is reflected in the surviving letters written by the troops. Not every combat was on a large scale. Many were small skirmishes, in which relatively small numbers of British troops fought. One of these was graphically described by Lance-Corporal William Eaton of the 14th Regiment in an undated letter to his brother. It tells of the suddenness and brutality of close combat, as well as the hardships the troops had to endure whilst pursuing the enemy.

They [the Afghans] began slowly to retire until they got to the foot of the hill, then they made a dogged resistance, we had to force them at the point of the bayonet then they began to retreat with their face to us, up the hill. I noticed one of the Afghans particularly, he was dressed in white and was weildin a great long sword, I think he must have been their commander by the way he was leading them on, our captain saw him and he said to us, leave him to me men. A few minutes after I saw him engaged in a desperate sword combat with the Afghan chief. And another Afghan was running with his sword uplifted to strike our captain in the back, there was not a moment to lose, I knew I could not get to him before he struck, I presented my rifle, I knew if I missed the Afghan would kill the Captain. I took aim and the Afghan dropped dead almost at the same time the Captain dropped the Afghan Chief. I now saw two more rush at the captain, he fought desperately with them, in a while one of them cut the captain badly in the hand and he dropped his sword in a instant he had his revolver out but it missed fire. It would have gone badly for the captain, but by this time I had got up to him, and I shot one and ran my bayonet through the other.

Eaton's letter then provides some detail as to the British tactics on the day.

Just then the bugle sounded the lie down. We kept laid down until the artillery got up the hill, then they fired a few shells amongst the trees this soon brought them out there was a lot of mud huts about a mile off and they all ran towards them, we were ordered to pursue them, but we could hardly walk, we had marched 8 hours, and then five hours hard fighting, with the Indian sun blazing onto us all day, and without anything to eat. It was no wonder that we could not run after them with our feet blistered so that we could hardly put them down but we followed as well as we could, the artillery sent a few shells among the huts and blew them down, they fled with their lives all that could towards Herat, the cavalry followed them and killed plenty of them. The assembly was then called, all the men came in and we buried our dead. A guard was then mounted for the night; I then laid on the ground. I remembered no more until I awoke this morning. The reveille was just going I got up and looked around, the scene looked desolate, there were hundreds of dead Afghans lying about. I found that I had slept all night with a dead Afghan for my pillow.[45]

For saving his life, Eaton's Captain presented him with the Afghan Chief's sword.

Private John Facer of the 30th Regiment was part of Stewart's force that marched to Kabul in April 1880 and he fought at the Battle of Ahmed Khel. Facer's diary of 19 April 1880 described the battle in which the Afghans nearly succeeded in breaking the British line.

Very soon the enemy began to feel the effects of our bullets. As each shell burst you could distinctly see twenty or thirty, sometimes more, fall to the ground. At length with a heavy cheer they rushed down the hills to meet us in hundreds, and in perfect disorder. Our skirmishing line was at once thrown out, it is reinforced by supports and reserves, and you may guess a tremendous fire was kept up for a few minutes, and our Martini Henris did frightful execution. As they approached, the men instantly fixed bayonets for a death struggle. The enemy were now within ten or twenty yards of us the effect the volley made on them I shall never forget. They were now receiving a tremendous fire both from us and the Regiment on the right, and it was here the men of the 59th Regiment got wounded during the action, as there were bullets in hundreds whistling over our heads and striking the ground in front of us.

Facer went on to reflect upon the luck needed to survive.

It is scarcely credible, the many who had narrow escapes of being either killed or wounded. For instance, one man received a scratch, and another had his shoulder cut off, and another got the lid of his pouch shot off, while I myself, during the retirement, stumbled and there I had to stay for I could not get up again, I was that exhausted. So I was surrounded by the enemy; but luckily only one man chanced to spot me out, and he was making a cut at me with a sword when he also stumbled, and my bayonet entered his navel and came out of his throat which put the fix on him. The line was now again advancing, and I heard a voice from my company calling me to lay down, which I did, and there I stayed until they got up to me and I was able to rejoin them.[46]

The British defeat at Maiwand (27 July 1880), in which over 1,000 men were lost, was the most comprehensive of the Afghan conflict and was as shocking to the British public as the defeat at Isandlwana the year before. Captain J. Slade of the Royal Artillery fought at Maiwand and wrote a description of the fighting in a letter to his mother.

The enemy got bolder and advanced closer and literally encircled us all. The firing got awfully hot especially the artillery and men and horses began to drop on all sides. The fire was now terrific and how any of us escaped I cannot tell, men were falling right and left of me and horses on all sides. When the Ghazis charged across I fired case shot and mowed them down in hundreds and really never came to within 10 or 15 yards of us until we had retired. How I escaped I cannot tell as they were all round us before I gave the word 'March'. My horse was shot, but fortunately for me did not fall.[47]

Private Thomas Lloyd of the 7th Royal Fusiliers was part of General Primrose's force besieged by the Afghans in Kandahar following the defeat at Maiwand. Lloyd wrote of his involvement in a number of sorties from the city, the first of which, on 15 August 1880, resulted in a narrow escape.

I was out with a party under Lieutenant Barlott, was in the skirmishing line under cover – saw an Afghan – left my cover to shoot him but I was very near receiving the vengeance of the Ghazies [Afghan tribesmen]. For no sooner did I showed my head then went bang 5 or 6 shots along the side of my earhole, returned to my former position as quiet as possible and considered I was much safer.

On 16 August, Lloyd joined a sortie to attack a strong enemy position to the northeast of the city. The British soon found themselves in difficulty as they were engaged in street fighting with an unseen enemy, who fired from loopholes and rooftops. Lloyd and his comrades had to fight a retreat, in which the British wounded had to be left to their fate. On 28 August Lloyd again left the shelter of Kandahar with a party of 100 men, to bury the dead and those that had been left behind on 16 August.

The sight we saw will never be forgotten by anyone that saw it. I am sure that no one would like to see it again. Poor Captain Cruckshanks R.E. had his body cut open and his intrails taken out and replaced by his clothes which were stuffed inside him.

Unfortunately, Lloyd was to see worse sights when he was part of a detachment that was sent out of the city on 15 September, after it had been relieved by Roberts. The troops were tasked with the burial of the dead from Maiwand, which had remained unburied since 27 July.

> It was a horrible sight to see the bodies of these poor fellows which were torn to pieces with Vulters and Jackalls. The skull and bones were lying about in all directions.

The task was so enormous that the burial party had to return the following day.

> A working party of a 100 men went out at 5.30 am to bury the remainder dead bodies of the 66th Regiment. There were thousands of cartridges laying where the firing line was and hundreds of solid shot from the enemies artillery buried in the ground.[48]

British forces were again engaged in South Africa in 1880–1, where they fought the Boers of the Transvaal, who had declared their independence from the Confederation of South Africa. In what can be safely be described as the only conflict lost by British forces during Victoria's reign, the British, under the command of General Colley, were to suffer three comprehensive defeats, and the men who survived were to suffer the ignominy of being a part of the only war for which a campaign medal was never issued, such was the shame of the defeat at the time.

In late 1880 the Boers besieged a number of British garrisons in the Transvaal, including one at Pochefstroom, and a British force sent to relieve the situation was attacked and defeated by the Boers at Bronkhorstspruit on 20 December 1880. Colley suffered a reversal at Laing's Nek on 28 January 1881, as he tried to force the pass into the Transvaal. Worse was to follow; on 8 February, Colley was surprised by a force of Boers at Schuinshoogte and was forced to flee the battlefield under cover of darkness, leaving his wounded to be taken prisoner. Finally, on 27 February, Colley secretly led a British force to the top of Majuba Hill, which dominated the Boer position at Laing's Nek. Colley assumed that this move would force the Boers to withdraw, however, the Boers attacked and a combination of too small a British force and

Boer marksmanship resulted in a rout of British forces and the death of Colley. Evelyn Wood assumed command and, whilst preparing a substantial force to restore British glory, he was forced to resort to a truce. This led to a treaty, due to pressure from Gladstone's government, and what many considered a rather ignominious peace.

Owing to the short length of the campaign and the relatively small number of British troops engaged, very few letters or diaries survive. However, Lieutenant Percy Marling, who was later to win a Victoria Cross in the Sudan campaign at the Battle of Tamaii (13 March 1884), did keep a diary and he recorded the solemn aftermaths of both the battles of Laing's Nek and Schuinshoogte. On 29 January, Marling made the following entry.

> Within 300 yards of my picket, when I was visiting the sentries just as day was breaking, I saw a man come out of the hospital tent and throw something as far as he could out into the veldt. I went to see what it was, and found a man's arm which had just been amputated above the elbow. I suppose the hospital orderly was too busy or too lazy to dig a hole and bury it, and thought the asvogels (vultures) would come and eat it as it was light, which they did. It was not an appetising sight on an empty stomach in the grey dawn. All night we could hear the wretched wounded groaning and crying out. At 6 pm the 9 dead officers were buried. It was a very sad and solemn sight.[49]

Marling also wrote of the horrors of a burial detail.

> On February 12th a party was sent out under a flag of truce to bring back to camp the bodies of the dead officers. The battlefield was covered by enormous numbers of vultures, who were feeding on both horses and human flesh. They were so gorged they refused to move. It was disgusting work having to dig up corpses which had been buried for four days in rainy weather in a tropical country like South Africa. The bodies were already decomposed and poor O'Connell was the only one who could be recognised by his features. Why the officers could not have been left in peace on the ground where they fought so gallantly I do not know ... The men would dig for quarter of an hour and then be violently sick. To show how fierce the fight had been, one helmet had five bullet holes in it, and many had two or three.[50]

In 1882 a British expeditionary force, under the command of Sir Garnet Wolseley, was sent to Egypt. British intervention was as a direct response to the increasingly vocal and violent nature of the nationalist movement in Egypt, under the leadership of Arabi Pasha, the minister of war. The movement focused on hostility towards European control of the Egyptian government of Khedive Tewfik and its finances, and it reached a crescendo when riots broke out in Alexandria in June 1882. Gladstone's government felt compelled to send a military force not only to protect its financial assets in Egypt – which included a share in the Suez Canal – but also its citizens. Having landed in Alexandria, Wolseley displayed masterful skills of deception and, whilst Arabi Pasha maintained a substantial force outside of the city, Wolseley travelled with the majority of his force via Ismailia to the Sweet Water Canal, from where he intended to attack the significant Egyptian defences at Tel-el-Kebir, which blocked the way to Cairo. An advanced division, under Major-General Graham, encountered the enemy at Kassassin on 28 August and a combined artillery and cavalry action won the day for the British.

In the aftermath of the battle, the Egyptians hastily improved the defences of Tel-el-Kebir and the British sent out numerous cavalry patrols to probe for weakness and gain intelligence. Alexander Tulloch took part in one reconnaissance, and rode over the same ground that the cavalry had attacked during the battle. He reported that, on 29 August

> … I made a reconnaissance over the desert towards Tel-el-Kebir, and came across the ground where the cavalry had charged. There were many dead, and, to my horror, I found several wounded men, some in a state of delirium, others very weak but still sensible … I sent at once for dhoolies from the Indian cavalry; and one poor fellow I helped to carry had his abdomen sliced open by a sword-cut. Fortunately the bowels had not been touched; but I had to put them back in their place before I moved the man. Another was a wounded officer – a huge fellow. As I lifted him, his head, badly cut and festering, fell on my shoulder; the broken bone of his left arm was protruding through the cloth of his coat; this I did not notice until placing him flat in his dhooly.[51]

Wolseley's intelligence had informed him that the Egyptians at Tel-el-Kebir did not place sentries or pickets away from the fortifications at night, and thus he decided to resort to a night march, so as to be in place for an attack by his whole force at dawn on 13 September. The night march was accomplished with great skill and the British gained the element of complete surprise. The Egyptian defenders were only able to fire a few artillery shells – which passed harmlessly over the heads of the charging infantry – before the British were able to storm into the first line of defences. It was an overwhelming British victory, and one that was achieved at a relatively low cost; 480 British troops were killed or wounded, with the Highland Brigade – which encountered the strongest resistance from Sudanese troops in the first line of defence – suffering 45 killed and 188 wounded. Egyptian dead numbered several thousand.[52]

The confused and bitter nature of the fighting inside the Egyptian defences was recorded in a letter by Lieutenant L. Perry of the Royal Artillery to a fellow officer.

A cheer on our left told us of the assault of the first line of entrenchment's, which fell at once; and we then came up to it and found a parapet about 4 feet high with ditches on both sides. The gunners at once set to work to pull this down with pick and shovel, the enemy meanwhile firing heavily from the second line. As soon as I could get my horse over I did, and found myself in the enemy's camp, surrounded with dead and dying of both sides. To these we paid no attention, but threw their beds and furniture into the ditches to help fill it up. In about 10 minutes the battery crossed, and we advanced about 500 yards at a sharp trot to the 2nd line, against which we came into action, from rising ground, about 500 yards range. The enemy was now in full retreat and the utmost confusion, so that after a few rounds the 'cease firing' sounded.[53]

The comprehensive victory brought an end to the conflict and British troops soon occupied Cairo.

After the Egyptian war of 1882, the British maintained significant interests in the country; Sir Evelyn Wood was tasked with restoring and retraining the Egyptian Army along British lines, whilst political power was in the hands of Lord Dufferin, and economic stability was the responsibility of Sir Auckland Colvin, the British government's financial advisor to the Egyptian government. British troops remained, garrisoned in Cairo. These three men effectively ran the country and it was they who first brought to the attention of the British government the worsening situation in the Sudan, which at this time was a protectorate of Egypt. The disturbances were centred on the rise of the Mahdi, or chosen one. This unrest was, initially, underestimated by the Egyptian Governor of the Sudan and, when a force was sent to apprehend the Mahdi, his loyal supporters heavily defeated the Egyptian troops. From this victory, and by appealing to religious fanaticism, the Mahdi recruited a large and committed army which was able to defy Egyptian authority, and he defeated two more Egyptian armies that were sent to quash him.

The events of 1882, in which the British intervened directly in Egyptian affairs and defeated and disbanded its army, effectively meant that the Sudan was left to its own devices. The Mahdi used this opportunity to recruit tribal leaders from north and south of Khartoum and the revolt spread ever closer to the Egyptian border proper.

Gladstone's government viewed the Mahdist revolt as a purely Egyptian problem, despite increasingly worrying intelligence reports. Although London would not sanction the use of British troops in the Sudan, it did allow the Egyptians to recruit retired Indian Army officers and one of these, General William Hicks, led an army of 8,000 Egyptians against the Mahdists in the Sudan. Unfortunately, Hicks allowed his force to be lured by the Mahdi into the deserts of Kordofan, where it suffered from lack of water and exhaustion. At Shaykan, on 4 November 1883, the Mahdi descended upon Hicks' ragged force and annihilated it. Hicks and other former British officers, as well as British newspapermen, were amongst the dead. The British public was shocked and there was a general call for a British force to be sent to the Sudan and for Hicks to be avenged. Gladstone resisted such calls, but mounting pressure meant that the government had to be seen to be taking some action to secure the safety of Egyptian nationals in the Sudanese capital of Khartoum, which was under imminent threat from Mahdist forces. After much procrastination, the British government settled on the despatch of Charles Gordon R.E. to Khartoum.

Gordon had previously been a Governor in Sudan working for the Egyptian government, and probably understood the country and the people better than any other Englishman. However, he was a driven man with a strong religious belief and a conviction as to his own destiny; he was certainly used to having his own way. For various reasons, including the need for haste, the reluctance of the government to face up to the danger of the situation and Gordon's own limited understanding of the actual mission, the task given to Gordon was rather unclear. While he was instructed to brief the government as to the seriousness of the situation on the ground, the need to prepare for an evacuation of Khartoum was also impressed upon him, as was the firm warning that Gordon would not receive any British military assistance.

Once Gordon had safely arrived in Khartoum, he became convinced that evacuation would be impossible and he consequently bombarded the British government with requests for British troops to be sent to defend the city. While London refused such demands, British troops were finally drawn into action along the Red Sea coast, where a follower of the Mahdi, Uthman Diqna, had attacked the Egyptian outpost at Suakin. This region was of very great strategic importance to Britain and, with the defeat of an Egyptian force sent to relieve the Suakin outpost, Major-General Graham was despatched with nearly 3,000 infantry, with cavalry and artillery support, to pacify the region.

The British reoccupied Suakin and Graham then marched his force on to Uthman Diqna's base at El Teb. Here, on 29 February 1884, the British met the charging Beja tribesmen in square formation. The bravery of the enemy astonished the British, as they were forced to repel wave after wave of rushing warriors, many of whom reached the British square and engaged the troops in fierce hand-to-hand fighting. Lieutenant Percy Marling described the Bejas as 'the pluckiest fellows I have ever seen'.[54] Two charges by the British cavalry were met by the Beja falling flat to the ground and attacking either the man or his horse as they passed over the prone warrior. Cavalry casualties – 20 killed out of 30 British fatalities – were relatively high. Over 1,500 warriors were killed and Utham Diqna withdrew his force. Whilst the British had won and had held the port of Suakin, the enemy still controlled most of the countryside, and Graham once more led his force out to confront the Mahdist force near the village of Tamaii.

Lieutenant Perry of the Royal Artillery was present at the Battle of Tamaii (13 March 1884), in which the British, under the command of General Graham, had advanced with two separate infantry brigades in square formation, supported by mounted infantry. Unfortunately, one of the squares broke as the Black Watch advanced too quickly. The Scotsmen became isolated and suffered heavy

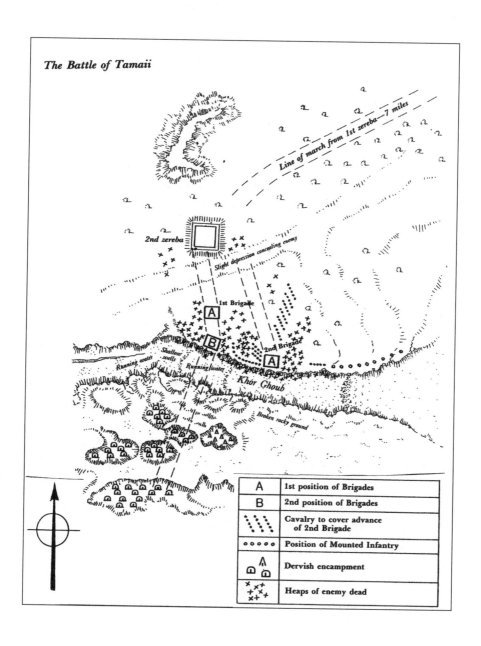

The Battle of Tamaii

Line of march from 1st zereba—7 miles

2nd zereba

Slight depression concealing enemy

1st Brigade

A

B

2nd Brigade

A

Shallow wells

Running water

Running water

Khor Ghoub

Broken rocky ground

A	1st position of Brigades
B	2nd position of Brigades
⋮⋮⋮	Cavalry to cover advance of 2nd Brigade
○○○○○	Position of Mounted Infantry
⌂ ⋀ ⌂	Dervish encampment
×ₓ⁺ ⁺ˣ₊ ×⁺ ⁺	Heaps of enemy dead

casualties, with over 60 killed out of a total of 109 British fatalities. The dervishes attacked wildly and the short battle was won, once again, by the ordered and controlled firing from both the infantry and the artillery. During one part of the battle the artillery were seriously threatened by rampaging dervishes, but, in a letter to a fellow officer at Woolwich, Perry made no mention of this threat. He instead gave details of the British artillery fire upon the dervishes in a coolly objective manner.

> The battle of Tamaii was not half such a good one [as El Teb] although we fired 22 rounds per gun but they had no artillery. We found common shell both time and percussion had most splendid effect over the boulders and granite rocks where the Johnnies were.[55]

Strategically, these two British victories had little importance. Although defeated in battle, the Mahdists still controlled the countryside and thereby blocked any advance along the Suakin to Berber route to Khartoum. A now outraged British public cried for a British force to be sent to relieve the Sudanese capital and, in August 1884, a reluctant government approved the funds for a relief expedition, commanded by Wolseley, of 7,000 British regulars. Wolseley decided to send his whole force down the Nile, but numerous delays and obstacles meant that by January 1885 the relief expedition had only reached Korti, still 200 miles across the desert from Khartoum. Messages smuggled out of the besieged city informed Wolseley of the plight of Gordon and of Khartoum's imminent fall. Wolseley therefore decided to despatch a flying column of 1,800 men, under the command of Brigadier Herbert Stewart, across the desert, in the hope of reaching Khartoum in time. This force encountered numerous hardships, both from the harsh desert environment and fierce opposition from Mahdist forces. The British were forced into battle at Abu Klea on 17 January and again on 19 January at Metemmeh. These battles shared many of the features of the earlier encounters with the Beja warriors and both were extremely violent struggles. At Abu Klea, the Mahdists broke the British square formation, which was only restored after the bitterest of life and death struggles. Stewart, who had been killed during the advance, was replaced by Sir Charles Warren. The latter, after many difficulties, was able to arrive by steamer off Khartoum on 27 January, only to discover that the city had fallen two days earlier. Warren and his force returned, exhausted and dejected, to Korti.

Lord Charles Beresford was at the centre of the British square at Abu Klea when the dervishes charged. In his memoirs he recalled the bravery of the enemy as they advanced to be met by a wall of British fire.

> They [Mahdists] were tearing down upon us with a roar like the roar of the sea, an immense surging wave of white-slashed black forms brandishing bright spears and long flashing swords; and all were chanting, as they leaped and ran ... the terrible rain of bullets poured into them by the Mounted Infantry and the Guards stayed them not. They wore the loose white robe of the Mahdi's uniform, looped over the left shoulder, and the straw skull-cap. These things we heard and saw in a flash, as the formidable wave swept steadily nearer. As I fired [the Gardner Gatling Gun], I saw the enemy mown down in rows, dropping like ninepins ... Their desperate courage was marvellous. I saw a boy of some twelve years of age, who had been shot through the stomach, walk slowly up through a storm of bullets and thrust his spear at one of our men. I saw several Arabs writhe from out a pile of dead and wounded, and charge some eighty yards under fire towards us, and one of them ran right up to the bayonets and flung himself upon them and was killed.

Beresford also recorded the destructive firepower of the British.

> I observed that the rows of bullets from the Gardner gun, which was rifle calibre .45 inch, with five barrels, had cut off heads and tops of heads as though sliced horizontally with a knife.[56]

Sir Charles Wilson, who, on the death of Stewart was to assume command of the flying column, was it appears inside the square when the dervishes broke through and left a remarkably vivid account of the melee that ensued.

> When the enemy commenced the advance, I remember experiencing a feeling of pity mixed with admiration for them, as I thought they would all be shot down in a few minutes ... As they advanced, the feeling was changed to wonder that the tremendous fire we were keeping up had so little effect. When they got within eighty yards, the

fire of the Guards and Mounted Infantry began to take good effect, and a huge pile of dead rose in front of them. Then, to my astonishment, the enemy took ground to their right rapidly, but in order, as if on parade, so as to envelop the rear of the square. I remember thinking, 'By Jove, they will be into the square!' and almost the next moment I saw a fine old sheikh on horseback plant his banner in the centre of the square, behind the camels. He was at once shot down, falling on his banner. Directly the sheikh fell, the Arabs began running in under the camels to the front part of the square. Some of the rear rank now faced about and began firing. By this time Herbert Stewart's horse was shot, and as he fell three Arabs ran at him. I was close to his horse's tail, and disposed of the one nearest me, about three paces off, and the others were, I think, killed by the Mounted Infantry officers close by … There was one strange incident. An unwounded Arab, armed with a spear, jumped up and charged an officer. The officer grasped the spear with his left hand, and with his right ran through the Arab's body, and there for a few seconds they stood, the officer being unable to withdrew his sword until a man ran up and shot the Arab. It was a living embodiment of the old gladiatorial frescoes of the Guards officers. I was much struck with the demeanour of the Guards officers. There was no noise or fuss; all orders were given as if on parade, and they spoke to the men in a quiet manner, as if nothing unusual was going on.[57]

The British had come close to being overwhelmed and, in reality, it was probably only the quick thinking of Percy Marling – who ordered the men of his rear rank to turn around and fire across the breached British square – that stopped the British from being swept away.

Colonel Talbot commanded the Heavy Camel Regiment at Abu Klea, and described the moments after the British were able to reform the square and the Gatling guns took effect.

When the square was re-formed a lot of the Mahdists were inside, but you may be sure that none of them lived to get out again … At last the Gatling guns were got into action, and that practically ended the battle. The Soudanese were simply mowed down. Their bodies flew up into the air like grass from a lawn-mower. But their pluck was astonishing. I saw some of the natives dash up to the Gatling guns, and thrust their arms down the muzzles, trying to extract the bullets which were destroying their comrades! Of course, they were simply blown to atoms.[58]

Despite Gordon's death, Wolseley was prepared and willing to carry on the fight, but the British government thought otherwise and decided to abandon the Sudan to the Mahdi. Wolseley came home and an Anglo-Egyptian army remained to discourage the Mahdi from invading Egypt proper. The Mahdi died in June 1885, and was succeeded by Khalifa Abdullahi, one of his senior followers. Abdullahi's early hopes of invading Egypt were dashed at the Battle of Ginnis (30 December 1885), when – for the last time dressed in scarlet – British troops and their Egyptian allies decisively defeated the Mahdists.

Private T. Reader, of the East Surrey Regiment, remained in Egypt and fought against the Khalifa's forces. He wrote a letter home to a friend after his first taste of action in the Sudan.

Dear Chum, I was at Haseen the first time in action and was glad when it was all over for the bullets came whistling overhead like so many birds, but its all over now and I am ready for another turn.[59]

Captain Gibb, of the Worcester Regiment, also remained in the Sudan after the failure of the relief expedition. Here, in June 1886, he was in command of a small force that engaged a party of dervishes. In a letter home, Gibb described a particularly close combat and discusses the merits of the pistol as compared to the revolver.

I took 5 camel men and went round their left flank and potted at them for an hour and then they began to move northwards, so we went at them with the result of two killed and two prisoners on their side and myself and one man scratched. I have secured the spear as a trophy. It first went through my jacket and made a small mark like a scratch from a pin. I blew the man's head off however for doing it. The pistol is a beauty and at close range is like a small cannon. It fires as easily as a gun and you can aim with it, which is more than one can do with a revolver.[60]

Lieutenant Bertram Mitford of the Buffs was seconded to the Egyptian Army at Wadi Halfa, which saw considerable action against marauding

Mahdist forces. In his diary of 1 May 1887, Mitford wrote of one action in which he was fortunate to survive.

> I went down the cliff followed by men of both companies – 2 and 3 were all broken up into small parties among the rocks, with parties of the dervishes in between them who reached out and attacked our parties. We gradually joined up, as well as we could among the rocks, and tried to form line from the cliff to the river, and then moved forward searching the rocks. We had just had a rush by 8 or 10 dervishes on the party of men I was with, and I was standing behind a rock loading my revolver and discussing where the next rush would come from when an arm came round my neck and seized me by the throat: my sword was hanging by the hilt strap from my left wrist, and I without thinking put it up to protect my head, and as I did his sword came down hard on the hilt, at the same time with my right hand I pushed my revolver round until I felt something soft and then pulled the trigger: the dervish collapsed and I found afterwards I had shot half his neck away. A few minutes afterwards was when Healey was wounded, and I was in time to shoot his man. It was a pretty warm time.[61]

Throughout the attempted relief of Gordon and the subsequent smaller operations along the Sudanese-Egyptian border, British troops were also engaged in Burma in the protracted Third Burmese War (1885–9) and in the less intense expeditions which lasted from 1889–92. Although Britain had been triumphant in the Second Burmese War (1851–3), the reality was that, although British troops had captured Rangoon, their control over the countryside was limited and the Burmese never really accepted defeat. The British would frequently launch expeditions into the jungle to destroy Burmese stockades and then return to Lower Burma, the area of the Irrawaddy delta around Rangoon, which they had annexed and in which they maintained an army of occupation. The accession of the independently-minded King Thibaw in 1878 saw a gradual worsening of relations between Britain and Burma. Thibaw was neither reluctant to use violence against his own subjects, nor was he slow to encourage economic ties with other European powers. The crisis came in 1885, when Thibaw signed a commercial treaty with the French, which alarmed the British government, for they could not possibly tolerate French influence so close to their Indian border. The

British launched a pre-emptive strike at Thibaw and declared their intention of annexing his kingdom.

The main British incursion was aimed at the royal court based at Mandalay. Commanded by General Prendergast, 12,000 men, consisting of several Indian regiments and three battalions of British troops including the Royal Welch Fusiliers and the 67th Hampshire Regiment, sailed up the Irrawaddy in an armed flotilla. The Burmese made a stand behind entrenchments at Minhla on 17 November, but the British, despite intense fire, pressed on, and the Burmese position collapsed. Prendergast's forces entered Mandalay on 28 November 1885. Thibaw surrendered and he and his family were sent into exile. Supposedly the campaign was over, but this was not to be the case as thousands of troops from the Burmese Army simply melted into the jungle, from where they continued their resistance to British rule.

From their jungle bases the Burmese resistance fighters, or *dacoits*, continued the fight, not just against the British, but also the local inhabitants who were forced to supply them under pain of death. The British were involved in numerous jungle expeditions, which gradually wore down resistance as the number of fighters dwindled. Even so, the *dacoits* did manage to threaten Mandalay and, in January 1891, they besieged the town of Kwalin, which necessitated the despatch of a relief column. In 1889, expeditions, one even commanded by Wolseley himself, were sent to the Ponkan and Wuntho regions. By 1890 the steady British military pressure, and the deaths of Burmese fighters, gradually saw resistance fade, although a substantial British presence remained.

The future Field Marshal, Sir George White, was present at the only significant battle of the Third Burmese War, at Minhla. In his diary of 17 November 1885, he left an account of the British artillery fire from their boats the *Irrawaddy* and the *Kathleen* and of the storming of the Burmese stockades. White wrote that the British artillery had had little success in destroying the Burmese guns, but that they had set alight the town of Minhla. He recorded that he saw the British troops sweep over the stockades and attack the Burmese redoubt.

> While I had my glasses up our sepoys drove a crowd of Burmans out of the fort to the edge of the river and they were verily between the devil and the deep blue sea. Many of them took to the river and swam, and the sepoys fired volleys at their heads. I think all were shot or drowned.[62]

Captain Hay, of the 1st Bombay Lancers, served in the aftermath of the Third Burmese War and kept a diary, which recorded the difficulties of operating in the countryside against the elusive *dacoits*. In this extract from 3 January 1887, Hay wrote of one particular operation;

> [We] surrounded the village of Palangan where Sawtura [resistance leader] was reported to be staying. Just as we were approaching the place at dawn about 500 yards from the village – a crack of a rifle was heard close to our left front. The bullet passed close to me. I heard the whizz most distinctly. I immediately order 'front form' to be extended at 20 yards intervals continuing a most cautious forward at a trot and walk alternately. Then I halted 200 yards or so from the village and rode close up with a couple of scouts to ascertain whether resistance was intended but seeing nothing ordered the troop to surround while we entered the village and searched for our man whom needless to say was 'not there'. We however made prisoners of all the men we could find (about 30) and took them in to camp.

Hay also wrote of the difficulty in controlling the local police militia, stopping them from inflicting their own punishment upon the local inhabitants, and of the measures that had to be taken to maintain discipline.

> I caught a Burmese Policeman beating a poor woman and stealing a lot of things. I had him strung up at once and gave him a good round dozen lashes making him prisoner. Took him before Reg on return who tried and sentenced him to 3 months HL [Hard Labour].[63]

The clamour from the British public to avenge Gordon remained intense, but Anglo-Egyptian forces were not to go on the offensive again until 1896. By then, the Liberal government had been replaced by a Conservative administration, who were concerned about possible French and Italian imperial expansion in the region. To check this possibility, General Sir Herbert Kitchener was given command of a combined British and Egyptian force and tasked to conquer the Sudan by entering Khartoum. To avoid the transport headaches encountered by Wolseley, Kitchener decided upon the construction of a railway along stretches of the Nile and into the Sudan. Mahdist forces were despatched to oppose the advance at Firket, but Kitchener easily defeated them on 7 June 1896. By 1897, Kitchener realised he would need a stronger British force for the final confrontation with the Khalifa, and requested extra troops.

With his force now complete, Kitchener advanced into the Sudan in 1898. At Atbara, on 8 April 1898, Kitchener's army faced a Mahdist army under the command of Mahmud wad Ahmad, who decided to fight the British behind a defensive entrenched stockade, or *zareba*, of thorn bushes. Several accounts survive from this battle, which tell of the brutal nature of the fighting once the British infantry had penetrated the Mahdist defences.

The Battle of Atbara was a particularly bloody one. After an artillery bombardment, the British troops charged and entered the *zareba* of the dervishes. Then a slaughter began, as Private Teigh of the Lincolnshire Regiment recorded in his diary.

> ... [we] were soon inside [the *zareba*] amongst the Dervishes, slaughtering them. Everyone they saw they had a shot at or stabbed them with our bayonets, whether he was alive or dead, for we thought of the hardships they had put us to, and also the long dreary marches across the desert before we came to them.[64]

Similarly, Lieutenant Meiklejohn, also of the Lincolnshire Regiment, wrote in his diary of the moment his men entered the *zareba*.

> The dervishes were few and outnumbered, but fought bravely. I glimpsed one man in the ditch raise his rifle at me. I spun round and fired at him with my revolver at about 10 yards, and saw a spirt of dust fly up just beside his shoulder. Simultaneously a flash came from his rifle, which seemed to pass just by my head with a loud whizz. I was just going to fire again when two of my men were on him, their bayonets flashed and went in up to the hilt, and he sank down into the ditch. Then one of my men and a dervish had an exciting struggle. The latter was grasping the bayonet in one hand, while trying to draw his knife, and the two were going round in a circle. I was going to the rescue but the Tommy recollected that his rifle was loaded and managed to pull the trigger, with the result that the dervish was blown away a foot or so.

Meiklejohn was then himself involved in a close struggle as a dervish thrust a large spear at him. He was able to parry the thrust and then 'the point of my sword caught him full in the chest, and I felt nothing till the hilt came against his ribs.'[65]

The aftermath of the battle was also pretty gruesome, as Meiklejohn recorded.

> The sight inside the zariba was really appalling. The trenches were piled up in places with dead or dying, while men, camels, donkeys, and horses, dead or badly wounded, lay thick on the ground, or struggled to get up. To make things more ghastly, several of the straw tukkles [huts] were on fire, and dense clouds of black smoke made a pall over parts of the ground. Many bodies were burning, and there was a horrible smell of roasting flesh. Unfortunately some women and children had been involved in the carnage. One poor wretch lay dying on the ground with a very young baby beside her.[66]

Lieutenant FitzGibbon Cox was keen to get away from the scene of devastation, and he also reflected on a possible change of career.

> We were very glad to get away from the battlefield as it was beginning to smell 'orrid, dead bodies and wounded dervishes all along the route. After my experiences today I have come to the conclusion that a married civilian is the life for me. Of course – the dressing station had no chloroform![67]

After receiving further reinforcements, Kitchener was able to continue the advance towards Omdurman. The Khalifa decided not to oppose the British on the march, but instead he assembled a huge army, 40,000 strong, which attacked the British outside the city on 2 September 1898. This was just what Kitchener had been hoping for, and, as the Mahdists charged across ground devoid of cover, the British artillery, gunboats and infantry opened fire and cut them down in their hundreds. It was a stunning and comprehensive victory, for the British lost just over 100 men, but inflicted nearly 10,000 fatalities upon the Khalifa's men. Of the British causalities, most occurred during the charge of the 21st Lancers, which was a minor action that did not affect the result of the battle in any way. The British were able to enter the city on the day of the battle and two days later a religious service was held in the ruins of Gordon's palace across the river in Khartoum. Gordon had been avenged. The Khalifa disappeared into the wastes of Kordofan with what remained of his force, and he was never to challenge the British again.

Lieutenant Robert Napier Smith took part in the famous charge of the 21st Lancers at Omdurman and wrote of his experience of the charge in a letter to his sister:

> Manoeuvre well carried out and I am left troops leader. Looking round see nullah (ditch) 8 feet wide, four feet deep in front. Every side a compact mass of white robed men, apparently countless, still firing and waving swords. Find myself at nullah. Man bolts out leaving 2 donkeys in my way, catch hold of horse hard by head. Knowing to fall would be fatal. He blunders against donkey, recovers and scrambles out. Am met by swordsman on foot. Cuts at my right front. I guard it with sword. Next, man with fat face, all in white having fired, missed me, throws up both hands. I cut him across the face. He drops. Large bearded man in blue, with two edged sword and two hands cuts at me. Think this time I must be done for but pace tells and my guard carries it off. Duck my head to spear thrown which just misses me. Another cut at my horse, miss guard, but luckily cut is too far away and only cuts through my breastplate and gives my horse a small flesh wound on neck and shoulder. Then I remember no more till I find myself outside with four or five of my troop … Rally my troop as well as I can. Horrible sights. everyone seems to be bleeding, including my own horse … It seems to be blood, blood, everywhere. Horses and men smothered with either own or other peoples, wounded men being carried off by others as one sees in pictures. Horses dropping down and running away. See Nesham led away with left hand hanging down.

The impact of the charge upon Napier Smith is evident from the final extract of the letter.

> After we saw complete success of work, we revisited the scene of the charge. I was told off to get 6 men of my troop and collect our dead. The less said or written about that the better. It was ghastly. The tears streamed down my cheeks and I was physically sick. It was terrible. At this present moment I don't wish the morn repeated. [68]

The Northwest Frontier of India called upon the services of soldiers from the Indian Army as well as the Queen's battalions throughout the 1880s and 1890s, although in surprisingly small numbers. It was not until the Pathan Revolt in 1897 that substantial numbers of British troops were engaged in this border region. Resentment of British authority and growing religious fundamentalism amongst the tribes-men saw an outbreak in the Tochi Valley, which rapidly spread to the Malakand Pass where two British garrisons were besieged at Malakand and Chakdara. The Malakand Field Force, under the command of General Sir Binden Blood, was raised and despatched, but as the relief operation was underway, further risings occurred, including amongst the Afridis tribesmen of the Khyber Pass, which was lost to the British in August 1897.

To regain both the Khyber Pass and their lost prestige, the British mustered men from garrisons all over India and a force of 12,000 British and 22,000 Indian troops, under the command of Lieutenant-General Sir William Lockhart, was tasked with ravaging the Afridis' productive Tirah Valley and thus forcing them into submission.

The so-called Tirah Field Force entered the Tirah valley in October 1897 and was first engaged at the village of Dargai. The dominating ridge which overlooked the Dargai was first taken by advanced British troops on 18 October, but without support they were forced to withdraw. Once the British had massed, orders were given to retake the heights on 20 October. By then, however, the Afridis tribesmen had reinforced the position with 8,000 men and the British met stiff resistance. The leading companies were pinned down by a withering fire. The Gordon Highlanders were ordered to advance and take the hill at all costs. Despite suffering 32 fatalities, the Gordons succeeded, winning two Victoria Crosses for their efforts. The ferocity of the fire was illustrated by the high number of close-run things; a bullet passed through one Major's helmet without injuring him and Lieutenant Dingwell was hit four times, one bullet hitting his revolver and another his cartridge case, but he only received minor scratches. The British force pressed on, only to be met by Afridis resistance from behind every ridge top. Although the British were able to achieve their objective of burning villages and crops and slaughtering livestock, the tribesmen inflicted numerous casualties by their sniping fire.

In a letter home, the British commander Lockhart-Maxwell wrote of the skill of the enemy, the losses of the British and the horror of the wounds inflicted by the enemy.

> The enemy have now taken the proper line of action – looked at from their point of view – and are harassing us badly. Not a day passes now without a convoy being cut, an officer or two killed or wounded, guards attacked and the nightly rest disturbed by heavy firing. The amount of ammunition and rifles they are getting hold of also is horrible. Their last catch [taken from the British baggage] was 99,000 rounds of Lee-Metford Dum-Dum cartridges. These Dum-Dum bullets, used for the first time during the present Malakand show are simply diabolical in their results, they blow men to pieces and I am sure ought not to be allowed in civilised war.[69]

Any straggling baggage column or unwary rearguard presented easy pickings for the Afridis, who also crept upon the British camps at night to shoot at any illuminated target. In an amazing understatement, Colonel Hutchinson wrote that 'It is extremely unpleasant, this whizz and spatter of bullets while you are at dinner or trying to enjoy a pipe around a camp fire before turning in.'[70]

The British were forced to fortify each camp site, as Private Walter Ware described in a letter to his parents.

> Afridis used to come down on the low hills in the night. Thousands of them, and fire in our camps, in fact we had to sleep in our trenches all night long. I say sleep, but it was very little of that … We are being fired on every night now but they can't hurt us much as we have built fortifications all round the camp and they won't come too near us so we don't take any notice of them.[71]

By early December, the British force began to make a fighting withdrawal back along the Khyber Pass. Although there were another two months of fighting, the 'scorched earth policy' of the British proved ultimately successful and the Afridis accepted Lockhart's terms of surrender. By using similar tactics, Binden Blood had been able to pacify the Malakand Pass. Although little more than a punitive expedition, the Tirah campaign had been a bloody one in which 287 troops were killed and another 853 wounded. The number of Afridis dead ran into thousands. The British soldier had been victorious over a most determined enemy, who fought on their own terrain and were perhaps the best shots and skirmishers in the world. General Sir George White offered the following praise to all those involved:

> The country was physically most difficult, and the enemy were well-armed and expert in guerilla warfare. Severe punishment was, however, inflicted on them. The officers and men conducted themselves in a manner thoroughly befitting the traditions of the Queen's army.[72]

War against the Boers was, perhaps, an inevitable result of the unsatisfactory peace of the First Boer War in 1881, and the economic pressures brought to bear between Britain and the Boers with the discovery of goldfields in the Transvaal. The resultant influx of thousands of foreign miners, or *uitlanders*, caused political difficulties and tensions between London and Pretoria and this spilled over into war in October 1899. The Boers seized the initiative and opted for an offensive strategy, with the aim of a quick strike into Natal, so as to inflict defeats upon the British and bring them rapidly to the negotiating table. British troops were besieged at Ladysmith, Kimberley and Mafeking, forcing the commander of the newly-arrived British Army of 47,000 men, Redvers Buller, to concentrate his plans on the relief of these towns. Buller split his force into three, with Methuen tasked to march on Kimberley, and, in the first battles of the war, the British soldier faced and frequently died at the hands of entrenched Boer riflemen.

At the Modder River, on 28 November 1899, Methuen frontally attacked the Boers, who were unseen across the river. The assault became pinned down by heavy enemy fire and stalled. The Boers abandoned their positions under cover of darkness, which enabled Methuen to claim a costly victory. Colonel B. Lang of the Argyll and Sutherland Highlands wrote of his experiences at the Battle of Modder River.

> We had not gone very far when we came under fire, so we got into extended order and continued to advance. There was no cover of any sort and we soon began to suffer casualties. Finally the firing line was brought to a standstill by the Boer fire from the deep banks of the

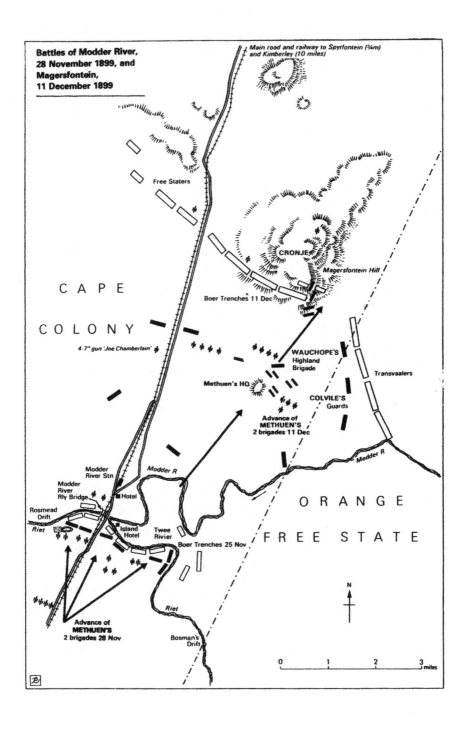

Battles of Modder River,
28 November 1899, and
Magersfontein,
11 December 1899

Main road and railway to Spytfontein (¾m)
and Kimberley (10 miles)

Free Staters

CRONJE

Magersfontein Hill

Boer Trenches 11 Dec

C A P E

C O L O N Y

4·7" gun 'Joe Chamberlain'

WAUCHOPE'S
Highland
Brigade

Transvaalers

Methuen's HQ

COLVILE'S
Guards

Advance of
METHUEN'S
2 brigades 11 Dec

Modder R

Modder
River Stn

Modder R

Modder
River
Rly Bridge

Hotel

Rosmead
Drift

O R A N G E

Riet

Island
Hotel

Twee
Rivier

F R E E   S T A T E

Boer Trenches 25 Nov

N

Riet

Advance of
METHUEN'S
2 brigades 28 Nov

Bosman's
Drift

0   1   2   3 miles

River which gave them excellent cover, and completely concealed them from us. Our firing line thus was almost stationary the whole day, and all ranks suffered from the blazing sun on the backs of our exposed legs. Eventually, in the afternoon, either by order or by our own initiative some of us moved off to the left flank to try and get round the Boer right flank. I was in this party and when crossing the river on the well of the weir, I fell into the river on the deepside. My kilt got soaked, and as it was already very dusty and the backs of my knees very sore from the sun, I suffered for some days after the battle from very sore and broken blisters, which completely put me out of action.[73]

The second week of December 1899 became known as 'Black Week', for the British suffered a series of humiliating defeats. General Gatace was repulsed at Stormberg Junction on the night of 10/11 December, and then Methuen's attack at Magersfontein was beaten back. Buller, leading the bulk of the Army, aimed to relieve the British at Ladysmith and attempted to force a river crossing of the Tugela at Colenso on 15 December, under the watchful eye of the unseen, dug-in enemy. The result was predictable and the losses immense. Private J. Lasby of the Devonshire Regiment fought at Colenso and left an account of the action, and its aftermath, in his diary.

After 2 hours very heavy shelling by our artillery, we were told to try and cross the other side of the Colenso Bridge, we got within 500 yards of this bridge when the enemy opened up a most tremendous rifle fire upon us, which caused us to lie flat down upon our stomachs, as if one got up, it meant death, we made S [South] advance but we found it impregnable to cross over the Bridge, our advance was done upon the flat of our stomachs, but the further we got up, the worse it got for us and it meant that we were getting further in 'death's hands'. We had about 8 hours of this kind of work amidst a most heavy shell and rifle fire, falling like hail stones around and about us, it was a picture of slaughter to see men laid out dead on the ground, who a few hours before were singing and quite joyful to meet the attack, and now knocked down, never to rise again, it was a most horrible sight …

Lasby wrote of his feelings after the defeat.

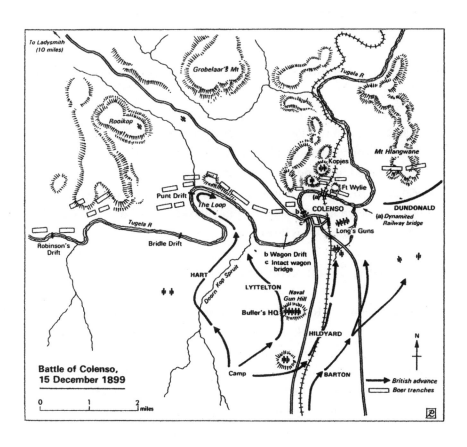

To Ladysmith
(10 miles)

Grobelaar's Mt

Tugela R

Rooikop

Mt Hlangwane

Kopjes

Ft Wylie

Punt Drift

The Loop

DUNDONALD

(a) Dynamited
Railway bridge

b COLENSO

c

Tugela R

Robinson's
Drift

Bridle Drift

Long's Guns

b Wagon Drift
c Intact wagon
bridge

HART

Doorn Kop Spruit

LYTTELTON

Naval
Gun Hill

Buller's HQ

HILDYARD

N

**Battle of Colenso,
15 December 1899**

Camp

BARTON

➤ British advance

☐ Boer trenches

0   1   2
|————————|————————| miles

On that day seeing that all hopes were given up for a bad job to try and get to our besieged comrades. So we had to retire back to our camp again, leaving many of our dead upon the veldt, after our retirement, our men with stretchers under the Red Cross, went out to fetch our wounded men in, and to bury the dead, which was a large number. As we retired back to our camp very downhearted at the very thought of being so unsuccessful, we reached camp at 6.30p.m. being very tired and almost parched up.[74]

Private Charles Gibson, also of the Devonshires, fought alongside Lasby at Colenso.

... when we got into rifle range the Boers let us have it, it was like being in a hail storm, thousands of bullets flying all around us, and men falling every minute killed and wounded, it was an awful sight ... we had to advance on to the open plains, there was not any cover, only small ant hills to get behind, I saw men dropping like flies, some shot through the head arms and legs, it was heartbreaking to see.

After the battle, Gibson recorded:

The Colonel of my Regiment and about 100 of my Regiment got captured, when we got back he had a roll call and there was about 20 men of my section away killed wounded and captured out of 55 of us that started the morning, there was not a man on the field that day that was not thinking about ones Chum, as I asked God to spare my life I thought often how my Chums was getting on, and when we got into camp, and called the roll there was a lot of my chums missing, a sergent in my tent being killed and one Private and several missing, the next day the 16th Dec the hospital was full up with wounded, some of us went over to see some of our comrades, it was a sight Doctors hard at it attending the wounded and sending them down to the base by train, it was a sight I never shall forget men layed out in line dead ready for burying.[75]

On Christmas Day 1899, Earl de la Warr was able to look back at the first, largely unsuccessful, battles of the war and reflect on how the nature of warfare had been changed by the tactics and weapons adopted by the Boers.

The battles in this campaign do not consist of a few hour's fighting then a grand charge, resulting in the rout of the enemy, when men can see the effect of their work. No; this is very different. Think of it, a two-mile march under the fire of an invisible foe, then perhaps eight or ten hours' crouching behind any available cover – an anthill or a scrubby bush – when the slightest movement on a man's part at once enables the hidden enemy to put him out of action, whereas he never has a chance of retaliating. Certainly this is fighting in circumstances which require extraordinary good nerve and courage. And when the day is over 'Tommy' has not even the satisfaction of knowing what he has accomplished.[76]

After the defeat at Colenso, Roberts was sent out from Britain to replace Buller, who retained a field command with the intention of relieving Ladysmith. After a series of minor engagements, on the night of 23/24 January 1900 Buller ordered his men to assault the position of Spion Kop, in the hope that, by taking and holding this hilly position, the Boers would be forced to withdraw. Unfortunately, dawn revealed that the British were badly exposed and vulnerable to both Boer rifle and artillery fire. After a day of torture and loss, the British withdrew at nightfall. Private Ernest Stanton of the Somerset Light Infantry wrote in his diary of the aftermath of the battle and the stoicism of the British soldier.

The majority of the fellows were wounded in the legs, or arms, but looked very weary, and worn out. Some of them that were wounded did not forget to smoke their pipes, just as if nothing had happened. Some as they past would pass a remark to the effect that it was rather hot up there, pointing to Spion Kop. Another poor unfortunate who was wounded in the arm, held his Rifle up for inspection, and the butt was simply shattered to pieces, remarking that he was going to keep it for a relic.[77]

Repulsed once more, Buller again attempted to relieve Ladysmith. An unknown Private of the Devonshire Regiment wrote an account of the ferocity of the British artillery on the Boer positions and its aftermath.

Relieved from the firing line at daybreak, had a little breakfast and then advanced to another hill which the Lancasters had taken, here we saw some of the worse sights I have ever seen in my life, Boers lying dead on the field, others lying in the trenches they fought in partly buried and around some big trees, which some of the Boers had been seeking shelter, the brains of two men were bespattered on the rocks. Dead horses lying all over the place and a few women's graves. One young married woman died shortly after we reached the position and our troops buried her body.[78]

One unidentified soldier wrote of the sensation of being under fire from Boer artillery.

… they dropped a lot of shells in our camp … it makes one feel queer when they can be heard screaming in the air and not know if they are going to drop on us or not and burst, and bowl a few of us over, a Kaffir had his head blown off and another his leg … The Boers fired at us off a hill with rifles we were lying down on the plain and the bullets cut the earth up round me but not one was hit.[79]

Sergeant Richard Hayward of the Rifle Brigade was besieged in Ladysmith and, on 6 January 1900, the Boers launched an all-out attack, temporarily capturing the two outlying defences of Wagon Hill and Caesar's Camp. Hayward was ordered with his men to recapture Caesar's Camp, and with scarcely any cover from the intense rifle fire and under a blazing sun, they hung on grimly all day to the advanced positions. In the evening they finally drove the Boers from their vantage point. Hayward wrote of the horrific sights he witnessed after this clash.

Early next morning, I had to go over the whole of the principal part of the battlefield, and a most awful sight it was. Bodies were in many cases, literally torn to pieces, limbs contorted horribly, heads flattened against rocks, bodies disembowelled and other sights which to think of, make one feel weak. Our men did not look so bad, most of them being shot in the head; but on every face was a look of pain. One bugler crawling along on all fours was killed in that position; a corpse was pointing at the enemy when a bullet entered his head, and remained in that position in death, and in all such cases they had to be buried in that position.[80]

Lance Corporal A. Rose of the Duke of Cornwall's Light Infantry fought at the Battle of Paardeberg (18 February 1900) and wrote an account of his role in the battle in his diary the following day. Kitchener, the British commander on the day, seemed to have learnt nothing from the two other attempts to advance upon a Boer position by crossing a river: Methuen's costly victory at the Modder River and Buller's failure at Colenso. In each case, the British commanders had tried to force a river crossing against an entrenched Boer position, and the British soldier had paid a heavy price. Kitchener simply repeated the tactics, and again the British were halted. Frontal attacks met with heavy casualties for no gain, so towards the end of the afternoon Kitchener launched a right flank attack, but, with so many earlier casualties, only half a battalion of the Duke of Cornwall's were available. Rose took part in this last attack, which again was doomed to failure and soon stalled. The British troops sought cover from the Boer rifle fire.

> We lay there for about an hour and dared not move. If you did it was a sure bullet so I had a smoke. I was behind a small ant heap which is a small mound of earth just sufficient to hide my head.

When darkness came, Rose and his comrades were able to leave their refuges and Rose himself recorded that he crossed the Modder three times to bring back British wounded to the main camp. The battle had cost Kitchener's command 1,270 casualties, including 24 officers and 279 men killed, one of whom was Rose's best friend. However, the British maintained their position and the Boer force, immobilised by fatigue and lack of horses, surrendered on 27 February. On 25 February, Rose had been assigned to a six-man burial party, which under cover of darkness had managed to bury men of the West Riding Regiment who had remained on the battlefield for a week and who were, as Rose recorded, 'smelling very bad'.

During the Boer War, it was rare for the British infantrymen to come in close contact with the enemy. Boers were felled by long range volley fire as they retreated, or by artillery fire, and certainly it was unusual for a British soldier to be able to get close enough to record, for certain, that his rifle fire had claimed a Boer's life. Rose, however, was to write in his diary of one engagement in which he could make such a claim. Following the Battle of Paardeberg, and after a brief illness, Roberts had resumed command, and he marched his men towards Pretoria. Rose remained part of this advance and he wrote the following on 4 June 1900:

Moved out of camp intending to get to Pretoria today. We had gone
about 14 miles when we were fired on from some very high hills in front
of us. We quickly opened out and up the hills we went and soon drove
them out of it. It was here I avenged my chum, shooting 2 Boers dead
and wounded three.

After the short skirmish, Rose recorded his exhaustion.

Here I first saw Pretoria – my feet were that sore I could hardly put
my feet to the ground, I feel properly done up – had to sleep on
the ground we had won without anything to eat and only one thin
blanket – sleep out of the question. This is the hardest day's work
I have ever done.[81]

The advance on Pretoria produced many horrific scenarios, such as
the one recorded by Private W.E. Milton of the Buffs, who wrote in his
diary of 10 March 1900

We were about 500 yards from the Boer position with fairly good cover
when we were shelled, still we had to push on – a sergeant and a private
of our line met a sad death both were struck by shellfire their clothing
at once caught fire and their ammunition exploding kept back all those
who were inclined to extinguish the flames. We buried their charred
remains later. Fix bayonets advance – heavy losses bayonet busy Boers
surrendered. Our losses were 1 officer killed, 2 wounded, NCOs and
men killed 21 and 79 wounded. We slept on the Battlefield, round our
camp fires after many regrets expressed for the number of gallant fellows
lost that day.[82]

Under such conditions, the troops could be very philosophical about
their fate. Writing home on 20 October 1900, Private Wellington of the
Devonshires wrote 'Tomorrow is the first anniversary of Elandolaagte,
just fancy being fired at for twelve months and missed!'[83] In a similar
vein, Sergeant Watterson of the West Riding Regiment wrote in his
war diary on 7 March 1900

My lucks out. Went on all right until about 3 p.m., when a sniper who
had me set for a long while but could not hit me, managed it alright, he

hit me in the hand and chest. Went to sit on an ant heap till they found a doctor, when he wasted another 50 rounds on me, but I moved out of his reach then.

Watterson also wrote of the care he received after he had been wounded and that he was required to make his own way to the hospital.

Doctor bandaged me up as I lay down with a few more waiting for ambulance, one poor fellow shot through the stomach. Ambulance arrived about 5p.m., trekked about 3 miles then they pitched tents for the hospital at dusk. Treated well, had some bovril, milk and stew.[84]

By 1900, despite Kitchener at Paardeberg, the frontal attacks against entrenched Boer positions were becoming a thing of the past. In his diary of 26 May 1900, Captain G. McSceales of the Argyll and Sutherland Highlanders wrote of an attack in which he and his men scouted the Boer position in advance of a battalion flanking movement. The extract also records the Boer tactic of drawing in the British, inflicting casualties and then fleeing from overwhelming British strength, so as to repeat the process another day.

Marched off early as advance guard. Found the Boers occupying a semi-circular group of hills in front of Lindley. 91st sent to make a flank attack on our right. I was sent with half my company to some low kopjes [hills] on our right. I advanced with one section in front and the other section about 100 yards behind in support, scouts being thrown out in front. The Boers allowed the scouts to advance almost up to the foot of the kopje and opened fire when the leading section and myself were about only 150 to 200 yards away. I immediately ordered the section to lie down and open fire, and sent back orders to the other section to work round our right. I had 2 men killed McGillivray and Rushforth and one Allett wounded while Murphy had the toe of his boot shot off and I was slightly grazed in the finger, a total of 5 casualties out of 9 men altogether. The rest of the Battalion coming up in about a quarter of an hour, the Boers fell back and the Battalion making a wide turning movement fired long range volleys at large numbers of them galloping away.[85]

With the fall of Pretoria to Roberts' forces and the relief of Ladysmith, Kimberley and Mafeking, the war, viewed by many as almost over, entered a new phase. Gone were the large clashes of arms, often over a day or more, in which the British were either repulsed or gained costly victories. The war entered a 'guerrilla phase', in which the mobile Boers were able to continue their hit and run tactics of engaging the British when either numbers or surprise favoured their success. After Roberts' return to England, overall command was given to Kitchener, who adopted a plan of containment in which thousands of blockhouses, garrisoned by sometimes as few as three British soldiers, were constructed across the veldt, in a successful attempt to restrict the movement of the Boer forces. The ability of the enemy to acquire supplies was reduced by the British policy of destroying farmsteads and crops. Boer families, known to support their fighters in the field, were rounded-up and placed in the world's first 'concentration camps', the conditions in which were frequently appalling and resulted in many civilian deaths. The Boers were worn down by such approaches and, in May 1902, they finally agreed to surrender. The Queen had died in January 1901, and it is perhaps fortunate that she did not live to see the worst excesses of the 'war of attrition', in which the British Empire and her soldiers could claim little glory.

The future British Prime Minister and wartime leader, Winston Churchill, fought at the Battle of Omdurman (2 September 1898) and was also present as a reporter during the opening year of the Boer War. He was thus able to witness two very contrasting conflicts. At Omdurman, Churchill saw all the pomp and magnificence of the advance of solid lines of enemy infantry, and he later described 'the mighty Dervish array, bright with flashing spears and waving flags'. Churchill saw literally thousands of dervishes felled by artillery fire and volley after volley of disciplined infantry fire; he witnessed the devastating effects of the machine-gun as the British, under Kitchener, gained their revenge over Mahdism for the death of Gordon in Khartoum. Yet, in just over a year, upon the same continent, Churchill could describe the following in his newspaper column:

> A modern action is very disappointing as a spectacle. There is no smoke except that of the bursting shells. The combatants are scattered, spread over a great expanse of ground, concealed wherever possible, clad in

neutral tint. Rows of tiny dots hurried forward a few yards and vanished into the brown of the earth. Bunches and clusters of brown things huddled among the rocks or in sheltered spots. The six batteries of artillery unlimbered, and the horses, hidden in some safe place, were scarcely visible. Once I saw in miniature through glasses a great wave of infantry surge forward along a spur and disappear beyond a crest line. The patter of the Mauser rifles swelled into a continuous rumbling like a train of waggons passing over a pontoon bridge, and presently the wave recoiled; the minute figures that composed it squeezed themselves into cover among some rocks, a great many groups of men began carrying away black objects. A trickle of independent dots dispersed itself. Then we groaned. There had been a check. ... The distant drama continued. The huddling figures began to move again – lithe, active forms moving about rearranging things – officers, we knew, even at the distance. Then the whole wave started again full of impetus – started – went forward, and never came back. And at this we were all delighted, and praised the valour of our unequalled infantry, and wished we were near enough to give them a cheer.

In describing the Battle of Pieters (27 February 1900) Churchill wrote

The head of the column reached the exposed ground, and the soldiers began to walk across it. Then at once above the average fusillade and cannonade rose the extraordinary rattling roll of Mauser musketry in great volume. If the reader wishes to know exactly what this is like he must drum the fingers of both his hands on a wooden table, one after the other as quickly and as hard as he can.[86]

Churchill's contrasting experiences of Victorian conflict in such a short space of time were at the extremes, but serve to illustrate the variety of combat to be found in colonial warfare. For most of the nineteenth century the British soldier was to be tested against a vast array of foes, in a number of hugely different environments, and these conflicts bear witness to the courage of the British troops. Whether, the Soldiers of the Queen were engaged in the 'Napoleonic' style bloody battles of the Sikh wars, in which large numbers of men hurled themselves at artillery positions with only a musket for protection, or the battlefields of the Boer War, that looked forward to those of the twentieth century, where the use of cover, mobility and artillery barrages were so crucial, the British soldier was, ultimately, victorious. He demonstrated an ability to be flexible, in which he was able to fight very different foes, over contrasting terrain. He could cope with the jungles of Ashantiland and the mountainous passes of the Northwest Frontier, which would see him adopt and adapt tactics and weapons to overcome the enemy. As Ian Heron has written of the Victorian soldier; 'Without them no Empire would have been won, whatever the genius of generals and strategists, whatever the ambitions of monarchs and politicians.'[87] The fortitude and courage of the Victorian soldier was remarkable and deserves to be honoured and remembered even if, today, we may condemn the motivations of such colonial conflicts.

Notes

1. J. Black, *Tools of War: The Weapons that Changed the World*, (Quercus, London, 2007), p.118.
2. D. Featherstone, *Khaki & Red: Soldiers of the Queen in India and Africa*, (Arms & Armour Press, London, 1995), p.10.
3. J. Spilsbury, *The Thin Red Line: An Eyewitness History of the Crimean War*, (Weidenfeld & Nicolson, London, 2005), pp.87–88.
4. B. Farwell, *Queen Victoria's Little Wars*, (Allan Lane, London, 1973), p.1.
5. Letter Lt. Thomas Gaisford, 20 August 1839, REF: NAM 1983-11-28.
6. J. Duncan & J. Walton, *Heroes for Victoria*, (Spellmount, Tunbridge Wells, 1991), p.32.
7. Letter Lt. Dennys, 12 January 1842, REF:NAM 1979-01-95.
8. Lt. Col Stephens, letter to wife, 22 July 1842, REF:NAM 2004-03-37.
9. B. Farwell, p.29.
10. Journal of Lt. Kirby, REF:NAM 1999-05-31.
11. Journal of Pvt. J. Hewitt, REF: NAM 2005-12-24.
12. B. Farwell, p.47.
13. Pvt. Perkes, letter to brother, 10 August 1846, REF:NAM 1975-05-57.
14. J. Duncan & J. Walton, p.39.
15. A. Swanson & D. Scott, (eds.), *The Memoirs of Private Waterfield*, (Cassell, London, 1968), p.37.
16. Ibid, p.101.
17. Ibid, p.166.
18. Lt. Dyneley, letter to parents, 26 September 1848, REF:NAM 2001-10-26.

19. Lt. Dyneley, letter to parents, 31 August 1848, REF:NAM 2001-10-25.
20. Memoirs of Lieut-General W. Whitlock, REF:NAM 9601-69.
21. Reminiscences of Charles Gray, REF: ASHM N-C93.GRA.
22. Diary of Donald Cameron, REF: ASHM N-B93.MOL.
23. Reminiscences of William Nairn, REF: ASHM N-C93 NAI 15176.
24. Memoirs of Major Macleod, REF: RAM MD/2410.
25. Reminiscences of Pvt. Burrows, REF: ASHM N-C93.TRA.
26. J. Spilsbury, p.107.
27. Diary of Serg. J. Taylor, REF: ASHM NC93 TAY.
28. Diary of Capt. M. Walker, REF:NAM 1968-07-85-1.
29. Gnr J. Cousins, RA, Memoirs, REF: RAM MD 2207.
30. Lt.Col. Sir Francis Tucker, (ed.), *The Chronicle of Private Henry Metcalfe*, (Cassell, London, 1953), p.29.
31. Memoirs of Pvt. Potiphars, REF: NAM 7201-45-1.
32. Diary of Capt. Ramsden, REF: RAM MD 1185/1.
33. Lt. Col. W. Gordon-Alexander, *Recollections of a Highland Subaltern*, (Edward Arnold, London, 1898), pp. 102 and 256.
34. Diary of Sgt Cooper, 2 May 1862, REF: NAM MD/1269.
35. J. Duncan & J. Walton, p.29.
36. Letter from Pvt. J. Oates, 25 November 1863, REF:NAM 1984-01-98.
37. Capt. Barker, letter to father, 17 April 1868, REF:RAM MD/1615.
38. Journal of Ensign W.A. Wynter, 33rd Regiment, REF: Bankfield Museum RMDWR.
39. B. Farwell, p.200.
40. J. Strawson, *Beggars in Red: The British Army 1789–1889*, (Pen & Sword, Barnsley, 2003), p.194.
41. F. Emery, *The Red Soldier: The Zulu War of 1879*, (Hodder & Stoughton, London, 1977), p.50.
42. Capt. F. Slade, letter to mother, 30 March 1879, REF: NAM 6807-235.
43. F. Emery, p.201.
44. Diary of R. Wolrige Gordon, REF: ASHM N-C91. GOR.W.
45. L.C. Eaton, letter to brother, undated, REF:NAM 1992-04-115.
46. Diary of Pvt. J. Facer, REF:NAM 8301-131.
47. Capt. J. Slade, letter to mother, 21 August 1880, REF: NAM 6807-235.
48. Diary of Pvt. Lloyd, REF:NAM 9404-86.
49. Colonel Sir Percival Marling, V.C., *Rifleman and Hussar*, (John Murray, London, 1931), p. 41.

50. Ibid, p.49.
51. Major-General Sir A.B. Tulloch, *Recollections of Forty Years Service*, (Blackwood, Edinburgh, 1902), p. 309.
52. P. Smith, *Victoria's Victories*, (Spellmount, Tunbridge Wells, 1987), p.166.
53. Lt. Perry, letter to 'my dear Synge', 16 September 1882, REF: RAM MD 22.
54. F. Emery, *Marching over Africa: letters from Victorian Soldiers*, (Hodder & Stoughton, London, 1986), p.133.
55. Lt. Perry, letter to home, 21 March 1884, REF: RAM MD 22.
56. *Memoirs of Lord Charles Beresford*, (Methuen, London, 1914) Vol.I, pp. 263, 265, 267.
57. P. Warner, *Stories of Famous Regiments*, (Arthur Baker, London, 1975), p.87.
58. J. Strawson, p. 227.
59. Pvt. Reader, letter to a 'Chum', 24 July 1885, REF: NAM 8506-6.
60. Letter Capt Gibb, 1 June 1886, REF: NAM 7411-52-4.
61. Diary Lt. Bertram Mitford, 1 May 1887, REF: NAM 8711-127-3.
62. A. Stewart, *The Pagada War*, (Faber, London, 1972) p.87.
63. Diary of Capt. Hay, 3 January 1887, REF: NAM 1969-09-43.
64. J. Meredith (ed.), *Omdurman Diaries 1898: Eye witness accounts of the legendary campaign*, (Leo Cooper, Barnsley, 1998), p.85.
65. Ibid, p.93.
66. Ibid, p.94.
67. Ibid, p.87.
68. P. Harrington & F. Sharf (eds.), *Omdurman 1898: The eye-witnesses speak*, (Greenhill Books, London, 1998), p.128.
69. Letter Lockhart-Maxwell, 14 November 1897, REF:NAM 7402-28-82
70. I. Hernon, *Britain's Forgotten Wars: Colonial Campaigns of the 19th Century*, (Alan Sutton, Stroud, 2003), p.436.
71. Ibid, p.437.
72. Ibid, p.449.
73. Diary of Col. Lang, REF: ASHM N-D1.LAN
74. Diary of Pvt. Lasby, REF: DRM Acc 2029.
75. Diary of Pvt. Gibson, REF: DRM Acc 1323.
76. D. Judd, *Calamities of the British Army in the Victorian Age*, (Phoenix, London, reissue 2007), p.152.
77. Diary of Pvt. Ernest Stanton, REF: SRO DD/SLI 17/1/32.
78. Account of Unknown Private, 28 February 1900, REF: DRM Acc No.5.
79. Account of Unknown Soldier, REF: Unidentified soldier: NAM 1980-03-17-1.

80. Account of Sgt. Haywood, REF:NAM 1998-01-130
81. Diary of Lance-Corp. Rose, 19 February, 25 February and 4 June 1900, Duke of Cornwall's Light Infantry Museum, Bodmin.
82. Diary of Pvt. Milton, REF:NAM 2006-04-09.
83. Memoirs of Pvt. A.W. Wellington, REF: DRM Accession No.2255
84. War Diary of Sgt. Watterson, REF: Bankfield Museum RMDWR.
85. Diary of Capt. McSceales, 26 May 1900, REF: ASHM N-D.1.ScE.3.
86. W.S. Churchill, *London to Ladysmith via Pretoria and Ian Hamilton's March*, (Pimlico Edition, London, 2002), p.146 and 187.
87. I. Hernon, p.8.

CHAPTER SIX

FOR THE GLORY OF THE EMPIRE

A soldier's duty is a soldier's life. A soldier's life is to lay it down, against the enemies of his Queen, against the invaders of his home, against slavery, cruelty, tyrants.

but these things cannot be done without great sacrifice, and what has been done is done for the British Empire.

Two quotes, both of which point to the reasons why Victoria's soldiers fought and died in the campaigns of her reign. The first is fictitious; it is taken from the play *Sergeant Musgrave's Dance* by John Arden, which was first performed at the Royal Court Theatre, London, in 1959, and is spoken by Sergeant Musgrave in Act III, Scene I. The second was reported to have been said by General Sir George White – commander of the besieged British forces at Ladysmith – to General Ian Hamilton, when the siege had been lifted. Whilst this book has concentrated so far on the experiences of the Soldiers of the Queen from when they left their barracks to travel on campaign until the aftermath of distant battles, little mention has been made as to whether the soldiers themselves held any beliefs as to what they fought for, whether they considered they were serving to enhance the glory of the British Empire, or if they held any views on death. Yet the soldiers did write of such things.

The British Victorian soldier may have been reluctant to write home with details of his sexual exploits, but he was not so hesitant to chronicle actions in which British troops either experienced atrocities committed against them, or which they committed them-selves. When writing of such acts, the British soldier was not, apparently, ashamed of what may have been done in the name of the Queen, nor did he consider that his actions might bring dis-honour upon himself, his regiment or his country. Whilst not necessarily proud of the atrocities he may have committed, the Victorian soldier wrote of them with something approaching indifference and a degree of callousness, which was surely caused by the situations in which he found himself in.

However, it should not be thought that atrocities were only com-mitted by the Victorian soldier, for such acts have a long history. Major Wolfe, the future General Wolfe and victor of Quebec in 1759, served as part of the British garrison in Stirling, and was involved in the hunting down of rebel Highlanders after the Battle of Culloden (15 April 1745), one of the most infamous slaughters in the annals of the British Army. In a letter to a friend, Wolfe wrote of one action in which the enemy was butchered by the British, an action that Wolfe justified by the fact that the Highlanders had treated the British in a similar fashion.

> The cavalry charge was done with wonderful spirit, and completed the victory with much slaughter … The rebels, besides their natural inclina-tions, had orders not to give quarter to our men. We had an opportunity of avenging ourselves for that and many other things, and indeed we did not neglect it. As few Highlanders were made prisoners as possible.[1]

It is well known that British troops committed atrocities against the Indian mutineers during the Mutiny (1857–59). The motivation for them was obvious enough, revenge for the murderous actions of the mutineers. Throughout Victoria's reign, British troops had been on the receiving end of atrocities committed against their comrades by the 'savage foes' that they faced. The central premise of John Arden's play is that the choices made by Sergeant Musgrave and his small band of comrades were made because their experiences of colonial war-fare had brutalised them, making them unhinged. Certainly, the sight of a butchered friend would have instilled a desire for revenge in the Victorian soldier, or at least made him fear and despise his foe. During the many conflicts in which troops fought there are many examples of British soldiers showing an apparent indifference to the fate of the enemy, including the wounded, and this callousness seems to have been greater when the adversaries that they faced had either committed earlier atrocities, or worse, had the insolence to defeat the British in battle. Thus, guidelines issued by the British commander during the Zulu War of 1879, Lord Chelmsford, before the conflict began, as to the treatment of prisoners, civilians and property, were frequently ignored, even by Chelmsford himself, once the Zulus had defeated the British at Isandlwana and a lust for vengeance had pervaded the British force. Similarly, during the various campaigns in the Sudan, the British soon learnt by bitter experience that a wounded dervish would likely attack any British troops who tried to capture him or offer him any comfort such as water. After the Battle of El Teb (29 February 1885) Lieutenant Marling recorded that 'We killed nearly all the wounded, as it wasn't safe to leave them, as they would knife you like a shot.'[2]

That the Victorian soldier witnessed terrible acts perpetrated by the enemy on his friends and comrades is beyond doubt. Private George Brown of the 44th Regiment fought in Afghanistan in 1841, and presumably was killed during the retreat from Kabul. In a letter to his parents, Brown did not hesitate to describe, in grim detail, the fate of one of his comrades at the hands of the Afghans. The man was on sentry duty when he was taken by the enemy. Brown wrote that his body was found the following day, 'cut all to pieces by the enimy wile on his watch. His head was cut in three places, his bowels in two, his fingers cut off and several more wounds in the body.'[3]

In his diary of the First Sikh War (1843–5), Lieutenant Walter Kirby recorded on 20 December 1845, the eve of the Battle of Ferozeshah, that 'To-day the body of Carey, one of our officers was brought in. He was greatly disfigured and his throat cut. These brutes mangle the wounded disgracefully.'[4] In his memoirs of the Second Burma War (1851–3), Ensign Whitlock recalled that the British wounded at the Battle of Pegu were attacked by the Burmese. He witnessed the attack upon one man of his own company, who had been shot through the thigh and was lying helpless.

> Some of the Enemy caught sight of him, and three or four of them waded across the ditch and attacked him as he lay on the ground and sliced his head off carrying his head across the ditch to their comrades who were on the other side and who heartily cheered the act.[5]

The Third Maori War (1863–6) was one in which the enemy frequently used ambush tactics upon the British troops, following which the dead soldiers would be mutilated by the Maoris. Writing in his diary on 8 May 1863, Sergeant James Cooper of the Royal Artillery described one ambush in which the British had been mauled and eight had been killed. Cooper wrote that 'it is high time to put a stop to these blood thirsty savages.'

Later in the month, when the British had managed to kill several Maoris, Cooper described their deaths as 'tit for tat'. In April of the following year, Cooper recorded that a Private Stewart had been attacked when attempting to get water from beyond the British redoubt. The Maoris had fired a volley which had broken his thigh bone and then Stewart had been 'tomahawked most brutally'. Four days later, Cooper wrote of the news that men of the 57th Regiment had been ambushed and that several men, including Captain Lloyd, had had their heads cut off.[6]

Such Maori brutality continued into the next year. In his diary of service in New Zealand, Private Thomas Tatlock of the 43rd Light Infantry detailed another mutilation that the enemy inflicted upon slain British soldiers. Writing on 22 April 1865, Tatlock described how an unarmed work party from the British camp had been ambushed and a J. Hawks had been killed. His body was found the next day, 'lying quite naked with his left eye, which had been cut out, lying on his cheek'.[7]

In his diary of the siege of Eshowe, during the Zulu War of 1879, Sergeant Hooper recorded one incident in which Private Kent of the 99th Regiment was attacked by Zulus whilst on vedette duty.

> 5 Zulus who had concealed themselves in the bush near by cruelly murdered him – the boy only to be recognised by the Regimentals [his emblems, badges etc], he had been horribly mutilated, 18 assegais [spear] and 1 bullet wound were found, each eye had been stabbed, the nose and ears split, the other wounds in the abdomen.[8]

Writing from Kabul in the same year, Major Woods of the 9th Lancers wrote to his wife and described to her the fate of two of his brother officers. Woods' letter could not have done much to reassure his wife, but this clearly did not occur to Woods.

Poor Hearsey and Ricardo's bodies were found but so frightfully mutilated that they were unrecognisable except for the clothes they were wearing. It is thought that Ricardo was killed through his horse running away with him. He was an indifferent rider and he only told me four days before, he never could hold his horse when galloping.[9]

Colonel George Kellie of the Indian Medical Service served during the Third Burma War (1885–9), and wrote of the tortures that the Burmese fighters, the *dacoits*, would inflict upon the civilian population, and how this behaviour influenced the British soldiers when they were able to engage or capture any of them.

> The next day I went to see the wife of the Thugyi of a village near us. This place had been attacked by dacoits. They had got ahold of the woman and wanted her to tell where her husband's money and her jewels were hidden. She refused to tell. They proceeded to torture her. She was a pretty young thing but in a terrible state when I saw her, and died in a short time. The dacoits had stripped her naked. They then lighted a fire under her abdomen, having first smeared it with kerosine oil and then asked for the money. She would not say, so they left her to burn while they looted the place. She was terribly injured. The burman was a brute. When they got a prisoner they crucified him alive, and cut open his abdomen. They used to slice open the pregnant women, and cut off the breasts of the virgins, and do other horrible things which I can not mention. It is easy to imagine that we were not soft hearted when our turn came.[10]

Lieutenant Dennys served in General Nott's force, which emerged from Kandahar in 1842 to seek revenge upon the Afghans for the murder of the British forces on the retreat from Kabul. It is clear from Dennys' memoirs that the British troops under his command had been brutalised by the news of events from Kabul. On 12 January 1842, Dennys recorded that he

> … led party to storm village of Kaleeshuk – the enemy fled at once and we occupied the village without losing a man; but the blood of the European troops was up and many of them had lost sense of humanity. I saw the body of a really pretty Afghan woman lying dead on the ground, and almost lost my life in my indignation freely expressed to an

English soldier who was dishonouring the body in a shameful manner with his bayonet.[11]

The bloody Battle of Mudki (18 December 1845) during the First Sikh War (1843–5) set the pattern for brutality in this conflict, and also in the subsequent Second Sikh War (1848–9). Both wars became renowned for the atrocities committed by both sides. At Mudki many of the British wounded and those that had been unhorsed and captured were slaughtered by the Sikhs, prompting a similar ruthless response from the British. Lieutenant George Cookes of the 3rd Light Dragoons wrote home to say that he had spared several Sikh prisoners and that in retrospect he considered that he was 'foolishly merciful'.[12] Certainly, after Mudki the Queen's troops would show little mercy and in subsequent battles they would cry 'Remember Mudki' to remind each other of what was expected.[13]

Private Waterfield recorded in his diary the action to drive a Sikh force back into the besieged city of Multan on 7 November 1848. He described the horrors that the sepoys inflicted upon the Sikhs.

The Native Cavalry now took up the charge and drove the enemy into the city (they who could reach as far), for hundreds kissed mother earth in making the attempt. There was a large dry nullah covered with the dead and dying of the enemy, and the crimes which were there enacted, over the poor fallen foe, was a disgrace to human nature. The sepoys were so embittered against the enemy, that they tortured the poor wounded in all kinds and shapes of ways; heaping dry rubbish against them and setting it on fire; prinking them with the bayonet; and even killing many who might have recovered from their wounds.[14]

Later Waterfield was included in the storming party that entered the city of Multan, one of the final acts of the Second Sikh War. He described how no prisoners were taken by the British troops:

On breaking into the houses of these unfortunate creatures, a volley of shots were fired amongst them, as they were huddled in a corner, regardless of old men, women and children. All shared the same fate. One of my fellow-corporals … was guilty of cold-blooded murder. He shot a poor, grey-headed old man, while he was begging that he would spare, and not hurt, his wife and daughters; nor take away the little property they possessed, consisting of a few paltry silver rings, upon their fingers and in their ears. The fellow pulled the rings off in the most brutal manner.

Waterfield also wrote of what he described as, 'another crime, more horrible, perhaps, than murder', that of rape, an act which he considered tarnished the glory of British arms. Finally Waterfield concluded that the acts he saw committed by British troops inside Multan were 'the most dreadful sights I have seen, that made the blood run chill in my veins'.[15]

Despite the cruelty of the Sikh wars, it was, perhaps, the Indian Mutiny that provoked the most terrible response from the British, in which brutality bred brutality. Cities captured by the rebels, such as Delhi and Lucknow, became focal points for the British and their recapture was considered essential to re-establish their authority. As news of the outrages committed by the mutineers against the British became well-known, so the retribution taken against captured rebels became swifter and more brutal. This was especially true after the news of the massacre of 125 women and children in Cawnpore became widespread. The fury of the British is, perhaps, best illustrated by the following extract from a letter written by John Nicolson to Herbert Edwardes shortly after the outbreak of the Mutiny.

> Let us propose a Bill for the flaying alive, impalement, or burning of the murderers of the women and children at Delhi. The idea of simply hanging the perpetrators of such atrocities is maddening.[16]

Similarly, Captain John Ramsden of the Royal Artillery was outraged when the Governor-General of India, Earl Canning, suggested that mercy should be shown to those mutineers who could not be found guilty of murder. Ramsden found this idea of leniency appalling. On 21 October 1857, he wrote

> I think 2 months hence would have been quite soon enough to talk about mercy. The more of the ruffins that are killed the better. They have all committed a crime punishable by death in mutinying, independent of other atrocities they have committed.[17]

Private Charles Gray, of the 93rd Regiment, justified his actions against the mutineers thus:

> When bayoneting the savage Indians who murdered innocent women and children … we knew we were avenging blood which had been wantonly shed, and had a particular satisfaction in doing so.[18]

One practice that has become associated forever with the crushing of the Mutiny was the execution of mutineers by tying them to an artillery piece, which was then fired. The future Lord Roberts recalled one incident when he was a Lieutenant serving during the Mutiny. His commanding officer, Brigadier Chamberlain, sentenced two sepoys of the 35th Native Infantry to death for being in possession of loaded muskets. Roberts was in charge of the detail that carried out the execution in front of the Regiment. He recalled that the order was given and the two artillery pieces fired simultaneously and shreds of cloth, bone and bloody hunks of flesh were spewed all over the parade ground. 'It was a terrible sight, and one likely to haunt the beholder for a long day, but that was what was intended.'[19] The manner of the execution did seem to have the desired effect, for the 35th never mutinied.

Captain John Ramsden memoirs recorded an incident that was all too common during this conflict.

> On the way … we found Goodenough's 60 men with 3 prisoners whom the magistrate had ordered to be hung – it is only necessary to mention one affair of this kind as an example of the primitive way of executing rebels caught 'Flagrante Delicto'. The three culprits stood under a tree. A gunner climbed up into the tree and put a thick rope over a bough, a man below put a clumsy running knot round the neck of one of the men, the patient offering no resistance, when everything was ready 3 or 4 men at a signal pulled at the other end of the rope and ran the man up nearly to the branch. This had little effect upon the patient than choking him severely; he was then let down again with a jerk two or three feet to try and dislocate his neck, which did not succeed – then a gunner got hold of his legs and swung by them. The man meanwhile being horribly distorted and contorted and screwed up into all kinds of shapes. I was so disgusted that I was on the point of riding up and shooting the other two men on the spot to release them from a like agony. They

stood beneath the tree contemplating their companion's dying throes and spasms with the most philosophical unconcern. But instead of following out my previous intention which was certainly a humane one, I ordered the men to leave the man on the tree and to bring on the other two prisoners and dispose of them in a more judicial manner, when they had better means.[20]

The execution of prisoners in those conflicts which were typified by brutality on both sides was not uncommon. Private Tatlock recorded in his diary of service against the Maoris in New Zealand that at Warra River 'an engagement took place, which resulted in the reported loss for the enemy of 28 killed and 30 wounded, 3 prisoners who were taken were shot for refusing to walk to our camp.'[21] Tatlock made no mention of whether the wounded were dealt with in the same manner. Private John Facer of the 30th Regiment described in his diary of the Second Afghan War (1878–80) the fate of prisoners captured at the bloody and hard-fought Battle of Ahmad Khel (19 April 1880). '4 prisoners were shot this morning; they were told to go away; and then a volley went after them; this is the easiest way, it saves the trouble of burying them.'[22] Also writing from Afghanistan, Lieutenant William Bernard William, who was present with Roberts' force besieged in Kabul in 1879, wrote in his diary

> On return to camp found our patrol had brought in eight men, some evidently of high degree. Sent in telegram about them and in accordance with reply shot them all in the evening.[23]

Similarly, Captain Gibb of the Anglo-Egyptian Army wrote a letter home in which he described an action against the dervishes and of the fate of the prisoners taken by his men. In writing of the lack of prisoners, Gibb admitted, 'I did not enquire about that as I can guess what became of them.'[24]

It is clear that the execution of prisoners was not simply undertaken to avoid further British casualties, as in the numerous battles with the dervishes. Lieutenant Robert Napier Smith was present at the battle of Omdurman and in a letter written just two days after the battle he leaves a clear impression of how the need for revenge motivated the thinking of some.

I believe the Soudanese [allies] raided and slaughtered, the night after the great battle. I am very glad. If I had my way, every man we captured on the battlefield should have been shot at once then and there, cold blood or not. If you had seen the condition of our dead you would have said the same.[25]

Lieutenant S. FitzGibbon Cox of the Lincolnshire Regiment was present at the Battle of Atbara (8 April 1898) and wrote in his diary of the conduct of the British troops once they had penetrated the dervishes' defensive position. He recorded that the frenzied British soldiers were hard to control and that few prisoners could be saved. Finally, he tries to justify the atrocities committed by stressing the evil acts of the dervishes.

The so-called humane conduct of the Englishman, who except in a very few occasions, where officers were on the spot to prevent it, spared nothing except the animals. Funny that the animals should be spared, perhaps it was animal instinct. However, not a man got off. Wounded or no, bayonets were shoved through anything human in the most brutal and cold-blooded fashion. Instance – a man [dervish] dropped his weapons and threw up his arms for mercy in front of one of the 79th who turned round and appealed to a sergeant who said, 'Put him out of misery, Sandy. We don't want none of these buggers 'ere.' The private turned round and bayoneted him through the neck and again through the back as he fell. However, there is only one thing to be said that one must remember what perfect devils these dervishes are – their frightful cruel habits – Gordon's murder.[26]

Violent conflict could make British troops indifferent to death, as can be seen in the writings of Private James Oates, who took part in the successful capture of the Maori *pah* at Rangiriri on 20 November 1863. After initial heavy British losses in a frontal attack, General Cameron resorted to an artillery bombardment which set the *pah* ablaze. The following day Oates

… took a look at the interior of their entrenchment. It was an awful sight, there they lay, dead and dying and some burnt to a cinder, victims of their own folly but it serves them right, they should stop at home and take care of the children.[27]

Should we be shocked that British troops could appear so callous and commit acts which, today, we would view as atrocities? Certainly it is true that brutality breeds brutality, and there is little doubt some of the sights seen by British troops must have, at the very least, made them vengeful. As Saul David has argued, throughout the nineteenth century the British soldier 'generally responded to their opponents' atrocities with the Old Testament mentality of "an eye for an eye".'[28] It was not until the Zulu War of 1879 that the British public really questioned whether these troops should be behaving as they did against civilians and the wounded enemy. And it was not until nearly another 20 years had passed that the dispatch of wounded dervishes at Omdurman caused widespread public outrage. In other words, public attitudes as to how the British public expected their soldiers to behave towards the enemy altered only slowly.

I believe that it is not possible for us to judge the acts of men from a different time and a different world with authority. Standards alter throughout history and it is unfair to judge the Victorian soldier by our own twenty-first century expectations.

Troops can only truly be condemned when their acts exceeded even the brutality of their own time. Thus whilst the killing of the wounded enemy was common during the Zulu War, and the various campaigns in the Sudan and Afghanistan, the killing of wounded Zulus who offered no resistance after the Battle of Rorke's Drift was exceptionally barbaric. Atrocities were not just limited to the murdering of the wounded; the widespread destruction of Zulu kraals was cruel and unnecessary and caused much hardship for the civilian population. Nineteenth-century colonial conflict was harsh and it is not surprising that examples can be found where the British soldier behaved in a brutish fashion, or in a way which many would find hard to understand today.

Despite all the hardships and horrors that were experienced on colonial service it is clear that for many, especially the officers, there was some enjoyment to be had. Captain Edward Hutton of the 60th Rifles wrote a letter to his father whilst on service in Abyssinia (1867–8).

> I am rather ashamed to own it, but I like this life, and I am as happy as the day is long. It is to me like a shooting expedition, with just a spice of danger thrown in to make it really interesting.[29]

Similarly, David William Stanley, 9th Earl of Airlie, was a career soldier with the 19th Hussars. He served in the Sudan in 1884–5 in the attempted relief of Khartoum, and remained in the army until his death in battle at Diamond Hill (11–12 June 1900). Here, charging upon a white horse, as his own was injured, he made an obvious target for the Boer riflemen and was shot dead. He wrote numerous letters home which provide a very evocative impression not just of his surroundings but also as to his thoughts on what motivated him. After the Battle of Magersfonein (11 December 1899), he wrote of the experience of conflict as well as his own firm belief in God, and it is clear that he enjoyed some thrill in the fight.

> I feel so different in a fight to what I do at a tactical field day. It is like riding to hounds compared to riding in a show ring. One's heart is the other side of the fence, and you can but do your best and pray to God. Not that I am not afraid. I hate the bullets and the shells, and the poor sad wounded make me unhappy, and I feel no desire for wounds or death. But God is there all the time, and I pray to Him to help me and give me the skill and courage if the sad wound comes, which I see others bearing so bravely that the tears sometimes come to my eyes.

In February of the following year, Airlie again wrote of combat.

> A man who has never been on active service has only half lived. I wish I could do justice to my subject, but I can't. How shall I put it? I imagine a most sensational novel, imagine the novel is true, and that you are in the novel yourself, and thereby get a look into yourself and other people, and feel as you never felt before. This is an exaggeration, but it will make you understand what I mean.[30]

It would also seem that religion and Empire motivated the Soldiers of the Queen. As Jan Morris put it

> The desire to do good was a true energy of Empire, and with it a genuine sense of duty – Christian duty, for though this was an Empire of multitudinous beliefs, its masters were overwhelmingly Church of England. Sometimes, especially in the middle of the nineteenth century, their duty was powerfully Old Testament in style, soldiers stormed about

with the Bible in their hands, administrators sat like bearded prophets at
their desks. By the 1890s it was more subdued, but still devoted to the
principle that the British were some sort of Chosen People, touched on
the shoulder by the Great Being and commissioned to do His will in
the world.[31]

Such attitudes were clearly expressed by Captain Alfred Edward
Hubbard in a letter to his wife, written on Sunday 28 August 1898, just
a few days before the decisive Battle of Omdurman.

> We had a stirring sermon from Mr. Watson this morning – His text was
> 'Fear not him who can destroy the body, but fear him who can destroy
> both body & soul' – He said that a soldier's death on the field of battle,
> fighting under his national flag was the greatest death possible & not
> to be feared by anyone – Regtal. colours, he said, are consecrated, &
> so may be taken to be banners blessed by God – the Union Jack, too,
> being composed of the Crosses of St. George, St. Andrew and St. Patrick,
> is essentially a holy flag – This too (the present Soudan campaign) is a
> crusade – & so blessed by God – It is a campaign to avenge (not revenge)
> the murder of one of the finest Englishmen that has lived (Gordon),
> who was murdered because he would not forsake his trust & those who
> looked to him for guidance. It was a very fine sermon.[32]

Writing less than two months before his death, Airlie seemed to be
resolute that the war had to be won for the good of the Empire: 'This
is no business and no play – it is a question of the Empire, and, please
God, we will carry it through and finish it in His way, whatever that
may be. It is LONG.' There was a belief that the soldier's duty included
the need to uphold the honour of the Empire and on occasions this
required acts of revenge. Private Samual Clunie wrote home to his
brother from Jellalabad, in July 1840. Clunie was part of the force that
was to take part in the British advance on Kabul and it is clear what
motivated him: 'We expect to proceed to Cabul to wipe the stain from
the British Flag and to revenge the blood of our slaughtered country-
men.'[33] 39 years later, Private Oakes of the 9th Lancers wrote to his
mother and father of yet another massacre of British troops at Kabul
in September 1879. Again, it is revenge that motivated Oakes when he
stated 'We are now under orders to March onto Cabul at a moment's

notice and I expect we shall have a chance of wetting the points of our Lances this time.'[34]

Death, both the reality of it and the fear of it, was a feature of many of the letters home. Airlie considered the attempted relief of Khartoum to be 'a very romantic war', and in a similar tone he wrote of his possible death in a romantic fashion.

> If I should by chance not get home to England (we may talk of that now with our camp on the Nile and the enemy the other side of the desert), put me up a small stone near the dear father's, and say I was a lucky fellow to die as I wished. But I mean coming *home*.

In contrast, Sergeant Henry Williams wrote of his return from the failed attempted to rescue Gordon in Khartoum. Williams was clearly bitter that comrades had been lost trying to relieve the city. On his arrival back at Wadi Halfa he wrote

> I noticed that since our departure from here a large cemetry had come into existence; thus then besides the number of scattered graves on the river side and especially at hospital locations, is one result of the expedition for the relief of one man [Gordon] who thought he could quell, and then rule, an unruly people. I had previously read in a newspaper of the memorial services in England for The Hero [Gordon] who had sacrificed himself upon the Altar of Honour and Duty, but not one word could I find in that same paper of any mention of the men. What of these, who mourns their loss, not a nation, only a few, had they not also sacrificed themselves upon the Altar of duty and honour. Such is life's destiny.[35]

Gunner John Cousins of the Royal Artillery, who served during the Crimean War, also wrote of the sadness and bitterness of losing comrades. At the end of the conflict, and just as he was to return to England, Cousins paid a visit to one of the British cemeteries.

> Now I had a look round the graves where so many thousands of my comrades had been buried. It was hard to part even from them, – the graves to be left behind in a foreign land. So I said good-bye with tears in my eyes.[36]

The different feelings that men experienced when death was all around them were also a subject in letters home. In a letter to his mother, written after the Battle of Sobraon (10 February 1846), Lieutenant Thomas Haydon describes his feelings before the fight began, which included the certainty that he would survive the fight. 'It is perhaps odd, but certainly I went out that day with a certain conviction in my own mind that I was not going to be touched and I have heard many say they felt the same on similar occasions.'[37] Lieutenant Dennys served throughout the Indian Mutiny. Writing of his feelings on a particular day during the Mutiny, 4 July 1857, Dennys remembered his and his fellow officers' concern for their safety.

> As I led the force that day, riding as usual at the head, I was quite conscious the whole time that any moment might prove my last, but I had been for many weeks accustomed to that feeling. Now, however, I was absolutely conscious that whatever was to be the end it must be close at hand. All my officers, I fancy, must have had much the same feeling but it seems strange how very little at that time we used to speak of what might too probably be our fate at any hour. I imagine that, whatever may have been our individual thoughts, we all knew that they were not sufficiently cheerful to form a subject of conversation.[38]

Moments before he took part in the assault upon Delhi, Captain Charles Ewart of the 2nd Bengal Fusiliers wrote a letter to his mother which gives a telling insight into what was expected of a Victorian army officer, as well as leaving us with an impression of the fear and concerns that were racing through Ewart's mind.

> I believe we are to escalade. You know what that will be – rush up a ladder with men trying to push you down, bayonet and shoot you from above. But you must wave your sword and think it capital fun, bring up your men as fast as you can and jump down on top of men already with fixed bayonets to receive you. All this is not very pleasant to think coolly of, but when the moment comes excitement and the knowledge that your men are looking to you to lead them on and bring them up with a cheer makes you feel as happy as possible ... It will be fearfully exciting work. I hope it won't make me swear...[39]

For all the fear of death and the loathing of the enemy, the British soldier wrote of his admiration for some of the colonial foes that he faced. The staunch defence of the Burmese, the disciplined attacks of the Ashantis and the regimental bravery of the Zulus all received much comment. Sergeant Edward Jervis wrote of the Zulus who repeatedly attacked the prepared British position at Kambula (29 March 1879): 'I do not think that a braver lot of men than our enemies in point of disregard for life, and for their bravery under fire, could be found anywhere.'[40] However, the most comprehensive praise was directed at the dervishes of the Sudan, whom the British faced between 1884–1898.

Lieutenant Hamilton Hodgson, who was present at the Battle of Omdurman (2 September 1898), reported in a letter to his father that

> I was watching them [the enemy] occasionally with my glasses. I never could have imagined anything so cool and brave as those men were, especially one, the last but one to fall; he had been wounded in his arm and limped, yet his ambition was to get the flag, and he got it and carried it some 50 yards at a sort of slow trot, when he was shot, and as he fell his companion too it and came on a few yards, when he fell, with the flag. I was sorry for these men; they were simply wiped out.[41]

Airlie also recorded his views of the enemy, his love of war and the desire to win.

> I LIKE the Boers, and am very pleased to be fighting against them. I believe them to be perfectly marvellous soldiers, and I believe that if they had cavalry and bayonets they would be nearly invincible in their own country ... The amazing thing is, that the Boers want to get home just as much as we do; but also, they are just as determined as we are ... We MUST win. I am very happy ... I love soldiering more than ever.

When the battle was won and the war over, the Soldiers of the Queen could reflect back upon the campaign and their service. Whilst they might have held views as to the bravery, or even savagery, of the enemy they had faced, their memories would surely have been filled with the hardship of colonial service. The poor conditions to be found in their garrisons, the massive physical test of endurance that the march to war

presented, the brutal nature of colonial warfare and the loss of comrades in battle or to disease must have remained with them for the
rest of their lives. Their story was not a glamorous one. Major Carr
wrote of the 2nd Battalion the Devonshire Regiment's experiences in
Afghanistan in 1880 and this extract typifies what was the true story of
the Victorian soldier:

> Not a Great War story of thrills and gallant exploits, but one of suf-
> fering and hardship in the honest performance of duty. The death toll
> was heavy, much more than is represented by the Memorial under the
> Colours in Exeter Cathedral, for a large proportion of the men invalided
> never recovered.[42]

It seems right to end this tale by quoting Lieutenant Marling, whose
experiences we have followed across the South African veldt, into Egypt
and the Sudan.

> I take off my hat to Tommy every time. The men under the most desper-
> ate fighting, untold hardships, with only three pints of filthy water a day,
> 1lb. of bully beef, and 1lb. biscuits, have behaved extraordinarily well. I'll
> back the British soldier against anyone in the world.[43]

These words, and the letters and diaries that survive, are a fitting tribute
to the Victorian soldier's bravery and endurance.

Notes

1. C. Hibbert, *Wolfe at Quebec*, (Cooper Square Press, New York, 1999
   edition), p.6.
2. Colonel Sir Percival Marling, V.C., *Rifleman and Hussar*, (John Murray,
   London, 1931), p.104.
3. Pvt. Brown, letter to parents, 8 August 1841, REF:NAM 1999-09-53.
4. Diary of Lt. Kirby, 20 December 1848, REF:NAM 1999-05-31-47.
5. Memoirs of Lieut. General W. Whitlock, REF: NAM 9601-69.
6. Diary of Sgt. Cooper, 8 May, 25 May 1863, 10 April, 14 April 1864,
   REF: RAM MD/1269.
7. Diary of Pvt. Tatlock, 22 April 1865, REF:NAM 1996-09-78.
8. Diary of Sgt. Hooper, 17 March 1879, REF:NAM 2001-03-73.
9. Major Woods, letter to wife, 29 December 1879, REF:NAM 7205-80-4.
10. Reminiscences of Col. Kellie, REF:NAM 7507-56.

11. Letter Lt. Dennys, 12 January 1842, REF:NAM 1979-01-95.

12. B. Farwell, *Queen Victoria's Little Wars*, (Allan Lane, London, 1973), p.39.

13. S. David, *Victoria's Wars The Rise of Empire*, (Viking, London, 2006) p.94.

14. A. Swanson & D. Scott, (eds.), *The Memoirs of Private Waterfield*, (Cassell, London, 1968), p.67.

15. Ibid, pp.169–170.

16. B. Farwell, p.88.

17. Diary of Capt. Ramsden, 21 October 1857, REF:RAM MD 1185/1.

18. Reminiscences of Charles Gray, REF:ASHM N-C93.GRA.

19. B. Farwell, p.97.

20. Diary of Capt. Ramsden, REF: RAM MD 1185/1.

21. Diary of Pvt. Tatlock, 2 August1865, REF:NAM 1996-09-78.

22. Diary of Pvt. Facer, 20 April 1880, REF:NAM 8301-131.

23. Diary of Lt. William William, 13 December 1879, REF:NAM 1978-04-9.

24. Letter Capt Gibb, 1 June 1886, REF: NAM 7411-52-4.

25. P. Harrington & F. Sharf (eds.), *Omdurman 1898: The eye-witnesses speak*, (Greenhill Books, London, 1998), p. 130.

26. J. Meredith (ed.), *Omdurman Diaries 1898: Eye witness accounts of the legendary campaign*, (Leo Cooper, Barnsley, 1998), p.87.

27. Letter from Pvt. J. Oates, 25 November1863, REF:NAM 1984-01-98.

28. S. David, *Zulu*, (Viking, London, 2004), p.276.

29. F. Emery, *The Red Soldier: The Zulu War of 1879*, (Hodder & Stoughton, London, 1977), p.199.

30. *The Happy Warrior: A Short Account of the Life of David, 9th Earl of Airlie*, (Winchester, 1901).

31. J. Morris, *Farewell The Trumpets*, (Faber & Faber, London, 1979), p.26.

32. J. Meredith, p.55.

33. Pvt. Clunie, letter to brother, 28 July 1840, REF:NAM 2002-07-12-2.

34. Pvt. Oakes, letter to parents, 16 September 1879, REF:NAM 8108-18-1.

35. Sgt. H. Williams, *Reminiscences of a Soldier*, REF:NAM 9208-372.

36. Gnr J. Cousins, *Memories from the Crimea*, REF: RAM MD 2207.

37. Lt. Haydon, letter to mother, 21 February 1846, REF:NAM 1987-11-49.

38. Memoirs Lt. Dennys, 4 July 1857, REF:NAM 1979-01-95.

39. J. Duncan & J. Walton, *Heroes for Victoria*, (Spellmount, Tunbridge Wells, 1991), p.85.

40. F. Emery, pp.172–3.

41. P. Harrington & F. Sharf (eds.), p.81.

42. Diary of Major Carr, REF: DRM Box PO3 7.

43. Colonel Sir Percival Marling, p.149.

APPENDIX

VICTORIA'S CAMPAIGNS

1836–8	First Carlist War (Spain)
1837	Insurrection in Canara, India
1837–8	Mackenzie's rebellion in Ontario
1838–42	First Afghan War
1839	Operations in the Persian Gulf
	Kurmool Campaign
	Capture of Aden
	Jodhpur Campaign
1839–42	First China War
1840	Expedition into Kohistan
	Marri uprising in Sind
1840–1	Syrian Expedition
1841–2	Expedition against Walleng hill tribes on the Arracan frontier
1842	Expedition against Shinwaris
	Pirara Expedition
	Insurrection in Shorapore district, India
	Bundlecund Campaign
	Occupation of Port Natal, South Africa
1842–3	Operation in the Saugor and Nerbudda territories
1843	Sind Campaign (India)
	Gwalior Campaign (India)
	Campaign against Borneo pirates
	Disturbance in Malabar (India)
1843–5	First Sikh War
1843–7	First Maori War
1844	Mutiny of two native regiments on Sind frontier

1844–5	Campaign in southern Mahratta country
	Campaign against hill tribes on the northern frontier of Sind
1845	Expedition against Voortrekkers (South Africa)
	Suppression of pirates in Borneo
1846	Aden besieged
1846–7	Seventh Cape Frontier War ('War of the Axe' – South Africa)
1847	Capture of the Bogue forts, China
	Rebellion in Golcondah and Darondah in the Golcondah Zemindary
1847–8	Expedition to Goomsore
1848	Sherbo Expedition
	White Cloud Expedition against the Braves
	Rebellion in Ceylon
	Expedition against King of Appolonia on Gold Coast
	Action at Boomplaats against disaffected Boers
1848–9	Second Sikh War
1849	Expedition against Baizai
1849–50	Expedition against Afridis
1850	Mutiny of 66th Native Infantry
	Expedition against Kohat Pass Afridis
1850–53	Eighth Cape Frontier War (including BaSotholand campaign, 1851–2)
1851	Expedition against Miranzai
	Bombardment of Lagos
	Operations against Umarzai Waziris
	Siege of Dhasore
	Occupation of Bahadoor Khail
1851–2	Two expeditions against Mohmands
1851–3	Second Burma War
1852	Expedition against Afidis
	Expedition against Ranizais
	Expedition against Umarzai Waziris
1852–3	Expedition to Black Mountains to punish Hasanzais
1853	Expedition against Hindustani Fanatics
	Expedition against Bori clan of Jowaki Afridis
	Expedition against Kasranis
	Expedition against Shiranis
1854	Rebellion of Burmese in Bassein district
	Operations against Rohillas, India
	Chinese Riots, Singapore
	Eureka Stockade incident, Australia

	Operations against rebels in Tondiman Rajah's country, India
	Relief of Christenborg on Gold Coast
	Expedition against Mohmands
1854–5	Malageah expeditions
1854–6	Crimean War
1855	Expedition against Miranzai
	Insurrection of Bedeers of Deodroog
	Storming of Sabbajee
	Expedition against Aka Khel Afridis
	Expedition against Rubia Khel Orakzais
1855–6	Insurrection of the Sonthals
1856	Fighting against the hill Kareems in Burma
	Expedition against Turis
1856–7	Persian War (Iran)
1857	Operations against Shans and Kareens of Martaban Provence
	Expedition to the Bozdar hills
	Expedition against Beydur Beluchis
	Expedition against villages on the Yusafzai border
	Expedition against hill tribes in Rajahmundry district
	The island of Perim, near Aden, occupied
1857–9	The Indian Mutiny
1857–60	Second China War
1858	Expedition against the Crobboes
	Expedition against Hindustani fanatics and Khudu Khels
1858–9	Expedition against Singhbhum rebels
1859	Bundlecund campaign
	Expedition against the Dounquah rebels
	Expedition against Kabul Khel Waziris
	Great Scarcies River expedtion
1859–62	The 'Blue Mutiny' in Bengal
1860	Expedition against Mahsud Waziris
1860–1	Second Maori War (New Zealand)
	Baddiboo War on the Gambia
	Quiah War in Sierra Leone
1861	Sikkim Campaign (India)
	Storming and capture of Rohea
	Attack on Madoukia
	Destruction of Massougha on Sierra Leone river
	Disturbances in Honduras

1862–3	Cossiah Rebellion
1863	Umbeyla Campaign
	Action against Malay Pirates
1863–4	Ambela and Shabkadr expeditions (North-West Frontier)
	First Ashanti War
1863–6	Third Maori War (New Zealand)
1864	Japan Expedition
	Expedition against the Mohmands
1864–5	Bhutan Expedition
1865	Bombardment of cape Haitian in Haiti
	Insurrection of freed slaves in Jamaica
1865–6	Aden expedition
1866	Fenian raids from the United States into Canada
1867	Fenian disturbances in Ireland
	Expedition to Little Andaman Island
	Expedition to Honduras
1867–8	Abyssinian War
	Black Mountain expedition (North-West Frontier)
1868	Expedition against the Bizoti Orakzais
	Basuto War
1869	Expedition against Bizoti Orakzais
1870	Red River Expedition (Canada)
1871–2	Lushai Campaign
1872	Expedition against Dawaris
1873	Town of Omoa in Spanish Honduras bombarded
1873–4	Second Ashanti War
1874–5	Duffla Expedition (Naga Hills, North-West Frontier)
1875	Bombardment of villages on River Congo
	Rebellion in Griqualand
1875–6	Perak Expedition (Malaya)
	Rebellion of slavers against British imposed anti-slavery laws in Mombassa
1877–8	Jowakhi Expedition (North-West Frontier)
	Ninth Cape Frontier War
	First Sekhukhune Expedition (South Africa)
1878	Pirate strongholds in Borneo bombarded
	Expedition against Zakha Khel Afridis
1878–80	Second Afghan War
1879	Zulu War
	Second Sekhukhune Expedition
1879	Punitive expedition against Zaumukts

	Expedition against Mohmands
	Expedition against Suliman Khel Pawindahs
1879–80	Naga Expedition
1880	Expedition against Batanis
	Expedition against Mohmands
	Expedition against Malikshahi Waziris
	Expedition against Marris
1880–81	Fifth Basuto War (South Africa)
	First Anglo-Boer War or Transvaal Rebellion
1881	Expedition against Mahsud Waziris
1882	Egyptian War
1883	Bikaneer expedition, India
1883–4	Akha Expedition, India
1884	Zhob Valley Expedition
1884–5	Bechuanaland Expedition
	Sudan Campaign (Gordon Relief Expedition, Suakin campaign, defence of Egyptian frontier)
1885	Bhutan Expedition
	Suppression of Riel's Rebellion (Metis) in Western Canada
1885–89	Third Burmese War
1885–98	Wars with Arab slave traders in Nyasa
1888	Suakin operations (Sudan)
	Sikhim Expedition (India)
	Hazara and Black Mountain expeditions (North-West Frontier)
	Dinuzulu rebellion, Zululand
1889	Tonhon Expedition
	Expedition to Sierra Leone
1889–90	Chin Lushai Expedition
1889–92	Burmese Expeditions
1890	Mashonaland Expedition
	Malakand Campaign
	Punitive expedition in Somaliland
	Vitu Expedition
1891	Manipur Expedition (India)
	Samana or second Miranzai Expedition
	Hunza and Nagar Campaign
	Hazara Expedition
1891–2	Campaign in Gambia
	Operations in Uganda

1892	Tambi Expedition
	Isazai Expedition
1892–3	Kachin Hills Expedition (India)
1893	First Ndebele (Matabele) War (Zimbabwe)
	British and French exchange fire by mistake in Sierra Leone
1893–4	Arbor Hills Expedition
	Third Ashanti War
1894	Gambia Expedition
	British expedition to Sierra Leone
1894	Expedition against Kabarega, King of Unyoro, in Uganda
	Disturbances in Nicaragua
1894–5	Waziristan Expedition
	Nikki Expedition
1895	Defence and relief of Chitral (North-West Frontier)
	Brass River Expedition
1895–6	Jameson Raid
1895–1900	Conquest of Ashanti
1896–7	Second Matabele War
1896	Bombardment of Zanzibar
1896–7	Bechuanaland Expedition
1896–8	Reconquest of the Sudan
1897	Samana or Affreedee campaign (North-West Frontier)
	Malakand Field Force
1897–8	Punitive expedition into Tochi Valley
	Tirah Campaign
	Uganda mutiny
1897–1903	Conquest of Northern Nigeria (capture of Benin City in 1897)
1898	Riots in Crete, bombardment of Candia
1898–1902	Suppression of the Mad Mullah in Somaliland
1899	Bebejiya Expedition, North-East Frontier
	Campaign in Sierra Leone
1899–1902	Anglo-Boer War or Second Boer War
1900	Boxer Rebellion (China)
	Rebellion in Borneo
	Aden field force supported Haushabi tribe fight off Humar tribe from Yemen

I would like to acknowledge the works of Brian Bond, Byron Farwell and Ian Knight in the construction of what I hope is a comprehensive list.

BIBLIOGRAPHY

Austin, Captain H, *With Macdonald in Uganda*, (Dawsons, reissue 1973).

Barthorp, M. *The British Army on Campaign 1856–1881*, (Osprey, 1988).

Beresford, Lord Charles, *Memoirs*, (Methuen, 1914).

Black, J. *Tools of War: The Weapons that Changed the World*, (Quercus, 2007).

Blake, G. *B.I. Centenary 1856–1956*, (Collins, 1956).

Blatchford, R. *My Life in the Army*, (Clarendon Press, Oxford, circa 1870).

Bond, Brian. *Victorian Military Campaigns*, (Hutchinson, 1967).

Bonner, R. *The Soldier's Pen: Firsthand impressions of the Civil War*, (Hill & Wang, New York, 2006).

Bowie, J. *The Empire at War*, (Batsford, 1989).

Boyden, P. Guy, A. Harding, M. *'Ashes and Blood': The British Army in South Africa 1795–1914*, (National Army Museum, 1999).

Brackenbury, H. *The Ashanti War of 1873–4*, (Frank Cass, New Impression, 1968).

Churchill, W.S. *The Story of the Malakand Field Force*, (Longmans, Green & Co., 1898).

Churchill, W.S. *London to Ladysmith via Pretoria and Ian Hamilton's March*, (Pimlico Edition, 2002).

David, S. *Zulu*, (Viking, 2004).

David, S. *Victoria's Wars: The Rise of Empire*, (Viking, 2006).

Duncan, J. & Walton, J. *Heroes for Victoria*, (Spellmount, Tunbridge Wells, 1991).

Edmondson, R. *Is a Soldier's Life Worth Living?* (Twentieth Century Press, 1902).

Emery, F. *The Red Soldier*, (Hodder & Stoughton, 1977).

Emery, F. *Marching Over Africa: Letters from Victorian Soldiers*, (Hodder & Stoughton, 1986).

Farwell, B. *Queen Victoria's Little Wars*, (Allan Lane, 1973).

Featherstone, D. *Khaki & Red: Soldiers of the Queen in India and Africa*, (Arms & Armour Press,1995).

Foot, M.R.D. (ed.), *War and Society: Historical Essays in Honour and Memory of J.R. Western 1928–1971*, (Paul Elek, 1973).

Fuller, J. *The Last of the Gentleman's Wars*, (Faber and Faber, 1937).

Gann, L.H. & Duignan, P. *The Rulers of British Africa, 1870–1914*, (Croom Helm, 1978).

Gordon-Alexander, Lt. Col. W, *Recollections of a Highland Subaltern*, (Edward Arnold, 1898).

Harding, M. (ed.), *The Victorian Soldier: Studies in the History of the British Army 1816–1914*, (National Army Museum, 1993).

Harrington, P. & Sharf, F. (eds.), *Omdurman 1898: The Eye-witnesses Speak*, (Greenhill Books, 1998).

Hernon, I. *Britain's Forgotten Wars: Colonial Campaigns of the 19th Century*, (Alan Sutton, Stroud, 2003).

Hibbert, C. *Wolfe at Quebec*, (Cooper Square Press, New York, 1999 edition).

Holmes, R. *Dusty Warriors*, (Harper Collins, 2007).

James, L. *The Savage Wars: British Campaigns in Africa, 1870–1920*, (Robert Hale, 1985).

Judd, D. *Calamities of the British Army in the Victorian Age*, (Phoenix, reissue 2007).

Knight, I. *Go to Your God Like a Soldier: The British Soldier Fighting for Empire, 1837–1902*, (Greenhill, 1996).

Knight, I. *Marching to the Drums: From the Kabul Massacre to the Siege of Mafikeng*, (Greenhill Books, 1999).

Manning, S. *Evelyn Wood: Pillar of Empire*, (Pen and Sword, Barnsley, 2007).

Manning, S. 'Foreign News Gathering and Reporting in the London and Devon Press: The Anglo-Zulu War, 1879, A Case Study'. Unpublished PhD, University of Exeter, 2005.

Manning, S. 'Private Snook and Total War,' *Journal of the Anglo-Zulu War Historical Society*, XIII, June 2003, pp.22–26.

Marling, Colonel Sir Percival, V.C., *Rifleman and Hussar*, (John Murray, 1931).

Maxwell, L. *The Ashanti Ring: Sir Garnet Wolseley's Campaigns 1870–1882*, (Leo Cooper, London, 1985).

Meredith, J. (ed.), *Omdurman Diaries 1898: Eye Witness Accounts of the legendary campaign*, (Leo Cooper, Barnsley, 1998).

Morris, J. *Farewell The Trumpets*, (Faber & Faber, 1979).

Morris, P, (ed.), *First Aid to the Battlefront: Life and Letters of Sir Vincent Kennett-Barrington,* (Alan Sutton, Stroud, 1992).

Murray, M. *Union-Castle Chronicle*, (Longmans, 1953).

Pakenham, T. *The Boer War*, (Weidenfeld & Nicolson, 1979).

Rogers, H. *Troopships and their History*, (Seeley Service & Co., 1963).

Ryder, J. *Four Year's Service in India*, (Leicester, 1853).

Skelley, A. *The Victorian Army at Home: The Recruitment and Terms and Conditions of the British Regular, 1859–1899*, (Croom Helm 1977).

Small, E.M.(ed.), *Told from the Ranks*, (Andrew Melrose,1897).

Smith, P. *Victoria's Victories*, (Spellmount, Tunbridge Wells, 1987).

Spiers, E. *The Army and Society 1815–1914*, (Longman, 1980).

Spiers, E. *The Victorian Soldier in Africa*, (Manchester University Press, 2004).

Spiers, E. *The Scottish Soldier and Empire, 1854–1902*, (Edinburgh University Press, 2006).

Spilsbury, J. *The Thin Red Line: An Eyewitness History of the Crimean War*, (Weidenfeld & Nicolson, 2005).

Stanley, D. W, *The Happy Warrior: A Short Account of the Life of David, 9th Earl of Airlie*, (Winchester, 1901).

Stewart, A. *The Pagada War*, (Faber, 1972).

Stewart, P. *The History of the XII Royal Lancers*, (Oxford University Press, 1950).

Strawson, J. *Beggars in Red: The British Army 1789–1889*, (Pen & Sword, Barnsley, 2003).

Swanson, A. & Scott, D. (eds.), *The Memoirs of Private Waterfield*, (Cassell, 1968).

Tucker, F. (ed.), *The Chronicle of Private Henry Metcalfe, H.M. 32nd Regiment of Foot*, (Cassell, 1953).

Usherwood, P. & Spencer-Smith, J. *Lady Butler Battle Artist, 1846–1933*, (Alan Sutton, Gloucester, 1987).

Warner, P. *Stories of Famous Regiments*, (Arthur Baker, 1975).

Whitman, W. *Memoranda During the War*, (Oxford University Press, 2004).

Wood, E. *From Midshipman to Field Marshal*, Vol.I & II (Methuen, 1906).

INDEX